Praise for *Software Development Pearls*

"This is a collection of lessons that Karl has [...] honestly, distinguished career. It is a retrospective o[...] e bad) he picked up along the way. However, this is r[...] my day' aphorisms, but lessons that are relevant and [...] ngentially, in software development today. The book is surprising. It is not simply a list of pearls of wisdom—each lesson is carefully argued and explained. Each one carries an explanation of why it is important to you, and importantly, how you might bring the lesson to your reality."

—**James Robertson,** *Author of* Mastering the Requirements Process

"Wouldn't it be great to gain a lifetime's experience early in your career, when it's most useful, without having to pay for the inevitable errors of your own experience? Much of Karl Wiegers's half-century in software and management has been as a consultant, where he's often been called upon to rectify debacles of other people's making. In *Software Development Pearls,* Karl lays out the most common and egregious types of maladies that he's run into. It's valuable to know where the most expensive potholes are and which potholes people keep hitting time and time again.

"Not just a disaster correspondent, Karl is well versed in the best techniques of business analysis, software engineering, and project management. So from Karl's experience and knowledge you'll gain concise but important insights into how to recover from setbacks as well as how to avoid them in the first place.

"Forty-six years ago I was lucky enough to stumble onto Fred Brooks's classic *The Mythical Man-Month,* which gave me tremendous insights into my new career. Karl's book is in a similar vein, but broader in scope and more relevant for today's world. My own half-century of experience confirms that he's right on the money with the lessons that he's chosen for *Software Development Pearls.*"

—**Meilir Page-Jones,** *Senior Business Analyst, Wayland Systems Inc.*

"Karl has created yet another wonderful book full of well-rounded advice for software developers. His wisdom will be relatable to all development professionals and students—young and old, new and experienced. Although I've been doing software development for many years, this book brought timely reminders of things my team should do better. I cannot wait to have our new-to-the-job team members read this.

"*Software Development Pearls* is rooted in actual experiences from many years of real projects, with a dose of thorough research to back up the lessons. As with all of Karl's books, he keeps it light and engaging, chock-full of relatable stories and a few funny comments. You can read it from front to back or just dive into a particular section that's relevant to the areas you're looking to improve today. An enjoyable read plus practical advice—you can't go wrong!"

—**Joy Beatty,** *Vice President at Seilevel*

"Karl's *Software Development Pearls* achieves the challenging goal of capturing and explaining many insights that you're unlikely to be exposed to in your training, that most practitioners learn through the school of hard knocks, and yet are critical to developing great software.

"While the book's structure compels you to connect with your experience and identify how to shift your behavior as a result, it's the content that shines: a collection of 59+1 lessons that cover the broad landscape of the software development ecosystem. These insights will help you save time, collaborate more effectively, build better systems, and change your view on common misconceptions. *Software Development Pearls* is an easy read and is backed by a wide range of references to other experts who have discovered these same insights in their travels.

"These lessons truly are Pearls: timelessly valuable elements of wisdom to make you better at developing great software, regardless of your role. Consider getting two copies of the book: one for yourself, and one to leave where others on the team can pick it up and discover their own pearls."

—**Jim Brosseau,** *Clarrus*

"This is an excellent book for anyone involved in software development. One of the brilliant (and unusual) aspects of the book is the way it is organized into self-contained lessons. Once you read them, they work like memes—memorable chunks of distilled knowledge that spring to mind when you need them. This happened to me recently when I was discussing the need for a requirements competency on agile projects with a senior executive and immediately thought of Lesson 8, 'The overarching objective of requirements development is clear and effective communication.'

"From personal experience, I can attest to the value of lessons like #22, 'Many system problems take place at interfaces,' but only because I was burned badly by not paying enough attention to them. Anyone in software development eventually accumulates hard-won lessons like these about what to do—and not do—in the future. This book will get you there with much less pain. As Karl says in Lesson 7, 'The cost of recording knowledge is small compared to the cost of acquiring knowledge.' Not only is that good advice for practitioners, it also neatly captures why you should buy this book."

—**Howard Podeswa,** *Author of* The Agile Guide to Business Analysis and Planning: From Strategic Plan to Continuous Value Delivery

Software Development Pearls

Software Development Pearls

Lessons from Fifty Years of Software Experience

Karl Wiegers

♠♠Addison-Wesley

Boston • Columbus • New York • San Francisco • Amsterdam • Cape Town
Dubai • London • Madrid • Milan • Munich • Paris • Montreal • Toronto • Delhi • Mexico City
São Paulo • Sydney • Hong Kong • Seoul • Singapore • Taipei • Tokyo

For information about buying this title in bulk quantities, or for special sales opportunities (which may include electronic versions; custom cover designs; and content particular to your business, training goals, marketing focus, or branding interests), please contact our corporate sales department at corpsales@pearsoned.com or (800) 382-3419.

For government sales inquiries, please contact governmentsales@pearsoned.com.

For questions about sales outside the U.S., please contact intlcs@pearson.com.

Visit us on the Web: informit.com/aw

Library of Congress Control Number: 2021942545

Copyright © 2022 Karl E. Wiegers

Cover image: Philipp Tur/Shutterstock

Key icon: LDDesign/Shutterstock

Person reading book icon: VoodooDot/Shutterstock

Stairs icon: FOS_ICON/Shutterstock

ISBN-13: 978-0-13-748777-6
ISBN-10: 0-13-748777-0

1 2021

For Chris, as always

Contents

Foreword

After Karl Wiegers received his PhD in organic chemistry, he took a job as a research scientist at Kodak in Rochester, New York. Karl had interviewed at Kodak before he accepted the job, and he thought he understood the nature of the work. He would be doing research related to photographic film, photo development, and related projects.

When Karl arrived at Kodak, he was escorted through a light lock, into the laboratory. A light lock is like an air lock in a submarine, except that it ensures that no light leaks into a room that is kept completely dark. After Karl went through the light lock, his eyes took several minutes to adjust to the barely lit laboratory. No one had told Karl that his research lab would be a photographic dark room.

Karl quickly realized he did not want to spend his career literally working in the dark, and so he transitioned to roles of software developer, then software manager, and eventually software process and quality improvement leader. Later, he founded his own company, Process Impact.

This practical book is Karl's attempt to lead others out of software darkness and into the light. As with his other books, there is more pragmatism than theory. The book concentrates on the areas in which Karl has direct experience: especially requirements, process improvement, quality, culture, and teamwork.

Karl doesn't explain why he titled the book *Software Development Pearls*. The process of growing a pearl begins when an irritant such as a grain of sand gets trapped in an oyster. In response, the oyster gradually accretes a substance to protect itself from the irritant. It takes a long time, but eventually the irritant results in a valuable pearl.

Karl is one of the most thoughtful software people I know. He has reflected deeply on the software development irritants he has encountered over his career, and this book contains 60 of his most valuable responses.

—*Steve McConnell, Construx Software and author of* Code Complete

Acknowledgments

Over a span of more than fifty years, I've learned how to do software development, project management, and process improvement from many sources. I've read countless books and articles, taken many professional training courses, and attended a multitude of conference presentations. I'm grateful to all the educators who passed along anything from one helpful nugget of knowledge to a whole new understanding of some part of our discipline. Two great trainers particularly stand out: Steve Bodenheimer and Dr. Joyce Statz. How many names of your professional instructors stick in your mind decades later?

The vast body of software engineering literature is a virtually endless source of enlightenment. Authors whose work I've found especially illuminating include Mike Cohn, Larry Constantine, Alan Davis, Tom DeMarco, Tom Gilb, Robert Glass, Ellen Gottesdiener, Capers Jones, Norm Kerth, Tim Lister, Steve McConnell, Roxanne Miller, James Robertson, Suzanne Robertson, Johanna Rothman, and Ed Yourdon. If you haven't read their work, you should. It's been a rare privilege to become friends with so many wise authors and consultants over the years.

I've had the good fortune to work with some talented software engineers. You can learn a lot from seeing how others work, because we all have complementary experiences. As the Principal Consultant at my company, Process Impact, I've provided about 150 companies and government agencies with training and consulting services. I appreciate all of the clients and students in my training courses who shared their horror—and success—stories with me. Those reports helped me learn what techniques do and don't work well in a multitude of real-world situations. I've distilled all that I learned from these numerous sources into the lessons in this book.

In preparing this book, I had valuable discussions with Jim Brosseau, Tanya Charbury, Mike Cohn, David Hickerson, Tony Higgins, Norm Kerth, Ramsay Miller, Howard Podeswa, Holly Lee Sefton, and particularly Meilir Page-Jones, Ken Pugh, and Kathy Reynolds. I thank them sincerely for their patience with my questions and the experience stories they shared. Thanks also to those people who provided insightful quotations to augment my personal observations.

I appreciate the helpful manuscript review input provided by Joy Beatty, Jim Brosseau, Mike Cohn, Gary K. Evans, Lonnie Franks, David Hickerson, Kathy Iberle, Norm Kerth, Darryl Logsdon, Jeannine McConnell, Marco Negri, Meilir Page-Jones, Neil Potter, Ken Pugh, Gina Schmidt, James Shields, John Siegrist, Jeneil

Stephen, Tom Tomasovic, and Sebastian Watzinger. Review comments from Tanya Charbury, Kathy Reynolds, Maud Schlich, and Holly Lee Sefton were particularly valuable. Thanks also to Gary K. Evans for permission to modify a useful figure on design interfaces.

I'm grateful to Haze Humbert, Menka Mehta, and the entire editorial and production team at Pearson for their fine work on my manuscript.

As always, I'm indebted to my wife, Chris, for patiently tolerating another book project.

About the Author

Since 1997, Karl Wiegers has been Principal Consultant with Process Impact, a software development consulting and training company in Happy Valley, Oregon. Previously, he spent eighteen years at Kodak, where he held positions as a photographic research scientist, software developer, software manager, and software process and quality improvement leader. Karl received a PhD in organic chemistry from the University of Illinois.

Karl is the author of twelve previous books, including *The Thoughtless Design of Everyday Things, Software Requirements, More About Software Requirements, Practical Project Initiation, Peer Reviews in Software, Successful Business Analysis Consulting,* and a forensic mystery novel titled *The Reconstruction.* He has written many articles on software development, management, design, consulting, chemistry, and military history. Several of Karl's books have won awards, most recently the Society for Technical Communication's Award of Excellence for *Software Requirements, 3rd Edition* (co-authored with Joy Beatty). Karl has served on the Editorial Board for *IEEE Software* magazine and as a contributing editor for *Software Development* magazine.

When he's not at the keyboard, Karl enjoys wine tasting, volunteering at the public library, delivering Meals on Wheels, playing guitar, writing and recording songs, reading military history, and traveling. You can reach him through www.processimpact.com or www.karlwiegers.com.

Chapter 1

Learning from Painful Experience

I've never known anyone who could truthfully say, "I am building software today as well as software could ever be built." Anyone who can't say that would benefit from learning better ways to work. This book offers some shortcuts for that quest.

Experience is the form of learning that sticks with us the best. It's also the most painful way to learn. Our initial attempts to try new approaches often stumble and sometimes fail. We all must climb learning curves, accepting short-term productivity hits as we struggle to master new methods and understand when and how to use them adeptly.

Fortunately, an alternative learning mechanism is available. We can compress our learning curves by absorbing lessons, tips, and tricks from people who have already acquired and applied the knowledge. This book is a collection of such pearls of wisdom about software engineering and project management—useful insights I've gained through my personal experiences and observed from other people's work. Your own experiences and lessons might differ, and you might not agree with everything I present. That's fine; everyone's experience is unique. These are all things I've found valuable in my software career, though.

My Perspective

Let me start with a bit of my background to show how I accumulated these lessons. I took my first computer programming class in college in 1970—FORTRAN, of course. My very first job—the next summer—involved automating some operations of the financial aid office at my college, all on my own. I'd had two credits of programming, so I was a software engineer, right? The project was surprisingly successful, considering my limited background. I took two more programming courses in college. Everything else I've learned about software engineering I've picked up on my own from reading, training courses, experience, and colleagues. That unofficial career path wasn't unusual some time ago, as people were drawn to software development from many backgrounds but had little formal education in computing.

Since that early start, I spent a lot of time doing a diverse range of software work: requirements development, application design, user interface design, programming, testing, project management, writing documentation, quality engineering, and process improvement leadership. I took some side trips along the way, like getting a PhD in organic chemistry. Even then, one-third of my doctoral thesis consisted of software code for analyzing experimental data and simulating chemical reactions.

Early in my career as a research scientist at Eastman Kodak Company, then a huge and highly successful corporation, I used computers to design and analyze experiments. I soon transitioned into full-time software development, building applications for use in the Kodak Research Laboratories and managing a small software group for a few years. I found that my scientific background and inclination guided me to take a more systematic approach to software development than I might have otherwise.

I wrote my first article about software in 1983. Since then, I've written many articles and eight books on numerous aspects of the discipline. As an independent consultant and trainer since 1997, I have provided services to nearly 150 companies and government agencies in many business domains. These interactions let me observe techniques that work effectively on software projects—and techniques that don't.

Many of my insights about software development and management came from my personal project experiences, some rewarding, but also some disappointing. I gained other knowledge from my consulting clients' experiences, generally on projects that did not go well. No one calls a consultant when everything is going swimmingly. I wrote this book so that you don't need to accumulate all those same lessons slowly and painfully through your personal project struggles. One highly experienced software engineer who read this list of lessons commented, "Every one of those items has a scar (or several) associated with it."

About the Book

This book presents fifty-nine lessons about software development and management, grouped into six domains, with one chapter on each domain:

Chapter 4. Project management

Chapter 5. Culture and teamwork

Chapter 6. Quality

Chapter 7. Process improvement

Chapter 8 provides one final, general lesson to keep in mind as you move forward. For easy reference, all sixty lessons are collected in the Appendix.

I haven't attempted to provide a complete list of lessons in those domains. There's so much knowledge in each category that no one could create an exhaustive compilation. Nor do I address other essential aspects of software development, most obviously programming, testing, and configuration management. Other authors have compiled comprehensive wisdom in those areas in books like these:

- *Programming Pearls* by Jon Bentley (2000)
- *Lessons Learned in Software Testing* by Cem Kaner, James Bach, and Bret Pettichord (2002)
- *Code Complete* by Steve McConnell (2004)
- *Software Engineering at Google* by Titus Winters, Tom Manshreck, and Hyrum Wright (2020)

The topics and lessons in this book are largely independent, so you can read them in any order you like without any loss of continuity. Each chapter begins with a brief overview of the pertinent software domain. Then several First Steps encourage you to reflect on your previous experiences with that domain before you dive into the chapter's lessons. The First Steps invite you to think about problems your teams have experienced in that area, the impacts of those problems, and possible contributing root causes.

Each lesson concisely states a core insight, followed by a discussion and suggested practices that teams can adopt based on the lesson. As you read through each chapter, think about how those practices might relate to your situation. A book icon in the margin, as shown here, indicates a true story drawn from my personal experiences, interactions with my consulting clients, or experiences that colleagues have shared with me. All the stories are real, though names have been changed to preserve privacy. In addition to the true-story icons, key points in each lesson description are flagged with a key icon in the margin, like the one shown here. Some of the lessons contain cross-references to other lessons, which are indicated with a margin icon like the one you see here.

The Next Steps section at the end of each chapter will help you plan how to apply the chapter's material to your project, team, or organization. No matter what sort of project you work on, what life cycle it follows, or what kind of product you build, look for the idea behind each lesson and see how you might adapt it to help your project be more successful.

Consider going through the First Steps and Next Steps with a group of your colleagues rather than doing them alone. At the beginning of the hundreds of training courses I've taught, I have small groups discuss problems their teams have experienced related to the course topic (the First Steps). At the end of the course, the same groups explore solutions to those problems, brainstorming ways to apply the course contents right away (the Next Steps). My students find it valuable to include a variety of stakeholders in those discussion groups. Different stakeholders bring diverse perspectives on how certain aspects of the project are going. Combining their perspectives provides a rich understanding of their current practices and a creative opportunity to choose practical solutions.

I hope many of my lessons resonate with you and motivate you to try something different on your projects. However, you can't change everything you do at once. Individuals, teams, and organizations can absorb change only at a certain rate as they strive to get their project work done concurrently. The final chapter in the book, "What to Do Next," will help you chart a path to translate the lessons into actions. That chapter offers suggestions about prioritizing the changes you want to put into motion and crafting an action plan to help you get from where you are today to where you want to be.

A Note on Terminology

I use the terms *system, product, solution,* and *application* more or less interchangeably in this book. In each instance, I'm simply referring to whatever ultimate deliverable your project creates, so please don't read any significance into whichever term I use in a particular place. Whether you work on corporate or government information systems, websites, commercial software applications, or hardware devices with embedded software, the lessons and their associated practices will be broadly applicable.

Your Opportunity

Unless you are indeed among that rare class of practitioners who are already building software as well as software could ever be built, you have some improvement opportunities. We all need to continuously enhance our capabilities: as individual practitioners, as project teams, and as organizations. We all want fewer scars.

A junior developer named Zachary Minott (2020) made some thoughtful observations about how he outperformed more experienced developers. Minott described an ethic of acknowledging what he didn't know, systematically going about learning, and putting the new knowledge into practice. He said, "If there is any superpower that I do have, it's the ability to learn fast and immediately apply what I learn to what I'm doing." Minott discovered the critical mechanism for continuously wending his way toward mastery of his discipline.

We all need to continuously enhance our capabilities. We all want fewer scars.

Perhaps you decide to take a class to learn a new skill or enhance your current way of working. While you take the class, the work continues to pile up. It's easy to ignore what you've learned and continue to work as you always have in the rush to get caught up. That's comfortable, as your current approach has sufficed so far. But that's not the way to improve.

I adopted the approach of identifying two areas on each project to get better at. I would set aside some time to learn about those topics and try to apply my new understanding. Not every technique worked out, but my approach allowed me to gradually accumulate skills that have served me well.

I encourage you to do the same. Don't merely read the book; take the next step. Decide how you and your colleagues can apply the practices you read about and what you hope they'll do for you. Build a list of practices that you want to learn more about and then put them into use. That way, you'll come out ahead in the long run.

Chapter 2

Lessons About Requirements

Introduction to Requirements

Every project has objectives—goals or outcomes toward which the work is directed. Every project also has requirements that define what is necessary to satisfy a business need or fill a product niche in the marketplace. Most projects begin with considerable uncertainty about requirements details. Those details become clearer incrementally as customers learn more and provide feedback on the project team's initial work of investigating the problem and exploring solutions. The requirements might be documented with precision, or they could exist only in stakeholders' heads. Either way, without a clear and shared understanding of requirements, it's unlikely that the team will achieve its objectives.

The team will discover all (or at least most) of the customer's requirements eventually. It's cheaper and less painful to discover them early—before the team thinks the development work is complete—rather than late.

Many Types of Requirements

Exploring requirements is far more involved than simply asking users what they want. (See Lesson 11, "People don't simply gather requirements.") The first challenge is that not everyone has the same idea of what a *requirement* is. The software

7

literature contains numerous definitions; this one is broadly inclusive (Wiegers and Beatty 2013):

> A statement of a customer need or objective, or of a condition or capability that a product must possess to satisfy such a need or objective. A property that a product must have to provide value to a stakeholder.

The term *requirements* encompasses numerous categories of information; several are defined in Table 2.1 (Wiegers and Beatty 2013, IIBA 2015). Software practitioners don't uniformly agree on what to call each type of information. What you call them is less important than recognizing the need to explore, record, and communicate these diverse classes of information to the people whose work depends on them.

Concisely put, business requirements describe *why* the organization is undertaking a project. User requirements describe *what* users will be able to do with the product. Functional requirements tell developers *what* to build. Aligning business, user, and functional requirements is an essential component of planning for success.

Table 2.1 *Several types of requirements information*

Requirement Category	Brief Definition
Business	Business objectives or goals that led to initiating the project. May be recorded in a vision and scope document, project charter, or business case.
User	Descriptions of activities, tasks, or goals that users must be able to accomplish with the product. Typically represented in the form of use cases or user stories. Sometimes generalized to *stakeholder* requirements, which encompasses a broader scope of needs beyond product usage.
Solution	Descriptions of the capabilities and qualities of a solution that meets the stakeholder requirements.
Functional	Descriptions of behaviors the product must exhibit under specified conditions. The bulk of the solution requirements are functional requirements. Developers implement code to satisfy functional requirements, which align with enabling specific user requirements.
Nonfunctional	An aspect of solution requirements that most commonly refers to quality and operational characteristics the product must exhibit, also called *quality attributes*.
External Interface	Descriptions of connections between the product and the outside world, including users, other software systems, hardware devices, and communication mechanisms.
Transition	Requirements that describe conditions the product must meet or activities that must be performed to enable a successful migration from a current state to a future state.

The core of requirements knowledge is a set of product—or solution—requirements that describe the product's features, functional behaviors, and characteristics. Projects often have additional transition requirements, which describe activities the project must complete beyond building the product itself (IIBA 2015). Examples of transition requirements include creating and delivering training materials, creating documentation for product certification, writing support documentation, migrating data, and other actions needed to help users move from the current state to a future state that includes the system.

Subdomains of Requirements Engineering

We can divide the broad domain of requirements engineering into the major subdomains of requirements development and requirements management. These subdomains encompass the five major sets of activities identified in Table 2.2 (Wiegers and Beatty 2013). Software teams don't perform the various requirements development activities sequentially. They are incremental and interwoven.

One of the central challenges of software requirements engineering is to ensure that the team understands and addresses the real problem, which might differ from the problem the customer initially presents. Customers often present solution ideas instead of needs. Those solution ideas can mask the actual problem and lead to implementing a solution that misses the mark.

Table 2.2 *Subdomains of requirements engineering*

Subdomain	Activity	Description
Requirements Development	Elicitation	Activities to discover and understand customer needs and the solution requirements needed to satisfy those needs.
	Analysis	Activities to reach a clear and rich understanding of requirements, refine them to an appropriate level of detail, prioritize them, and reveal relationships among them.
	Specification	Activities to represent requirements knowledge, store it, and communicate it to affected stakeholders.
	Validation	Activities to confirm that a solution that satisfies the specified requirements also will meet customer needs.
Requirements Management		Activities to track the status of requirements during development, respond to requirement changes, and trace requirements to subsequent development products.

Unlike most software work, requirements work is less about technical computing and more about interpersonal communication. Because requirements development is challenging, it's not realistic to expect every project team member to be fully proficient at it. Many organizations develop a cadre of people who are highly skilled at requirements activities: trained and experienced business analysts (BAs), product managers, or—on projects using agile development approaches—product owners. The term *business analyst* has largely replaced other terms for people who perform requirements functions on information technology (IT) projects, such as *requirements engineer, requirements analyst, systems analyst,* and simply *analyst*. Unless the role distinction is significant, I'll use *business analyst* to refer to whoever is conducting requirements activities on a project, regardless of their job title or other responsibilities.

> Unlike most software work, requirements work is less about technical computing and more about interpersonal communication.

The Business Analyst Role

In recent years, the importance of business analysis as a specialized project role has been recognized through the establishment of professional organizations, such as the International Institute of Business Analysis or IIBA (www.iiba.org). These organizations have developed bodies of knowledge and certification programs (IIBA 2015). Even if a project team doesn't include a dedicated BA, other team members who work with stakeholders to understand requirements and define solutions do perform the BA role.

Skillful BAs uncover the real stakeholder needs and craft specifications to guide the work of designers, developers, testers, and others. A dedicated BA has the system- or enterprise-level view necessary to evaluate requirements in a broad business context. When customers communicate their needs directly to developers, both parties have only a siloed view of the system from their limited perspectives. The BA offers a higher-level view that spans all the developers and their customers.

Different organizations task their BAs to perform various project functions. The BA typically leads requirements development and management activities for the project. They guide discussions with user representatives to elicit requirements through a variety of activities. Knowledgeable stakeholders provide most of the input, and the BA organizes, records, and disseminates the information.

Requirements Are Foundational

Requirements serve as the foundation for all projects. There's no single "right" way to handle requirements. Software development projects can choose among numerous life cycles and development models, which advocate various ways to represent requirements. The essential point is that developers need the same information to correctly build the right software regardless of the project team's development approach. (See Lesson 6, "Agile requirements aren't different from other requirements.") Not all project teams create written requirements specifications. Nonetheless, they all accumulate requirements knowledge of various kinds and store it in some container, which I'll call a requirements document or a set of requirements for convenience.

Several of my consulting clients have asked me, "How do companies that are really good at requirements handle them?" My answer is, "I don't know; they don't call me." It's hard to learn what organizations that have mastered the requirements process do unless they share their experiences through publications or presentations. I've also had more than one client tell me, "You're here because the pain has become too great." More often than not, shortcomings in requirements are a major cause of that pain.

All project teams should take requirements seriously, adopting and adapting established requirements engineering techniques to suit their project's nature and team culture. Software teams that neglect requirements increase their risk of project failure. I've been interested in improving how software and systems development projects handle their requirements since about 1985. This chapter describes sixteen valuable lessons I've learned in that time.

First Steps: Requirements

I suggest you spend a few minutes on the following activities before reading the requirements-related lessons in this chapter. As you read the lessons, contemplate to what extent each of them applies to your organization or project team.

1. List requirements-related practices that your organization is especially good at. Is information about those practices documented to remind team members about them and make it easy to apply them?

2. Identify any problems—points of pain—that you can attribute to short-comings in how project teams deal with their requirements.

3. State the impacts that each problem has on your ability to complete projects successfully. How do the problems impede achieving business success for both the development organization and its customers? The problems could lead to tangible and intangible costs from unplanned rework, schedule delays, product support and maintenance, uncomplimentary product reviews, and customer dissatisfaction.

4. For each problem from Step 2, identify the root causes that trigger the problem or make it worse. Some root causes are internal to the project team or organization; others arise from sources outside the team that are beyond your control. Problems, impacts, and root causes can blur together, so try to tease them apart and see their connections. You might find multiple root causes that contribute to the same problem or several problems that arise from a single root cause.

5. As you read this chapter, list any practices that would be useful to your team.

| Lesson 1 | If you don't get the requirements right, it doesn't matter how well you execute the rest of the project. |

A business analyst at one of my consulting clients related an unfortunate project experience. Their IT department was building a replacement information system for use within their company. The development team believed that they already understood the system's requirements without obtaining any additional user input. They weren't arrogant, just confident. However, when the developers presented the completed system to the users, their reaction was, "But seriously, folks, where's our application?" The users rejected the system as completely unacceptable.

The development team was shocked; they thought they were working in good faith to build the right product. However, neglecting to engage with the users to ensure that the development team understood the requirements was a serious oversight.

When you proudly present your new baby to the world, you do not want to be told, "Your baby is ugly." But that's what happened in this case. So, what did the company do? They rebuilt the system, this time with adequate user input. (See Lesson 45, "Organizations never have time to build software right, yet they find the resources to fix it later.") That was an expensive lesson in the importance of customer involvement in getting the requirements right.

Whether you're building a new product or enhancing an existing one, requirements are the basis for all subsequent project work. Design, construction, testing, documentation, training, and migration from one system or operating environment to another all depend on having the right requirements. Numerous studies have found that effectively developing and communicating requirements are critical success factors for any project. Conversely, common contributors to troubled projects include inadequate project vision, incomplete and inaccurate requirements, and changing requirements and project objectives (PMI 2017). Getting the requirements right is core to ensuring that the solution aligns with the developing organization's product vision and business strategy (Stretton 2018). If you don't get the requirements right, you will fail.

Without high-quality requirements, stakeholders can be surprised at what the development team delivers. Software surprises are usually bad news.

The Right Requirements—But When?

I'm not saying that you need a complete set of requirements before you commence implementation. That's not realistic for any but the smallest and most stable products. New ideas, changes, and corrections will always come along that you must fold into your development plans. But for any portion of the system that you're building—whether it's a single development iteration, a specific release, or the full product—you need to have the requirements as nearly correct as possible. Otherwise, plan on performing rework after you think you're done. Agile projects use development iterations to validate the requirements that fed into the iteration. The further away those initial requirements are from what customers actually need, the more rework that will be needed.

Some people claim that you'll never get the requirements right. They say customers always think of more to add, there are always worthwhile changes to make, and the environment evolves continuously. That may be true, but I counter with, "In that case, you might never finish the project." From the perspective that there's always something you could add, you might never nail the requirements perfectly. But for the agreed-upon scope of a given development portion, you've got to get them right, or success will elude you.

The situation is a little different if you're building a highly innovative product. If no one has ever made anything like it before, you're unlikely to get it right on the first try. Your first attempt is essentially a plan to test hypotheses and determine the requirements through experimentation. Ultimately, though, your explorations will lead to an understanding of your novel product's capabilities and characteristics—its requirements.

The Right Requirements—But How?

There's no substitute for ongoing customer engagement to develop a set of accurate, clear, and timely requirements. (See Lesson 12, "Requirements elicitation must bring the customer's voice close to the developer's ear.") You can't just hold a workshop early on and then tell the customers, "We'll call you when we're done." Ideally, the team will have customer representatives available throughout the project. The team will have many questions to ask and points that require clarification. They'll need to elaborate high-level requirements from early explorations into appropriate detail at the right time. The team needs frequent feedback from users and other stakeholders to validate their understanding of requirements and the solutions they conceive.

It can be challenging to get customers to sign up for this extensive level of participation. They have their own work to do; their managers might not want some of their best people to spend a lot of time on the project. "You can go to a workshop or two," the manager might say, "but I don't want those software people interrupting you all the time with questions."

One way to sell the case for ongoing engagement is to point out problems the organization has experienced because of inadequate customer participation. Even better, cite local experiences where customer engagement paid off. Another persuasion technique is to propose a structured framework for the requirements engagement instead of leaving it completely open-ended. This framework might include some combination of informal discussions, elicitation workshops, requirements reviews, and working with screen sketches, prototypes, and incremental releases.

Customers are more likely to be excited about the project and willing to contribute if they see signs of tangible progress, such as through periodic releases of working software. They'll also be more enthusiastic if they see that their input truly influences the project's direction. It's sometimes a struggle to persuade users to accept new and replacement software systems. User representatives who worked with the IT team and understand the new system and its rationale can greatly smooth the transition.

I've worked with several customer representatives who had an outsize impact on the project's success. Besides providing input on requirements, some of them also provided user interface sketches and tests to verify that portions of the software were implemented properly. I can't overstate the contribution such committed customers made to help the development team get the requirements right and deliver the right solution.

Without high-quality requirements, stakeholders can be surprised at what the development team delivers. In my experience, software surprises are usually bad news. When they see the product, the reaction I want from my customers is, "Wow, Karl, this is better than I ever imagined. Thank you!" That's the kind of software surprise we can all live with.

Lesson 2	The key deliverables from requirements development are a shared vision and understanding.

The tangible output from requirements development is a record of the findings in some persistent form. That form is often a written document, commonly called a software requirements specification, business requirements document, or market requirements document. Alternatively, you could represent requirements in the form of index cards, sticky notes on a wall, diagrams, acceptance tests, prototypes, or combinations of these. All of those artifacts are useful deliverables.

The most significant requirements development outcome, though, is a shared understanding and agreement among stakeholders regarding the solution the project team will deliver. That understanding provides a reality check on whether the project's proposed scope and budget align with the solution's needed features and characteristics.

Expectation management is an important aspect of project management. Requirements development strives to craft a shared expectation—a common vision—among the project stakeholders regarding the solution. The requirements artifacts mentioned earlier communicate the specifics of the agreement. That vision aligns all project activities (Davis 2005):

- The work that the project sponsor is funding
- The solution that customers expect will let them achieve their business objectives
- The software that testers verify
- The product that the marketing and sales teams are offering to the world
- The plans and task lists that project managers and development teams create

It's hard to determine whether multiple people share a common understanding of something as complex as a software development project. I've been in meetings where a group of people reached some agreement, but later we realized that we understood certain aspects of the agreement—and hence the outcome—differently. Those differences could lead the participants to work at cross-purposes.

A vision statement provides a common strategic target toward which all project participants should direct their efforts.

A vision statement helps to achieve shared understanding and aligned expectations. I've used the following vision keyword template to focus the thinking of project stakeholders (Wiegers and Beatty 2013, Moore 2014):

For	[target customers]
Who	[statement of the business need or opportunity]
The	[name of the product or project]
Is	[type of product or project]
That	[major product capabilities; core benefits it will provide; compelling reason to buy the product or undertake the project]
Unlike	[current business reality or alternative products]
Our product	[concise summary of the major advantages of this product over the current reality or the competition]

As a simple example, following is the vision statement I wrote for a website that I built to support a book I wrote. Even though that tiny project was all in my brain, writing a vision statement at the outset brought clarity to what I hoped to accomplish with the website.

> For readers who are interested in the book *Pearls from Sand*, PearlsFromSand.com is a website that will provide information about the book and its author, allow site visitors to buy copies in various formats, and facilitate building a community of people interested in sharing their life lessons. Unlike websites that merely describe and promote a book, PearlsFromSand.com will allow visitors to contribute their own life lessons and to read and comment on life lessons posted by others.

If your project doesn't have a vision statement, it's never too late to write one. In the training classes I teach on software requirements, I ask the students to write a vision statement for their current project using this keyword template. I'm always impressed by the concise summaries they generate in only five minutes. I can quickly understand what the projects are about from their vision statements.

When several people from a project team take a class together, sometimes their vision statements have significant differences. I suggest that multiple stakeholders who represent diverse perspectives write vision statements separately. Comparing those statements reveals whether the stakeholders share a common understanding, at the top level, of where the project is heading. Disconnects suggest that team members need to work on aligning their expectations.

A consultant friend had precisely that experience on a client project. She said: "I asked the four major stakeholders to write their own vision statements while we were all in the same room. The results were highly varied and incompatible in some ways. It's better to find that out early on."

A vision statement provides a common strategic target toward which all project participants should direct their efforts. If the vision changes during the course of the project, the project sponsor must communicate those changes to everyone affected so that they retain a common focus. A vision statement doesn't replace requirements analysis and specification. It provides a reference point to ensure that the team's solution requirements align to achieve that vision and, consequently, success.

Lesson 3	Nowhere more than in the requirements do the interests of all the project stakeholders intersect.

Consultant and author Tim Lister defines project success as "meeting the set of all requirements and constraints held as expectations by key stakeholders." This statement implies that a project team must identify its stakeholders and determine how to engage with them to understand those requirements and constraints.

A *stakeholder* is any individual or group that is actively involved in a project, is affected by the project, or can influence the project's direction. The relationships between stakeholders and the project span a broad spectrum. Some stakeholders simply have the project outcome imposed on them; others profoundly shape the requirements. And there will be someone who can change the project's direction or even terminate it.

A stakeholder is any individual or group that is actively involved in a project, is affected by the project, or can influence the project's direction.

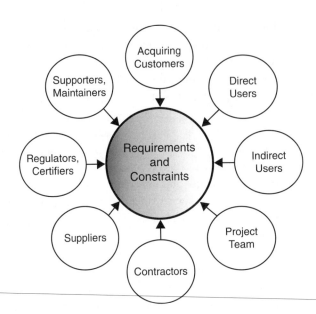

Figure 2.1 *Multiple stakeholders present requirements the project must satisfy and constraints it must respect.*

Stakeholders can be internal to the project team, internal to the developing organization, or external to the organization. Figure 2.1 shows some typical stakeholder communities that most software projects need to consider. There could be others, depending on the product category: corporate information system, commercial software app, government system, or a physical product that contains embedded software.

Stakeholder Analysis

The project team should cast a wide net early on to identify potential stakeholder groups. Don't be surprised if you generate a frighteningly long list. It will take some work to identify and understand your stakeholders. However, that's much better than overlooking a critical community and having to make adjustments late in the project.

End users and customers who acquire products for others to use are core sources of product requirements. A customer who specifies, selects, or pays for a product doesn't always use it—and might have misconceptions about what the user community needs to do their job. Many products have a diverse array of end users. To simplify requirements exploration, group your users into *user classes* that have distinct sets of needs (Wiegers and Beatty 2013). Users might not even be humans, but rather hardware devices or other software systems that interface with yours. You'll need to identify people who can provide requirements on behalf of those nonhuman components.

We usually think of *direct users* who will interact with the product hands-on, but you might also have *indirect users*. Indirect users could provide data that feeds into an information system, or they might receive the system's outputs even if they don't generate those outputs themselves. I was involved with a corporate project metrics system that consolidated data from dozens of projects and produced monthly reports that were distributed to many managers. Those managers were indirect users—they didn't touch the metrics application itself. As the audience for the system's reports, though, they were core stakeholders.

A colleague described an indirect user succinctly: "Your customer once removed is still your customer." To identify indirect users, you'll need to go out one or two layers beyond the application's immediate context to see what groups of people and other systems require representation. Also, identify disfavored user classes that you *don't* want using the system, such as hackers. They aren't stakeholders—they won't provide requirements or constraints—but you need to anticipate and thwart their evil intentions.

Consider the following questions about each stakeholder group you identify.

Who are they? Describe each stakeholder group so that all project participants understand who they are. Stakeholder descriptions might be reusable across several of the organization's projects.

How interested are they? Think about how strongly the project's outcome will affect the group and how much involvement they want with the project. You'll need to learn about each stakeholder group's expectations, interests, concerns, constraints, and fears.

What influence do they have over the project? Determine what decisions each stakeholder can and cannot make. Which groups hold the greatest power over the project? What are their attitudes and priorities? You'll particularly need to engage those groups that have both high interest in and a high degree of control over the project (Lucidchart 2021).

Who would be the best people to talk to? Identify appropriate representatives of each community with whom to work. They should be sources of definitive information.

Where are they? Elicitation is an iterative process that requires multiple encounters. It will be easiest to gather input from a stakeholder group if you have direct access to individual members. If you don't, you'll need to establish long-distance communication mechanisms and protocols.

What do I need from them? Determine the information, decisions, and data you'll need from each group. This understanding will help you choose the best ways to get that information at the right time. For user classes, you'll need to understand their user requirements—the things the product must let them do—and their quality expectations. Some stakeholder groups will impose constraints the project team must respect. Constraints could fall into several categories, including the following:

- Financial, schedule, and resource limitations
- Applicable policies, regulations, and standards (business rules)
- Compatibility with other products, systems, or interfaces
- Legal or contractual restrictions
- Certification requirements
- Limitations in the product's capabilities (that is, functionality *not* to include)

What do they need from me? Some stakeholders merely need to be informed about significant issues that affect them, so you'll have to know what project information is relevant for each group. Others might need to review the requirements to ensure that they don't clash with pertinent policies or restrictions. Work with your stakeholders to understand what they expect from you, just as you communicate your expectations to them. A big part of successful collaboration is to build and maintain mutual trust through effective communication.

How and when should I engage with them? Once you understand which stakeholder representatives you can interact with, consider the best ways to work with them to exchange the information you both need. If you can't access real representatives of a particular user class, consider creating *personas*, imaginary people to serve as stand-ins for the real human beings (Cooper et al. 2014).

Which stakeholders are most important when resolving conflicts? When resolving conflicting requirements and making priority decisions, assess which outcome aligns most strongly with the project's business objectives. Certain user classes may be favored over others; meeting their needs contributes more to business success than satisfying requirements from other user classes. Use early stakeholder analysis to understand these priority impacts instead of waiting until you confront your first conflict.

Who Makes the Call?

Identifying the decision makers helps to lay the foundation for a successful project. In some cases, the decision maker could be a single person, such as the project sponsor or product owner. That's the most efficient method, provided the individual has the information to make appropriate decisions and is accessible to make them quickly when needed. More often, you'll need to identify the right group of people to make each category of decisions. Group decisions take longer to resolve, but they better reflect a composite set of interests toward achieving the project's objectives.

Those responsible for making decisions that span multiple stakeholder communities should base their decisions on the project's business objectives. Objectives, a vision statement, project constraints, and other business requirements typically are recorded in a project's vision and scope document or a project charter (Wiegers 2007, Wiegers and Beatty 2013). A project without clear business requirements has little basis for making—and justifying—significant decisions.

We're All on the Same Side Here

It's not always possible to thrill all stakeholders with a project's outcome. Tensions between stakeholders can devolve into an adversarial situation, with people working at cross-purposes to protect their interests. Building a collaborative relationship with your key stakeholders goes a long way toward achieving project success. Since you might have to work with those same people in the future, it pays to establish communication pathways and mutual respect from the beginning.

Lesson 4	A usage-centric approach to requirements will meet customer needs better than a feature-centric approach.

One of our internal corporate users asked my team to add a new feature to an application his group used. He stressed how necessary the feature was, so we dutifully built in the capability. To the best of our knowledge, though, no one ever used that feature. I wouldn't have been very receptive to that customer's next request for an enhancement.

There's folklore in the software industry that—depending on the source you read—50 percent to 80 percent of software features are rarely or never used (The Standish Group 2014). Regardless of the exact figures, considerable delivered software functionality does provide little value to end users. Does your personal usage fully exploit every application's features? Mine doesn't. I've written numerous books and many articles using Microsoft Word, yet Word has many features I've never touched and never will. The same is true for other apps I use. Unless I'm an anomaly (which is always a possibility), the software industry puts considerable effort into delivering rarely used features that sit idle, patiently waiting for someone to call on them.

Why the Excess Functionality?

Focusing requirements explorations on features—the product itself—contributes to this proliferation of dormant functionality. Soliciting an open-ended list of functions from customers invites feature bloat. A feature-centric perspective can also lead to a product that seems to have the right capabilities yet doesn't let users accomplish their tasks.

I recommend shifting requirements conversations away from the product itself and toward what users need to do with the product. We change the emphasis from functionality to usage, from the solution to the need. A usage-centric strategy helps the BA and the development team quickly understand the user's context and objectives. From that knowledge, the BA can better identify what capabilities a solution must have, for whom, why, and when.

Both feature- and usage-centric approaches lead to identifying the functional requirements that developers must implement. However, focusing on usage helps ensure that we include all the functionality users need to perform their tasks. It reduces the problem of building excess functionality that seems like a good idea but doesn't help users achieve specific goals. The usage-centric perspective enhances usability because developers can thoughtfully integrate each bit of functionality into a task flow or a user objective (Constantine and Lockwood 1999).

I recommend shifting requirements conversations away from the product itself and toward what users need to do with the product.

Putting Usage First

Usage-centric requirements exploration involves a small but significant shift in the questions a BA might ask during an elicitation activity. Rather than asking, "What do you want?" or "What do you want the system to do?" the BA asks, "What do you need to do with the system?" The resultant conversation identifies tasks or goals the users need to accomplish with the help of the system.

Use cases are a good way to represent those tasks (Kulak and Guiney 2004). Users generally don't launch an app to use a particular feature; they launch an app to accomplish an objective. Each time I open my business accounting software, I have one or more goals in mind. Maybe I want to reconcile my credit card, transfer funds to my personal bank account, pay a bill, or record a deposit. Each of those goals is a use case—literally, a case of usage. I open the app with that intent in mind, and I follow a sequence of steps that invokes the functionality needed to accomplish the task. If all goes well, I complete my objective successfully and close the app— mission accomplished.

Use cases are appealing for several reasons. They're a natural way for user representatives to think about their needs. It's hard for users to articulate just the right set of functionality for a product, but it's easy for them to talk about usage scenarios from their daily lives. Use cases provide a structured way to organize descriptions of related functionality. A use case template has slots in which you can record information to provide as rich—or as slender—a use case description as your team finds valuable (Wiegers and Beatty 2013). The related functionality includes a description of the most typical or default interaction sequence for the task (the normal flow) and any variations on that typical sequence (alternative flows). The BA or developers will deduce the functionality the solution must provide so that users can perform those tasks. A proper use case description also identifies error conditions that could arise and defines how the system should handle them (exception flows).

Usage-centric analysis aids prioritization. The highest-priority functional requirements are those that enable the highest-priority user tasks. Some use cases will be more important and timelier than others, so implement those first. Within a single use case, the normal flow takes top priority, along with its accompanying exceptions. The alternative flows will have lower priorities and often can be implemented later, or perhaps never. An operational profile assessment can help you determine which use cases are performed most frequently and should have the highest priority. (See Lesson 15, "Avoid decibel prioritization when deciding which features to include," for more about operational profiles.)

Putting yourself in the user's shoes leads to better user experience designs. It can provide insights about limitations of an implementation that you might not get from a product- or feature-centric mindset. If users can't do what they need to do with the product or they don't enjoy using it, adding more features won't increase their satisfaction.

A User Story Concern

Many agile project teams record requirements in the form of user stories. According to agile expert Mike Cohn (2004), "A user story describes functionality that will be valuable to either a user or purchaser of the system or software." User stories generally are written according to a simple template:

As a <type of user>, I want to <perform some task> so that I can <achieve some goal>.

or

As a <type of user>, I want < some goal> so that <some reason>.

User stories are intended to be brief placeholders that remind team members to have conversations to fill in missing details shortly before implementing the story.

One concern I have with user stories is that they possess no intrinsic organizational scheme. Merely collecting a bunch of user stories, even if they were written following this pattern, is not much different from the age-old elicitation method of asking users, "What do you want?" You get many significant but random bits of information, all mixed up together, along with extraneous content.

One large project collected several thousand user stories from many stakeholders on yellow sticky notes. Some of the user stories were incomprehensible; many conflicted with other stories. Some looked like probable duplicates, and still others were tantalizingly suggestive but incomplete. The project had a big pile of unorganized information of many different kinds, all labeled as user stories. It was hard to tell from the pile which bits of functionality related to user tasks and aligned with the project's business objectives and which stories were just thoughts that people had contributed.

Some of these user stories were usage-centric; others were not. The stories spanned a wide spectrum of detail, size, and importance. They ranged from "As a user, I want the screen font to be sans-serif so that I can easily read it" to "As a payroll supervisor, I want the system to calculate state unemployment taxes for every state where we have employees so that we can pay the unemployment taxes correctly." Stories like these don't address users and their usage, but rather the system's features and properties.

Amassing an extensive collection of stories containing isolated functionality fragments requires that someone aggregate them from the bottom up to recognize themes related to user tasks. Organizing any pile of information from the bottom up is rather like assembling a jigsaw puzzle by picking up one piece at a time and saying, "I wonder where this piece goes." My brain works better when I take a top-down approach. I prefer to begin with broad strokes, like identifying user tasks, and then progressively refine and elaborate them into their details. I'm less likely to miss something significant that way, and it's less work than assembling the whole puzzle one isolated piece at a time.

On the surface, the simple user story template seems like a reasonable way to record user requirements. It's good to know which user class is requesting each bit of functionality so that you know whom to talk with to flesh out the story details at the right time. Deferring that exploration of details until the information is needed is an efficient way to allocate limited time. Statements written in this form can be usage oriented, describing a task and stating the goal the user wishes to achieve. However, author Raj Nagappan (2020a) points out some limitations of how people might misapply the user story pattern, such as by writing stories that focus more on solutions than on the problem, and the user story's deliberate lack of needed detail. An alternative is a *job story* template in the following form, which emphasizes the problem (situation) more clearly (Klement 2013):

When <situation>, I want to <perform some task>, so I can <achieve an outcome>.

Usage Rules!

I began taking a usage-centric approach to requirements development in 1994. I quickly recognized how focused and efficient it was compared to my previous elicitation approach. If properly written with a perspective on tasks and goals, use cases, user stories, and job stories all invite requirements participants to focus on how people will use the product instead of just its functional behaviors. Even if you take a lean approach, rather than fully populating a rich use case template, usage-centered thinking will lead to solutions that do a superior job of meeting customer needs.

Lesson 5	Requirements development demands iteration.

Early in my programming days, I would often begin coding with just a fuzzy notion of what I wanted the program to do. Sometimes I would begin to flail, writing and rewriting code, making lots of changes but little progress. I'd start to panic, knowing I was spinning my wheels. Eventually, I recognized the problem: I hadn't sufficiently thought through the program's requirements. My false starts resulted from iterating on the code, instead of iterating in my brain first; the latter is far faster. Once this light bulb came on, I always took the time to explore requirements carefully before diving into the source code editor. I never panicked while programming again.

Later, when I was writing software for other people, I would walk out of a customer discussion feeling that I understood what they had told me and that I had the information I needed to proceed. But as I worked with our initial requirements, questions came up and knowledge gaps revealed themselves. I often had to circle back to the customers to clarify issues, refresh my memory, and close those gaps. Sometimes they weren't happy to see me again, but we discovered that requirements development demands an iterative and incremental process.

Progressive Refinement of Detail

Once I appreciated the importance of understanding where I was headed before starting to code, I realized that I could never discover *all* of the requirements up front, even for a small application. Nor could I think of all the pertinent details for each requirement at the outset. But then I understood: that's okay. I didn't need all the details right away. I just needed enough knowledge to get my thinking started.

> You need to get enough accurate requirements information before you build each chunk of the product, or you're going to build it again.

Effective requirements development involves progressively refining your set of requirements, their details, and their clarity. You can't get all the requirements right with the first discussion. However, you do need to get enough accurate requirements information before you build each chunk of the product, or you're going to build it again. Here's a process I found to work well once the project's business requirements have been established.

Step 1.   Develop a preliminary list of user requirements (use cases or user stories). Learn enough about each to understand their scope, magnitude, and relative importance.

Step 2.   Allocate the user requirements to upcoming development cycles based on their priority. Some are up first; others can wait.

Step 3.   Further elicit and refine the details of those requirements that are planned for the upcoming development cycle, deriving functional requirements from the user requirements.

Step 4.   Reprioritize—including any new requirements that have come to your attention—and then move down the priority list as development continues.

Step 5.   Return to Step 2 and continue.

Ongoing prioritization is essential because there's little value in delving into the details of requirements whose implementation isn't imminent. As the project goes on, some anticipated needs may be deferred into the far future or disappear entirely. As Mike Cohn (2010) points out, "Teams should be careful to make sure there is a real need to better understand an item before putting more early effort into it than would otherwise be warranted...."

Emergent Functional Requirements

As people use a software application, they get ideas: "Wouldn't it be nice if..." or "What if I could...." Maybe a user thinks of an easier way to perform some action or discovers that, while performing action A, they'd like to drop into action B briefly. If those ideas are important enough, you'll need to modify the system to incorporate them. Those bits of functionality that you can't identify in advance are *emergent requirements* (Cohn 2010). Regardless of the development life cycle you're following, project plans must accommodate this natural—and beneficial—requirements growth.

Now, this doesn't mean we need to build a complete system—or even a complete iteration—based on what we already know and then patch in all the extra functionality that pops up. We can use various techniques to reveal some of these emergent requirements. One approach is to create multiple views of requirements. Instead of only writing use cases, functional requirements, or user stories, draw some pictures. Visual analysis models describe requirements at a higher level of abstraction that lets people step back from the details and see a bigger picture of workflow and interconnections.

Writing tests looks at requirements from a different angle. Tests define how to tell whether a system functions as we expect. Writing tests involves a different thought process from describing how we expect the system to behave under certain conditions. If we conceive tests early on, we'll find ambiguities and errors in our requirements and discover missing requirements, such as unhandled exceptions. We might even realize that we don't need certain requirements if we can't think of any tests that demand their existence. The concept of early test thinking was the foundation of the agile approach of test-driven development (Beck 2003).

Prototypes are a powerful way to bring requirements to life. They put in front of users something more tangible than a list of functional requirements or a stack of story cards. Prototypes can be simple or elaborate, conceptual or precise, paper or executable (Wiegers and Beatty 2013). Iterative prototyping advances the requirements conversation and helps users find requirements errors and omissions before you've invested much effort in building the product. See Lesson 17, "Design demands iteration," for more about prototyping.

Emergent Nonfunctional Requirements

As with functionality, parameters for some nonfunctional requirements also are hard to specify early on. Precisely what levels of availability, reliability, or usability does the application need? Plan on some learning cycles to home in on quantifiable, realistically achievable, and cost-effective target values for each significant quality attribute.

For instance, don't expect a meaningful answer the first time you ask some user, "What are your usability requirements?" You'll start with the basic understanding that usability is important. Over time, you'll extend that into understanding the various pertinent aspects of usability and ultimately determine each of those usability aspects' target goals. With quality attributes, though, the trick is to get sufficient information early enough that the team can make architectural decisions to achieve each attribute's objectives. It's a lot easier to paste in new functionality than to remedy foundational architectural flaws. (See Lesson 20, "You can't optimize all desirable quality attributes.")

Developing a useful set of requirements of any kind requires the patience to iterate, progressively acquiring more knowledge at the appropriate time so that developers can build the right product. I don't know of any shortcuts.

Lesson 6	Agile requirements aren't different from other requirements.

Many software organizations use agile development methods on at least some of their projects. Business analysts and product owners sometimes use the term *agile requirements* to describe their work (Leffingwell 2011). This term implies that an agile project's requirements are somehow qualitatively different from those for projects following other life cycles. In my opinion, they are not (Wiegers and Beatty 2016).

A developer needs the same information to correctly implement the right functionality no matter what development process the project uses.

The critical point is that a developer needs the same information to correctly implement the right functionality no matter what development or project management process the project uses. Agile and traditional projects handle requirements differently in various respects. Nonetheless, most established requirements engineering and business analysis practices are useful on agile projects when thoughtfully applied.

Agile approaches strive to adapt to the inevitable change that occurs, rather than imagining that all requirements can be well understood early on and remain stable throughout the project. However, all projects require the same fundamental requirements activities. Someone still needs to analyze stakeholders, elicit requirements from various sources, and validate that a solution based on those requirements will achieve the project's business objectives. The major differences between how agile and traditional projects handle requirements activities fall into several categories.

Roles and Responsibilities

Most traditional project teams include one or more dedicated BAs who perform or lead the project's requirements elicitation, analysis, specification, validation, and management activities. Many agile projects lack an official BA role. Instead, a product owner defines the project's scope and boundaries, creates and maintains the *product backlog* of pending work, and gets the user stories ready to be implemented (Cohn 2010, McGreal and Jocham 2018). Requirements development is a collaborative process that includes the product owner, suitable user representatives, and other stakeholders. (See Lesson 12, "Requirements elicitation must bring the customer's voice close to the developer's ear.") Developers, not BAs, are responsible for ensuring that the stories contain enough information before accepting them for development.

Terminology

Traditional project teams generally employ use cases and functional requirements. Instead of talking about requirements, most agile teams refer to user stories, epics (high-level features or tasks that are broken down into smaller user stories), acceptance tests, and other product backlog items, all of which represent pending work (Cohn 2004). But it's the same requirements knowledge, by any name. No matter how you represent it or what you call it, the team must produce and communicate that knowledge so that everyone can do their jobs effectively.

Documentation Detail

Agile methods embrace the principles of lightweight and just-in-time documentation. Customers' close collaboration with developers on agile projects generally means that requirements need less detail here than they do on traditional projects. Stakeholders will develop the necessary precision when they need it, through conversations and appropriate documentation. Certain user stories might have little detail provided. Risky, complex, or high-impact functionality might be elaborated into more detail.

However, relying primarily on verbal communication poses risks. Our memories are incomplete, inconsistent, and impermanent. People come and go on project teams. And, of course, the system continues to exist long after the initial development work is done. Someone must maintain it, update it, provide production support (sometimes in the middle of the night), and eventually decommission it. Each project team needs to create sufficient documentation to manage those issues without wasting time recording information that no one will use. (See Lesson 7, "The cost of recording knowledge is small compared to the cost of acquiring knowledge.")

Activity Timing

Starting with a broad exploration of requirements at a high level of abstraction lets you do some initial estimation, prioritization, and sequencing in any software development approach. Traditional approaches aim to create a fairly complete requirements specification early in the project. That works fine in some situations; it fails miserably in others.

In contrast, agile teams plan to generate the requirements details just before implementing a particular bit of functionality. This method reduces the risk of the information being obsolete or the requirement being unnecessary when developers and testers act on it. As shown in Figure 2.2, stakeholders and the product owner perform some initial elicitation and analysis. The product owner then allocates user stories and other backlog items to specific iterations for implementation. The product owner, developers, and customers will further clarify each story's details through the usual requirements development activities, creating no more written documentation than necessary. The team will continue to accept and implement requirements throughout the project.

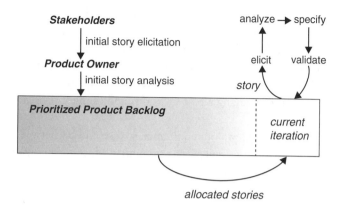

Figure 2.2 *Requirements activities occur within each agile iteration.*

A just-in-time approach reduces unnecessary effort, but that makes it harder to recognize requirement dependencies and architectural implications that should be addressed early to facilitate stable product growth. To mitigate the risk of a flawed architecture, agile teams should look at the broad scope in early iterations and consider what major architectural decisions might be necessary. Similarly, the team should begin exploring nonfunctional requirements early so that the design achieves critical performance, availability, and other quality goals that span the product.

Deliverable Forms

At the top level, user stories are analogous to use cases. The distinction is in how thoroughly you detail them and whether you record the information. The BA on a traditional project might work from use cases to develop a set of functional requirements. Many agile project teams flesh out each user story's specifics by writing acceptance criteria and tests that will indicate whether developers correctly implemented the story. If your project uses tests to represent requirements details, then as you read the other lessons about requirements in this chapter, think about how they might apply to your tests.

In reality, functional requirements and their corresponding tests are alternative ways to represent the same information. Requirements specify what to build; tests describe how to tell whether the system behaves as expected. Writing *both* requirements and tests provides a powerful combination. It works best when different people write requirements and tests from the same source of information, such as a use case.

Every time I've created and compared those two requirements views, I've found gaps, ambiguities, and interpretation differences. Correcting those errors during requirements exploration is far cheaper than finding them in the implemented software. An alternative strategy is to have developers record the user story details in the form of acceptance tests, which a tester then reviews. As with writing both requirements and tests, you're engaging a pair of brains and thought processes to look for problems.

If you create multiple views of requirements, disconnects between them reveal problems. If you create just a single view—no matter which technique you choose—you must trust it to be accurate.

When to Prioritize

Prioritization considers the relative value that each requirement contributes to the customer versus the effort, risk, and cost of implementing it. Traditional projects might prioritize requirements early and rarely look back. On an agile project, prioritizing the product backlog contents is an ongoing activity. You need to select which items go into upcoming iterations and which ones to ultimately discard from the backlog. The teams are always asking, "What's the most important thing to work on next?" In reality, all project teams, not just agile teams, ought to manage their remaining work priorities to deliver the maximum customer value as quickly as possible.

Is There Really a Difference?

For the most part, customers don't care how you build software applications. Customers just want the products to meet their needs, be efficient and easy to use and extend, and satisfy their other quality expectations. Most requirements development and management techniques that traditional projects employ are equally applicable to agile projects. As always, the team needs to adapt practices to best suit their objectives, culture, environment, and constraints.

In agile development, each bit of incremental change provides a stand-alone, usable piece of functionality. Your product is a system that you improve iteratively, learning from an unsuccessful change and rapidly pivoting to a better solution for that piece. Focusing on small requirements, each of which provides a complete, usable, small change, is a different analysis process than chopping a large, integrated solution into little just-in-time bites that fit into a development iteration.

The business analysis process is somewhat different on agile projects as well. While legacy BA techniques still apply—stakeholder and business rules analysis, process modeling, and many more—how you integrate them into an incremental agile process poses a challenge for many BAs (Podeswa 2021). As business analysis expert Howard Podeswa points out:

> Part of the transition is developing a new mindset. The BA role on an agile project is not as much about predetermining what will be done, but about continuously renegotiating during the development process. There's an ongoing assessment of what the work team should and should not do—the tradeoffs needed to maximize the delivered value.

Fundamentally, though, the requirements knowledge used on an agile project is not qualitatively different from that on a traditional project. Requirements development still boils down to discovering and clearly communicating the information to allow all project participants to build some portion of the right product well.

Lesson 7	The cost of recording knowledge is small compared to the cost of acquiring knowledge.

When I teach a requirements class, I ask whether any of the students ever had to reverse engineer information from an existing system to figure out how to modify it or add new functionality. Nearly everyone raises their hand. Then I ask whether they recorded what they learned for future reference. Few hands go up. That means if anyone has to go into that same part of the system in the future to make another change, they'll have to repeat the reverse-engineering process.

Recovering knowledge through reverse engineering is tedious. Doing it repeatedly is inefficient. If you write down what you learn, that information is available if you or anyone else needs to go back to it. This recording is a way to incrementally accumulate knowledge about an ill-documented system as you work on it. It nearly always takes less time to write down what you learned through reverse engineering than it took you to learn it.

I would decide *not* to record that newly recovered knowledge only if I were certain that no one—including myself—would ever need to work with that part of the system again. As I'm not skilled at predicting the future, I prefer to retain information in some shareable form. That's better than keeping it in my brain, where it will fade over time.

One of my consulting clients reverse engineered a full set of use cases from their poorly documented, mature flagship product. Then they developed a comprehensive set of test cases from those use cases, which allowed them to do thorough regression testing as the product continued to evolve. They found it was well worth their time to record that reverse-engineered knowledge.

Fear of Writing

Some people balk at taking the time to document requirements. But the hard part isn't writing requirements—it's figuring out what they are. Similarly, people are sometimes reluctant to write a project plan. Again, the hard part is thinking through all the activities needed to complete the project: identifying deliverables, tasks, dependencies, required resources, schedules, and so forth. Writing a plan is transcription. It takes time, yes. However, I argue that it takes less time than trying to verbally communicate the same information to multiple people in a consistent way throughout the course of the project. It's also less error-prone than everyone having to remember all that information accurately.

Perhaps teams that are reluctant to document their requirements are concerned about succumbing to analysis paralysis. A symptom of this trap is that requirements development seems to go on forever, yet construction cannot begin until the requirements are complete. Analysis paralysis is a potential risk, but good judgment will let you avoid it. Don't use the fear of paralysis as a rationale for not recording essential requirements information.

I once was the lead BA on the third team to undertake an essential corporate project. The two previous efforts had stalled out for some reason; I never learned why. When my fellow BAs and I asked the key customer whether we could talk with him about requirements, he resisted. "I gave my requirements to your predecessors," he said. "I don't have time to talk about requirements anymore. Build me a system!" That became our BA team's mantra: "Build me a system!"

Unfortunately, the previous teams hadn't documented any of the information they'd acquired. We had to start from scratch. Our customer wasn't happy, but he cooperated when we promised to use requirements techniques that we knew worked well and to write down what we learned. That project was highly successful. My company decided to outsource the system's implementation, and the contracting company found that our requirements provided a solid foundation for development. Had the first two teams recorded what they'd learned, we would have had a big head start on the project.

Benefits of Written Communication

Early in my software career, I led a project with two other developers. Two of us worked in the same building; the third sat a quarter-mile away. We didn't have a written project plan or requirements, though we had a good shared understanding of where we were heading. We met weekly to go over progress and plans for the next week. On two occasions, one developer walked out of our weekly meeting with a different interpretation of what we had decided than the other two of us held. He worked in the wrong direction for a week, and then he had to redo that work. It would have cost little for us to write down our plans and requirements as we went along to avoid wasting time like that. I never made that mistake again.

Agile teams following Scrum hold a brief meeting called the *daily scrum* to update status, identify impediments, and keep the team aligned on their project goal for the next twenty-four hours (Visual Paradigm 2020). That's easier to do when everyone is colocated or well connected electronically. However, even frequent touchpoints like a daily scrum don't retain any historical record and don't facilitate planning beyond the immediate future. If you're confident no one will ever need to revisit the decisions or information exchanged in a meeting, then there's no reason to record it. Otherwise, the time needed to document those useful bits of knowledge is a modest investment.

If every project stakeholder were privy to every discussion, interpreted information identically, and had a perfect memory, you'd never need to write anything down. Alas, this is not reality. Documentation serves as a persistent group memory, a resource to which team members can refer across space and time (Rettig 1990). During a retrospective, project records can refresh participants' memories about what was intended and what actually happened. If people other than the original developers need to modify a product, good documentation can save them time.

Instead of waiting until users can see working software to provide useful feedback for developers, reviews of written requirements invite domain experts to spot problems before they're cast into code. Many projects invoke complex logic or business rules that are best represented in decision tables or mathematical formulas. Record that information in persistent forms so that you can validate its accuracy and completeness. That documentation feeds nicely into test design as well.

If someone has gone to the trouble of preparing documentation, it behooves those who work on the system to exploit that knowledge. One project team developed a good set of requirements, but the contract team brought in to implement the system ignored them. The contractors elected to talk to the users again about their needs, thereby annoying them and wasting time.

If every project stakeholder were privy to every discussion and had a perfect memory, you'd never need to write anything down.

One of my consulting clients hired a team of contract BAs who created multiple three-ring binders of requirements for a very large project. The company then brought in a second contract team to build the product. That implementation team saw the binders and said, "We don't have time to read all those requirements. We've got software to build!" So they built the system based on what they thought it ought to be. Then they built it again, based on the actual requirements that the earlier BA team had created. No matter how pressed you are for time, it will be quicker to learn from a good set of requirements than to build the product twice.

Sometimes it's in the developer's best interest to have certain information documented. For instance, if a team is writing software for an organization that hasn't documented its business rules, the software code that applies or enforces those rules becomes the definitive source of that business-level knowledge. The developer who implemented the code around those business rules then becomes the subject matter expert to whom the business must turn when policies change. People shouldn't have to extract business-level knowledge from a particular application's code in yet another reverse-engineering process.

A Sensible Balance

Documents have their benefits and their limitations. Even the best-written requirements can't replace human dialogue, but they certainly help. Writing something down doesn't guarantee that it's accurate, complete, or immutable. It does increase the chance that people who access the information will reach the same understanding of it and can refresh their knowledge in the future. Documentation must be current, accurate, and accessible to those who need it. If readers can't readily find what they're seeking, it doesn't matter how good the documentation is.

Some people misinterpret the agile development philosophy and resist creating documentation. The Manifesto for Agile Software Development states, "We have come to value...working software over comprehensive documentation" (Beck et al. 2001). It does not state, "We don't need no stinkin' documentation." Agile expert Mike Cohn (2010) points out the shortcomings of written documents but advises, "Don't throw out the baby with the documentation":

> These weaknesses of written communication are not to say we should abandon written requirements documents—absolutely not. Rather, we should use documents where appropriate.... The goal in agile development is to find the right balance between documentation and discussion. In the past we've often been skewed way too far toward the side of documents.

Cohn's advice suggests that BAs, project managers, product owners, and developers should create written documentation judiciously. They should record information at an appropriate—not necessarily minimal—level of detail. When details are known and precision is necessary, write it down. This approach is more realistic than attempting to cast in stone volatile or preliminary information that someone must maintain over time. And it's safer than relying totally on people's memories.

With experience, you learn that the world is drawn in shades of gray. In almost any situation, any extreme position is silly. The two extremes of either writing every piece of project information in great detail or having no written documentation are both silly. If you remember that it's less expensive to record knowledge than to discover—or rediscover—it, you can decide what information is worth writing down.

Lesson 8	The overarching objective of requirements development is clear and effective communication.

Software development is partly about computing and partly about communication. Requirements engineering, though, is entirely about communication. In general, we're better at the technical side of software development than the human side. Those team members who lead requirements activities—who I'm calling business analysts, regardless of their job title—sit at the hub of a project communication network, as shown in Figure 2.3. They coordinate the exchange of requirements knowledge among all project participants.

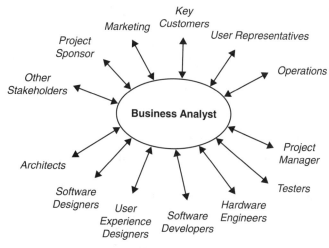

Figure 2.3 *The business analyst coordinates the communication of requirements knowledge among all project participants.*

The communication links in Figure 2.3 are all two-way arrows. Some participants primarily supply requirements input to the project from the customer domain: project sponsor, marketing, key customers, and user representatives. Other participants lie in the implementer domain and consume the requirements process outputs: architects, software and user experience designers, developers, and testers. If your product contains both software and hardware components, electrical and mechanical engineers also could be involved.

The BA must keep all participants informed about the body of requirements knowledge, priorities, status, and changes. Everyone could participate in requirements reviews; they'll see different kinds of issues from their diverse perspectives. Some people will make the many requirements-related decisions that every project faces. And everyone involved should contribute comments and ideas regarding the requirements to help the team reach and sustain a holistic understanding.

Multiple Audiences, Multiple Needs

The BA has a tough job. The other participants will communicate requirements input primarily verbally. The BA also might refer to documents, such as sources of business rules or information about related products. The BA must assess, classify, and record all that information in appropriate written forms. I say "written" because the BA needs to communicate the information back to the sources for verification and to those who will base their work on the requirements. With so many audiences who have diverse backgrounds and vocabularies, the BA must think carefully about the best ways to communicate with each of them. The people who receive requirements knowledge differ in several respects:

- What information they need to see
- When they need to see the information
- How much detail they need
- How they prefer to receive information
- How they want written information to be organized

Anyone who ever tried to create a single requirements deliverable that tells all project participants everything they need to know quickly learned that it's impossible to do. There are many kinds of requirements information, as we saw in Table 2.1. The BA must determine how to represent each type of information at the appropriate level of detail and organize it meaningfully for each audience.

The BA should ask the various audiences what information they need and how they want to receive it. For instance, developers and testers need the details about each requirement they work with, but the project sponsor doesn't care about those specifics. People who want only the broad strokes might favor pictures over words so that they don't get mired in details. A shared repository, such as a requirements management tool, can serve as the definitive location of requirements information for those who need all the specifics.

It helps to use standard templates for certain sets of information so that readers know where to find what they need. I've found templates for a vision and scope document, use case document, and software requirements specification particularly helpful (Wiegers and Beatty 2013). Document creators should work with the recipients of each deliverable to tailor a standard template that will best suit their needs. (See Lesson 57, "Adopt a shrink-to-fit philosophy with document templates.")

Document authors choose the vocabulary, level of detail, and organizational scheme that make sense to them. But maybe their choices aren't the most effective for some recipients. A senior systems engineer described the challenge of using language that speaks to the major requirements audiences:

> The implementer is the most critical customer of requirements because their interpretation of what they've read dictates what the product will be. A requirement written in the business customer's language might be full of terms and processes unfamiliar to the average implementer. The implementer will have a hard time understanding exactly what is being requested. Requirements are often written in the business customer's language to get contractual buy-off. Translating these perspectives into requirements that the implementer understands is an important step.

Consider creating a glossary so that everyone involved with the project shares the same understanding of relevant business terms, technical terms, abbreviations, and acronyms. A glossary can be reused across multiple projects in the same application domain, thereby enhancing consistency.

High-quality software development is based on high-quality requirements, crafted into usable forms and communicated to everyone who needs to know.

Choosing Representation Techniques

The most obvious way to represent requirements information is in natural language text. However, that gets bulky for a sizable system, whether you're writing requirements in a document, on index cards or sticky notes, or in a requirements management tool. Readers can get the details of the requirements, but it's hard to visualize an overview from all those details and see how the pieces fit together. Natural language is prone to ambiguity, fuzzy words that leave too much to the reader's imagination, and mistranslation. Still, natural language is how human beings communicate, so writing requirements that way is logical.

You can write requirements using various techniques. Some teams employ use cases and lists of functional requirements. Others rely on user stories, feature descriptions, and/or acceptance tests. The method you choose doesn't matter, provided the technique achieves the goal of clear and effective communication with the audience.

Of course, you're not limited to using natural language. You can supplement—though rarely fully replace—written requirements with different representations or views: visual models, prototypes, screen designs, tables, and mathematical expressions. Each view depicts part of what people need to know about requirements; combining multiple views provides a richer understanding (Wiegers 2006a). There are even formal requirements notations that can be proven to be correct, although they are rarely used other than on life-critical systems.

For those audiences who need only an overview, consider emphasizing diagrams rather than text. I took an excellent class on analysis and design modeling long ago that completely altered how I approached software development. Diagrams can illustrate process flows, data relationships, user interface navigation, system states and transitions between them, decision logic, and more. I enthusiastically incorporated visual modeling into my development practices.

To my disappointment, I soon learned that no single diagram could show everything I needed to know about a software system (Davis 1995). Instead, each model shows portions of system knowledge from a particular perspective. Business analysts have to choose appropriate models based on the information their audiences need to see.

Standard vocabularies and notations are central to clear communication. We can't work together if we don't share the same understanding of words and symbols. A consulting client once asked me to review a model that one of their BAs had drawn. I understood the diagram, but the BA had used some unconventional arrow notations. I had no idea what those arrows signified—there was no legend—or why they differed from the standard arrows used in other places.

Software methodologists have developed numerous standard notations for drawing analysis and design models, including these:

- Structured analysis (DeMarco 1979)
- IDEF0 (Feldmann 1998)
- Unified Modeling Language or UML (Booch et al. 1999)
- Requirements Modeling Language or RML (Beatty and Chen 2012)

I strongly advise using these, or other, standard models. Don't invent your personal notation unless you've concluded that no models exist that show what you want, which is unlikely. You'll need to educate the people who see the diagrams about how to read the notations; legends on the diagrams that explain the symbols used can help. Keep the models as simple as you can—focus on communicating clearly with your audience.

Can We Talk?

High-quality software development is based on high-quality requirements, elicited from the right people, crafted into usable forms, and communicated to everyone who needs to know. An effective BA is skilled at many forms of communication: listening, questioning, restating, writing, modeling, presenting, facilitating, and reading nonverbal cues. If you're functioning in the BA role, you'll need all these skills—plus the wisdom to know how and when to apply them—to unite all the project participants toward their common objective.

| Lesson 9 | Requirements quality is in the eye of the beholder. |

Just as beauty is in the eye of the beholder, so too is quality. Software requirements deliverables have an audience of people who will use them to do their parts of the project work, as well as representatives of customers who will receive or use the product. Those recipients—not the people who produce the deliverables—are the right ones to assess their quality.

If someone finds problems with my requirements, it doesn't matter how good I think they are.

I could create a set of requirements that seems perfect to me. It contains every-thing it should and nothing it shouldn't, the contents are organized logically, and all of the statements seem clear and understandable—to me. But if someone finds problems with my requirements, it doesn't matter how good I think they are. The creators (BAs) and recipients (architects, designers, developers, testers, and others) of these bodies of knowledge should agree on their contents, format, organization, style, and level of detail.

Many Requirements Beholders

The BA's challenge is that there are so many audiences for requirements information, as the previous lesson described. Those audience members have different notions of quality and what they want to see, because they use the information for different purposes. They come from diverse backgrounds, have differing perspectives, make various assumptions, and might prefer different communication mediums. This diversity makes it hard for a BA to meet everyone's needs.

A good way to tell whether your requirements are of high quality is to invite people who represent multiple reader perspectives to review them. (See Lesson 48, "Strive to have a peer, rather than a customer, find a defect.") Those review-ers will look for different kinds of problems. Table 2.3 lists some quality issues that various requirements audiences can look for in a review; they want to be able to answer "yes" to each question. The type of formal peer review called *inspection* is particularly good at finding certain classes of requirements errors (Wiegers 2002a). During an inspection, one participant describes each require-ment in their own words. The other participants can compare that interpretation to their understanding of the requirement. If the interpretations don't all match, they've found an ambiguity.

Requirements Quality Checklist

Business analysts should strive to build the following characteristics into their deliv-erables as they pursue high-quality requirements (Davis 2005, Wiegers and Beatty 2013).

- **Complete.** No requirements are missing. Each requirement includes all the information the reader needs to do their job. Any known omissions are flagged as TBD, To Be Determined. In practice, there's no way to be sure that you've found all the requirements. If you deliberately opt to write incomplete require-ments, expecting readers to acquire further details when needed, make sure the readers know that.

Table 2.3 *Some quality issues that different requirements readers can look for*

Requirements Reader	Some Quality Issues
Project Sponsor, Marketing, Key Customers	• Will a solution based on the requirements achieve our business objectives? • Do we understand the risks and business impacts associated with each requirement?
User Representative	• Do I understand each requirement? • Does each requirement accurately express a customer need? • Would a solution based on this set of requirements satisfy my needs? • Are all of the requirements necessary?
Project Manager	• Can the team construct a solution for the requirements with the available resources and within existing constraints? • Does the information provided for each requirement let me assess its complexity and impact on the project?
Business Analyst, Product Manager, Product Owner	• Does each requirement address customer value? • Are the requirements clear and unambiguous? • Is each requirement free from conflicts with others?
Designer, Developer, Hardware Engineer	• Do I understand each requirement? • Do the requirements contain, or point me to, all the information I need to design and build a solution? • Is a solution based on the requirements achievable both technically and with the resources and time available?
Tester	• Do I understand each requirement? • Are all exceptions identified and the ways to handle them described? • Can I think of ways to verify whether each requirement was implemented correctly?
Other Stakeholders	• Do the requirements respect all expectations and constraints that my perspective imposes?

- **Consistent.** A solution that satisfies any requirement should not be incompatible with any other requirement. Catching inconsistencies is difficult. It's hard to spot inconsistencies between different requirement types, such as a functional requirement that violates a business rule or clashes with a user requirement, if the two types of information are stored in different places.

- **Correct.** Each requirement accurately states a need expressed by a user or other stakeholder. Only the pertinent stakeholders can assess this characteristic.

- **Feasible.** Developers can implement a solution to address this requirement within known technical, schedule, and resource constraints.

- **Necessary.** Each requirement describes a capability or characteristic some stakeholder really needs.

- **Prioritized.** Requirements are classified as to their relative importance and the timeliness of their inclusion in the product.

- **Traceable.** Each requirement is uniquely identified so that it can be linked back to its origin and linked forward to designs, code, tests, and any other items created because of that requirement. Knowing each requirement's source adds context and shows whom to consult for clarification.

- **Unambiguous.** All readers will interpret each requirement in only one way and in the same way. If a requirement is ambiguous, you can't determine whether it is complete, correct, feasible, necessary, or verifiable, because you don't know precisely what it means. You can't remove all the ambiguities of natural language, but avoiding words like these can help: *best, etc., fast, flexible, for instance, i.e.* and *e.g., improved, including, maximize, optionally, several, sufficient, support,* and *usually* (Wiegers and Beatty 2013).

- **Verifiable.** There is some objective, unambiguous, and cost-effective way to determine whether the solution satisfies the requirement. Testing is the most common verification technique, so some people refer to this characteristic more narrowly as *testable.*

You're never going to create a perfect set of requirements. You don't need to, provided the project's development process includes mechanisms to quickly detect and rectify requirements errors before the team implements them. Soliciting feedback from the multiple requirements audiences helps you avoid excessive rework costs because of requirement defects.

Lesson 10	Requirements must be good enough to let construction proceed at an acceptable level of risk.

As I mentioned, you're never going to get a perfect set of requirements. Some requirements could be incomplete, incorrect, unnecessary, infeasible, ambiguous, or missing entirely. Requirements sometimes conflict with each other. But you still need to build software based on the available requirements information.

Practically speaking, your goal is to develop requirements that are *good enough* to allow the next development stage to proceed. It's a question of risk. You should invest enough effort into requirements development to reduce the risk of performing excessive unplanned rework because of requirements problems.

Unfortunately, no green light comes on when your requirements are good enough. It's hard for a BA to judge whether they've elicited all the pertinent requirements and stated them accurately. Yet, someone must decide when the next portion of the product's requirements provides a suitable foundation for construction. System architects, designers, and developers can help make this judgment.

Your goal is to develop requirements that are *good enough* to allow the next development stage to proceed.

Dimensions of Detail

Being good enough encompasses both the quantity of information presented and its quality. A minimal set of perfectly written requirements could lack details that developers and testers need, yet a comprehensive set of poorly written, inaccurate requirements is worthless. Requirements expert Alan Davis (2005) states the goal of requirements specification nicely: "To specify the desired behavior of the system, in sufficient detail that system developers, marketing, customers, users, and management are closely aligned in their interpretation." The key words here are *sufficient detail*. We can think of three dimensions of requirements completeness: the types of information included, the breadth of knowledge, and the depth of detail for each item.

- **Types of information.** Project participants naturally focus on the functionality that users need to accomplish their goals, but a useful set of requirements goes well beyond that. Developers also need to know about quality attribute requirements, design and implementation constraints, business rules, external interface requirements, and data types and sources. A simple collection of functional requirements or user stories isn't sufficient.

- **Breadth of knowledge.** This dimension encompasses the scope of requirements information contained in a specification. Does it include every user requirement known to be in scope or just the high-priority ones? Are all relevant quality attributes addressed or just those that are paramount? Would a reader know whether this is the complete spectrum of expectations or whether they'll need to close gaps? If it's not complete, will all readers see the same gaps? Implied and assumed requirements that no one writes down pose a high risk of being overlooked. (See Lesson 13, "Two commonly used requirements elicitation practices are telepathy and clairvoyance. They don't work.")

- **Depth of detail.** The third dimension addresses how much detail and precision is provided for each requirement. Do the requirements identify possible exceptions (errors) and specify how the system should handle them? Or do they cover only the happy paths of normal behavior? If the specification addresses a nonfunctional requirement such as installability, does it also cover uninstallation, reinstallation, repairing an installation, and installing updates and patches? Both functional and nonfunctional requirements must be precise enough to be verifiable in the implemented solution.

How Much Is Enough?

There's no single right answer to the question of how much information is enough in a given situation. However, anywhere that knowledge gaps exist, someone will have to close them. Part of deciding when the specified requirements are good enough is determining how much detail is needed, who will acquire it, and when. The Business Analysis Body of Knowledge from the IIBA contains a definition of solution requirements that states in part: "They provide the appropriate level of detail to allow for the development and implementation of the solution" (IIBA 2015). What constitutes "appropriate" is a judgment call whose interpretation will vary from person to person.

Many agile software development teams don't specify written requirements in detail, but that doesn't mean the developers and testers don't need those details. As we saw in Lesson 6, they do. If written information isn't available at implementation time, someone must track it down from the right source. Otherwise, the software team members must fill in the blanks themselves, possibly missing the mark from the customer's perspective. If that happens, the requirements weren't quite ready for prime time.

> **Lesson 11**   People don't simply gather requirements.

People often speak of gathering requirements on a software project, but this conveys an inaccurate impression. The word *gathering* suggests that the requirements are lying around out there somewhere, just waiting to be collected. When I hear someone say "gathering requirements," I conjure a mental image of picking flowers or hunting for Easter eggs. I'm afraid it's not that simple.

Gathering versus Elicitation

Requirements rarely exist fully formed in users' minds, ready to be passed on to a BA or development team on demand. Assembling a set of requirements does involve some collection, but it also involves discovery and invention. The term *requirements elicitation* more accurately conveys how software people collaborate with project stakeholders to explore how they work now and determine what capabilities a future software system should provide. Requirements experts Suzanne Robertson and James Robertson (2013) vividly refer to this process as "trawling for requirements":

> We use the term *trawling* to describe the activity of investigating the business. This term evokes the nature of what we are doing here: fishing. Not idly dangling a line while hoping a fish might come by, but rather methodically running a net through the business to catch every possible requirement.

According to *The American Heritage Dictionary of the English Language* (2020), elicitation means calling forth, drawing out, or provoking. The sense of calling forth and drawing out requirements describes the process better than merely *gathering*. (BAs aren't trying to provoke the stakeholders with whom they work, though I fear that happens inadvertently sometimes.) A big part of the BA's function during elicitation is to ask the right questions to stimulate the stakeholders' thinking and get beyond the superficial and obvious.

> When I hear "gathering requirements,"
> I conjure a mental image of picking flowers
> or hunting for Easter eggs. It's not that
> simple.

The least useful questions to ask when exploring requirements are "What do you want?" and "What are your requirements?" Such vague questions trigger a lot of random—yet important—input, blended with extraneous information and seasoned with unstated assumptions. A business analyst is not a mere scribe, writing down whatever stakeholders tell them. A skillful BA facilitates elicitation conversations, guiding the participants to discover the pertinent knowledge in a structured fashion.

The BA needs to analyze and organize the information collected—without the irrelevant bits—and then present it in useful forms to developers and other project participants.

When to Elicit Requirements

As we saw in Lesson 5, elicitation calls for an iterative and incremental approach with cycles of refinement, clarification, and adjustment. The discussions could move from fuzzy, high-level concepts into details, or they could begin with specific functionality fragments that the BA must then synthesize to a higher level of abstraction. Information from one source might conflict with that from another. Sometimes the BA obtains new input that forces them to revisit what the group thought was a resolved issue. Cycling back like this can be frustrating for participants ("Haven't we had this conversation already?"), but it's the nature of nonlinear human communication and exploration. Requirements elicitation is like peeling away the layers of an onion, revealing the interior as you go along—except that the more you peel, the bigger the onion appears.

In the hypothetical, pure waterfall life cycle, elicitation is performed only at the project's beginning. Ideally, a BA could assemble all the requirements up front, and they would remain stable throughout system development. Projects for which that approach works well do exist, but the time they must invest in the requirements phase is significant. Even traditional project teams know that requirements written early on must be revised and elaborated throughout the project's course.

Agile development projects deliberately address requirements in smaller chunks and expect the requirements set to grow and evolve during development. Each development iteration includes elicitation activities. The project begins with some requirements exploration, but there's no expectation of gaining a complete and detailed understanding at that point. Instead, the team accumulates just enough knowledge to prioritize and allocate requirements to the early development iterations. During each iteration, the team then refines its allocated requirements—typically represented as user stories and acceptance tests—to whatever level of detail the developers and testers need.

The Elicitation Context

A project's vision and scope document or project charter sets the stage for elicitation. It establishes the project's business objectives, scope (what's explicitly in), and limitations (what's explicitly out). To begin the elicitation process, identify stakeholders who might be sources of valuable information. Those stakeholders could have veto power over a requirement ("You can't do that") or the power to add a requirement ("You must also do this"). You'll work with those stakeholders to understand their business, their needs and concerns, and what they expect a new or modified system to do for them.

If you're the BA, plan your elicitation strategy before diving in. The interaction techniques you choose will depend on the access you have to the stakeholders, where they're located, whether group or individual discussions are most appropriate, and how much time they can spend. Plan each interaction to make sure you get the information the development team needs. You might need to adjust the interaction techniques depending on the level of constructive engagement you're getting from your stakeholders.

Elicitation Techniques

You can find requirements knowledge about the business or the project in many places and ways. Following are several elicitation techniques that most project teams would find useful (Davis 2005, Robertson and Robertson 2013, Wiegers and Beatty 2013).

Interviews

One-on-one stakeholder interviews are efficient and focused, letting you drill down into details without distracting side trips. However, they lack the synergistic interactions that often stimulate new ideas in group discussions. For both individual and group interviews, the BA should prepare a list of areas to explore and questions to ask (Podeswa 2009).

Group Workshops

Workshops in which a BA meets with several user representatives and other stakeholders are a common elicitation practice. Workshops usually explore user requirements to understand the tasks a system must let users perform. All group activities risk being diverted by discussions that are out of scope for the meeting's objectives. It's easy for the group to head down a rathole, mired in details when they should be thinking at a higher level. A skillful facilitator keeps the participants on topic so that the workshop produces useful information. (See Lesson 14, "A large group of people can't agree to leave a burning room, let alone agree on exactly how to word some requirement.")

Observations

Observing users as they work in their native environment yields information that they might not think to share if a BA simply asked questions about what they do. An observant BA can identify issues and bottlenecks that the new system could address to make the business processes more efficient. Users often compensate for shortcomings in a software system through workarounds, so observation can reveal improvements to make in a replacement system. User experience designers—who perform the BA role on some projects—also find it valuable to observe users as they work.

Document Analysis

Documentation on existing systems, products, and business processes can be a rich source of potential requirements. Studying such documentation helps a BA get up to speed on a new application domain. Documents provide information about relevant business rules: corporate policies, government regulations, and industry standards. Suzanne Robertson and James Robertson (2013) aptly term the process of reverse engineering new requirements from existing records "document archaeology." Information gleaned from historical sources needs to be validated to ensure that it is still current.

Surveys

In-person interviews and workshops can engage only a limited number of participants. Surveys let you solicit input and attitudes toward current products from a larger population. Online surveys are useful for commercial products in cases where the development team might not have direct access to representative users. There's an art to creating surveys that elicit the information you seek and increase the chance that users will complete them (Colorado State University n.d.). Surveys should ask the fewest questions that will tell you what you need to know.

Online surveys often force the user to answer every question to enable submitting them. I sometimes abandon surveys when I realize how long they are. I'm willing to share my opinions, but I don't want to spend a lot of time wading through pages of questions.

Wikis

Wikis and other collaborative tools let you collect input and ideas from more people than you could fit into a workshop. One person's post prompts another's endorsement, revision, extension, or dissent. The drawback to this freewheeling approach is that the BA will need to filter through the discussion threads to search for gems of information.

Prototypes

It's hard for people to visualize what a proposed solution might be like from abstract discussions and requirement lists. A prototype makes requirements more tangible. Even simple screen sketches can help workshop participants crystallize their thinking. It's risky to build prototypes too early during requirements exploration, because people can fixate prematurely on a particular—and maybe not ideal—solution.

Laying the Foundation

Elicitation is the core requirements engineering practice on a software or systems development project. Without a solid foundation of requirements knowledge acquired through effective elicitation, a project is on shaky ground.

Lesson 12	Requirements elicitation must bring the customer's voice close to the developer's ear.

During one of my most productive periods as a software developer, I created some applications for a scientist named Sean in Kodak's research laboratories. Sean was the only user; I was the entire software team. I performed all the activities needed to create an application: requirements development, user interface and program design, coding, testing, and documentation. One application was a complex spreadsheet tool that let Sean simulate the photographic results from numerous camera and film parameters. Another was a mainframe-based application to analyze his experimental data.

Sean and I sat ten feet apart. I was highly productive because Sean and I could interact frequently, informally, and quickly. I could show him what I was doing, get my questions answered, and obtain his feedback on user interface ideas. This proximity, and the fact that only Sean had input to the project, let us collaborate in tiny, fast cycles. We didn't need written requirements, because I could quickly get the details I needed from him.

My work with Sean was the ideal software development environment: one developer plus one customer, sitting close together. That's also rare. Most projects have many customers grouped into several user classes, numerous sources of requirements, and multiple decision makers. They have a development team that ranges from a few people in one place to hundreds in multiple locations. These vastly more challenging projects need other ways to get the voice of the customer close to the ear of the developer to elicit requirements, establish priorities, communicate changes, and make decisions.

Communication Pathways

Unless you're building software for yourself, you'll always confront a gap between customers who have needs and developers who build solutions. Each project team needs to establish effective communication pathways between the two communities early in the project. Your options depend on how many participants are involved, who and where they are, how well the communities understand each other, and the software team's skill set.

> Once you've identified your user classes, you need to determine who will serve as the literal voice of the customer for each group.

Figure 2.4 shows several communication models to connect the customer's voice to the developer's ear. My situation with Sean illustrates model A, a direct connection between users and developers. This direct connection presents the least need for detailed written requirements and the fewest miscommunication opportunities, provided the developer and user understand each other's terminology. More often, though, some intermediaries will be involved.

When you have many users with diverse needs, they can't all talk directly to developers. That's a recipe for chaos, as developers are bombarded with input without knowing which sources are authoritative. It burdens the developers to resolve conflicting input from multiple sources. To cope with that diversity, many of my consulting clients and I have successfully used the model labeled B in Figure 2.4.

Stakeholder analysis generally reveals multiple user classes that have largely distinct needs. Members of different user classes could use different product features,

Figure 2.4 *Several communication pathways can connect the voice of the customer to the ear of the developer (left image: Freepik.com; right image, Voronin76/Shutterstock).*

perform different tasks, vary in their frequency of use, or have other distinctions. Once you've identified your user classes, you need to determine who will serve as the literal voice of the customer for each group.

Product Champions

In model B, the primary conduit for requirements information involves one or more key user representatives, called *product champions,* who collaborate with one or more BAs (Wiegers and Beatty 2013). The product champions have the domain knowledge and understand the project's business objectives. They interact with their fellow user-class members to solicit requirements input and feedback on ideas and to inform the other users of the project's progress. The BA facilitates bridging the communication gap between product champions and the development team.

Note that communications also take place along the reverse direction of the arrows shown in Figure 2.4. As developers—or anyone else involved in the pathway—have questions or require clarification, they'll need to go back to the source of the requirement to resolve them. It's helpful to record where each requirement came from so that developers can quickly get the answers they need.

Other Requirements Communication Pathways

Companies that build commercial products often use communication pathway C in Figure 2.4. The marketing department assesses the market needs and sales potential for a new or improved product. Marketing may work with a product manager who has the lead responsibility for defining the product characteristics that will lead to business success. The organization can partition the responsibilities for defining the product in various ways across the marketing and product management functions.

The product manager performs the functions that a BA handles on an IT project. Here's a concise statement of the product manager role (280 Group 2021):

> The Product Manager is responsible for delivering a differentiated product to market that addresses a market need and represents a viable business opportunity. A key component of the Product Manager role is ensuring that the product supports the company's overall strategy and goals.

Projects that follow an agile development approach, particularly Scrum, often follow communication pathway D in Figure 2.4. The product owner establishes the product's vision and goal, and they create and communicate the contents of the product backlog (Cohn 2010). The product owner defines a road map by which the product will evolve incrementally from concept, through early releases, to a mature product that delivers customer value (McGreal and Jocham 2018). The product owner thus serves as the voice of the customer.

Unless they're already domain experts in all the areas the users represent, responsible product owners will seek input from people like the product champions I mentioned earlier. In Scrum, the product owner—a single individual—has sole accountability for managing the product backlog contents, even if they delegate some of the work to other people (Schwaber and Sutherland 2020). The product owner also interacts with marketing and business managers and takes their input into account in the prioritized story backlog.

As you can see, the product owner fulfills much of the role that a BA might otherwise perform on an IT project, and more. However, some agile project teams recognize the value of having a skilled BA on the team to work with the product owner. When both roles are present, they can collaborate in various ways. The BA often functions as an extension of—or surrogate for—the product owner. The product owner might delegate some areas of responsibility, such as working with particular user classes, to the BA. The BA then is responsible for everything about that area except the prioritization against requirements from other areas. Prioritization remains the product owner's purview.

Sometimes the product owner is more product and market facing, whereas the BA is more technical facing, crafting solution requirements from user requirements (Datt 2020a). This model appears as pathway E in Figure 2.4. In other cases, the opposite is true. The nature of their collaboration boils down to however the product owner thinks the BA can add the most value to the project.

Bridging the Gap

Whether the title is business analyst, requirements engineer, product manager, product owner, or something else—or even if developers perform requirements activities themselves—all projects need to connect a product's users with its creators. The job title is less important than the presence of the role and a clear definition of its responsibilities and authority. The individuals who perform this function need the right knowledge, skills, experience, and personality to work with both customers and developers. They must establish a relationship based on mutual trust and respect with both communities.

Effective requirements development ensures that developers hear the customers' voices loud and clear. Those connections can determine whether the project is a grand success or never makes it to the finish line.

Lesson 13   Two commonly used requirements elicitation practices are telepathy and clairvoyance. They don't work.

According to *The American Heritage Dictionary of the English Language* (2020), telepathy is "the supposed process of communicating through means other than the senses, as by the direct exchange of thoughts." Clairvoyance is "the supposed power to see objects or events that cannot be perceived by the senses." Those skills certainly would make software development far easier—if they were real. Although they don't exist, telepathy and clairvoyance appear to be the technical foundation for some projects.

Guess That Requirement!

People sometimes think that certain requirements are so obvious they need not be stated. Some users might be wary of coming across as condescending, not wanting to insult a BA's intelligence by stating something they think the BA already knows. I'd rather hear something that I already know a second or third time—thereby reinforcing its validity and my understanding of it—than to have someone assume that information is in my brain when it's not.

Some busy users don't want to spend the time discussing requirements with a BA, product owner, or developer. Their attitude seems to be, "You should already know what I need. Call me when you're done." That attitude assumes both telepathy and clairvoyance on the BA's part.

The two big risk areas are assumed requirements and implied requirements. *Assumed requirements* are those that people expect without having to say so. *Implied requirements* are needed because another requirement exists, but they aren't explicitly stated either. It's not reasonable to expect a BA to read minds or see beyond the horizon to acquire that hidden knowledge. As we've seen, you'll never have an entirely complete set of requirements, but the project participants must exercise judgment regarding what can safely remain unsaid.

Being Explicit

I prefer to communicate the expectations we know about explicitly instead of hoping that someone else knows what I'm thinking. It's great if all project stakeholders have a close enough mind meld to yield the right product without having to record requirements details. The more that those people have worked together, and the more the development team knows about the application domain, the easier that mind meld is to achieve. But my general philosophy is that if the requirements don't describe a particular capability or characteristic, no one should expect to find it in the product.

The BA should try to reveal and confirm unstated assumptions, as sometimes they're invalid or obsolete.

We sometimes express requirements informally because we assume the reader has a "sensibility filter" similar to our own, yet people might interpret the same statements differently. That ambiguity leads to mismatched expectations and surprises upon delivery. You might be operating under a different set of assumptions than I am. An *assumption* is a statement we regard as being true in the absence of definitive knowledge that it is true. The BA should try to reveal and confirm unstated assumptions, as sometimes they're invalid or obsolete.

 The risk of miscommunication increases when system implementation is outsourced. I once reviewed a requirements document for a project that was planning to outsource the development work. The document contained many requirements that began with "The system shall support...." I asked the document's author how the contracting company's developers would know precisely what functionality the word *support* implied in each instance. After a moment of thought, she gave the correct answer: "I guess they won't." She wisely decided to clarify just what she meant by *support* throughout the document to eliminate the ambiguities. That's much better than relying on telepathy or clairvoyance.

Here's an example of an implied requirement. You request an undo function for some application feature. The developer implements the undo function, and you test it. It works fine. You ask the developer where the redo operation is.

"You didn't ask for redo," the developer replies.

"I thought that asking for an undo function would obviously imply a redo capability as well. Could you put that in, please?" you ask. The developer adds the redo function, and it works. But then you wonder why there's only a one-level redo. That leads to further discussion: how many levels of redo do you want? Do you want to be able to jump to any point in the undo sequence and redo all of the undone actions from that point onward? When should the undo history queue be cleared? And on and on.

If the developers and users are in close contact, they could start with that simple undo requirement and discuss it to agree on exactly how the undo/redo function should behave. That way, it doesn't take multiple development iterations to rework your way to what the customer had in mind. However, if you're outsourcing development, you'd better do that thinking beforehand and include all the specifics in the requirements. Otherwise, don't be surprised if the faraway developer's interpretation of a scantily written requirement doesn't match the customer's expectation.

The contractor might even detect this implied functionality in a proposal but base their bid on only the original requirement, anticipating that you'll come back with the additional request. Then the contractor can request more money and time to accommodate your "scope creep."

Telepathy Fails

You can't work out the nuances of all functionality just through thinking and discussion. Sometimes only development cycles or prototypes will let users figure out just what they need. Assumed requirements and the resultant design choices can lead to expensive rework, though. I recently read about an inappropriate design decision that engineers made regarding the control stick in the F-16 Fighting Falcon fighter jet (Aleshire 2004):

> Originally, the engineers made the stick itself solid, unmoving, since the computer could translate the pressure on the stick from the pilot's hands as easily as the stick's actual movement. But the pilots hated that. They wanted to move the stick, to gain that sense of control.

There's no substitute for getting input on both requirements and proposed solutions from people who will use the product. And there's no excuse for not writing down the resultant knowledge to ensure that the product designers can satisfy the customer's needs.

Lesson 14	A large group of people can't agree to leave a burning room, let alone agree on exactly how to word some requirement.

I once was the lead BA on a medium-sized information system project. Two other BAs and I worked with members of different user classes to understand their requirements. One day my colleague Lynette called me, concerned. Her first elicitation workshop had covered far less ground than planned. The frustrated participants were concerned about how long this process would take. Lynette sought advice.

I asked her how many people were in the workshop. "Twelve," she replied. Ah, therein lay the problem. A large group of people has a hard time reaching agreements and making decisions. Group members are easily distracted by side conversations. Multiple people might have something to say on each topic, leading to longer— but not necessarily more fruitful—discussions. It's easy to get dragged into one participant's pet topic in considerable detail, which might not advance the day's objectives. Disagreements can escalate into lengthy debates. Certain individuals can dominate the discussion, while others might tune out entirely.

I suggested that Lynette cut the size of the group in half. She didn't need six user representatives, just two or three. Some people who were there as observers or to protect their interests weren't adding value to the requirements exploration. I recommend including people with software development and testing experience in elicitation discussions, as they bring insights regarding the feasibility and testability of proposed requirements. In this case, Lynette's background let her represent those perspectives herself. Lynette shrank the group for subsequent workshops, and everyone felt much better about their quicker progress.

Pay Attention!

Four people can have a productive discussion without getting distracted by sidebar conversations. As Figure 2.5 illustrates, there are few pairwise interactions in a group of just four people. However, the number of such connections snowballs with larger groups. Figure 2.6 shows how many more two-way connections there are in a group of ten. It's not surprising that some people will slip into private discussions, especially if they aren't interested in the current topic. The idea of keeping groups relatively small to make rapid progress applies to requirements elicitation workshops, peer reviews, and similar collective activities.

One strategy we found to help control group size was to hold separate workshops with members of different user classes. Different user classes have largely distinct requirements. If you collect all project stakeholder representatives into a single workshop, any topic that comes up will be of interest to only a subset of the group. The others may well be bored and feel that they're wasting their time. Conducting workshops with separate user classes helps ensure that all participants are interested in the agenda items. That said, judiciously combining members of different user classes can synergistically reveal connections, questions, and innovations that neither group might come up with independently.

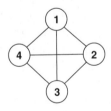

Figure 2.5 *Four people have just a few two-way connections.*

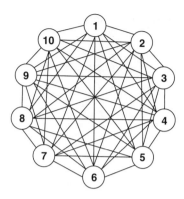

Figure 2.6 *The number of pairwise connections explodes in a large group, offering many opportunities for distracting side conversations.*

Facilitator to the Rescue

Keeping a large group on track requires skillful facilitation. Sometimes facilitation is ad hoc: someone in the group takes the initiative to stand at the whiteboard with a marker in hand and bring order out of chaos. The BA could serve as the facilitator, or the group could bring in an impartial outside facilitator. A facilitator should come prepared with objectives and an agenda for each session. Timeboxing discussions sustains progress so that the group doesn't get too tangled up with one topic and neglect others due to lack of time.

A facilitator can judge when to let a discussion go on longer than planned because of the value it's adding. They can assess when it's appropriate to drill down into more detail and when it's time to move on to the next topic. A good facilitator will notice if a discussion about requirements has slipped into solution explorations and bring the group back on track. Ellen Gottesdiener's book *Requirements by Collaboration* (2002) provides extensive guidance on planning and leading requirements workshops.

Focus, Focus, Focus

One of the biggest challenges with leading a large workshop is keeping discussions in scope. Figure 2.7 shows that the facilitator must first consider the horizontal scope, the subset of possible user requirements that the group should plan to discuss in a specific workshop. There's also a vertical scope, the depth into which the group should explore each of the selected items.

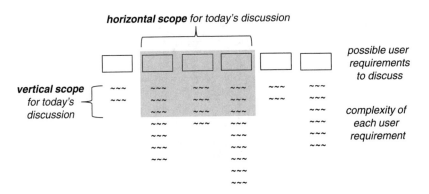

Figure 2.7 *An elicitation workshop needs to focus on a specific subset of requirements down to a particular depth of understanding.*

A workshop is not the time to try to define all the details of every requirement. Early in requirements exploration, you want to learn just enough about each one to let the team estimate their relative size and prioritize them for implementation. Spend only enough time debating the wording to ensure that all the participants share a common understanding of what each requirement means. The BA can flesh out the details offline with users at the right time, such as just before implementing a requirement that was allocated to a specific development iteration.

The facilitator must respect the input that workshop participants offer. While the facilitator needs to keep the discussion focused on the day's topic, they also must honor the basic human need to be heard. If someone raises an issue outside the discussion's scope, the facilitator should record the idea so that it's there for future reference and then quickly bring the discussion back in scope.

Reaching Outside the Group

You do miss something by having only a handful of workshop participants. Keeping the group small is not intended to exclude input from others, just to accelerate progress. To close the gaps, supplement your elicitation workshops with asynchronous methods, such as wikis, to solicit input from more people. I found it helpful to write up the information from each workshop and distribute it promptly to the participants for review and to a larger group for their comments, corrections, and elaborations. Engaging other stakeholders in the process broadens your knowledge, validates the workshop results, informs the community about the project's direction, and promotes buy-in.

Negotiating to reach consensus requires more discussion than a simple majority vote, delegating the decision to a single individual, or flipping a coin.

As you collect information from various stakeholders through multiple channels, someone has to resolve conflicting requirements. Even terminology can conflict. Two people might use different words to mean the same thing or overload a single term with multiple definitions that lead to confusion. Someone will also need to reconcile priorities across the requirements obtained from various user classes and decide which proposed changes to accept. Every project needs to determine who its decision makers are for these matters and how they'll make the call—their decision rules (Gottesdiener 2002). Some decision-making processes take longer than others. Negotiating to reach consensus requires more discussion than a simple majority vote, delegating the decision to a single individual, or flipping a coin.

Elicitation workshops are an effective way to explore requirements collaboratively. As a BA, it's rewarding to lead a team of engaged user representatives to a shared understanding of their requirements and a solution. If the group is too big, though, you can wind up in the proverbial herding-cats scenario, doing your best to keep people engaged and on topic and yet walking out tired and frustrated at the end. Small groups move much more quickly. And they'll always be able to agree on which fire exit to use should it become necessary.

Lesson 15	Avoid decibel prioritization when deciding which features to include.

You've probably heard the saying, "The squeaky wheel gets the grease." The software analogy suggests that the person who advocates the loudest for their requirements gets top priority. I call that *decibel prioritization*. It's not the best strategy.

Most teams confront a mass of functionality that's too large for the project box. Designated decision makers must choose what to include and what to defer or discard. Even if you can handle all of the requested work, you need to determine the most appropriate implementation sequence. Some requested capabilities are both important and urgent; they go first. Others are important but can wait for later implementation, and still others are neither important nor urgent. An essential aspect of project planning, prioritization guides the allocation of items from the backlog of remaining work to the most appropriate iteration, build, or release.

The objective of all prioritization exercises is to deliver the maximum customer value quickly and cheaply.

Every stakeholder likes to think that their needs are the most profound. Influential, strong-willed, or highly vocal managers and customers can exert a lot of pressure to address their needs first. However, the loudest customers aren't necessarily demanding the most significant features from a business perspective. The objective of all prioritization exercises is to deliver the maximum customer value quickly and cheaply. You don't want to waste effort on features that don't contribute much to the product's success. Thoughtful prioritization, therefore, should consider numerous factors besides speaking volume.

Prioritization Techniques

People have developed many methods for prioritizing software requirements. Several researchers have studied which requirements prioritization techniques are most practicable and effective (Hasan et al. 2010, Kukreja et al. 2012, Achimugu et al. 2014). Commonly used techniques include these:

- Three-level classifications, which all boil down to high–medium–low

- MoSCoW (Must, Should, Could, Won't) classification

- Pairwise comparisons of individual features, functional requirements, use cases, or stories to sort the items by priority

- Rank ordering the priorities of a set of similar requirement items

- Distributing 100 points among individual requirements, giving the highest-priority items the most points

- The planning game, commonly used on agile projects, in which customers and developers collaborate to list a set of user stories in order of their relative priority (Shore 2010)

- Analytical methods that rate requirements based on the value they contribute to the product and their implementation cost (Wiegers and Beatty 2013)

Prioritization Criteria

The same thought process applies whether you're prioritizing use cases, individual use case flows, features and subfeatures, functional requirements, or user stories.

Consider the following factors as you decide which of your requirements are imperative, which are desirable, and which are optional.

Business Objectives

The most decisive criterion is the extent to which each requirement will help the organization achieve its business objectives. The reference for making this judgment lies in the project's business requirements, which the project sponsor should establish early in the project. They describe the business opportunity being created or exploited and quantify the business's objectives for the project. Without clear objectives, it's hard to make rational decisions about which functionality to implement and when.

User Classes

Not all user classes are created equal. Satisfying the requirements from favored user classes contributes more to business success than meeting other groups' needs. Stakeholder analysis includes determining which user classes are most important—favored—so that you can grant their requirements a higher priority.

Usage Frequency

Understanding how often users will use certain functions helps to judge which capabilities to implement first. One way to assess the frequency of usage is to develop an *operational profile* for the application. An operational profile describes what percentage of the time users will perform each operation during a usage session (Musa 1993). For instance, what percentage of user sessions at an airline's website involves making a flight reservation, modifying or canceling a reservation, checking flight status, or tracking missing luggage? All other things being equal—and they aren't always—the most frequently used operations will have the highest implementation priority.

Regulatory Compliance

Requirements that allow the product to achieve regulatory compliance or certification must have high priority. It doesn't matter whether the right user functionality is present if you're not permitted to sell or use the product. A related consideration affects functionality that certain stakeholders need but which isn't visible to most users. Examples include security requirements, recording access history, and building audit trails. Some of these under-the-hood capabilities could have high priority even if no end user is clamoring for them.

Foundational Functionality

Certain functionality should be implemented early, even if it doesn't provide immediate user value, because it's foundational for later functionality. That is, you need to consider the dependencies between requirements when you determine the implementation sequence. Some functionality might establish a complex product's architectural soundness. It can be disruptive to shoehorn in this kind of functionality later in the project, so build it earlier rather than later.

Risky Functionality

Requirements that present high risk from an implementation point of view should be implemented early to verify their feasibility and reduce the overall technical risk of the project.

Analysis over Volume

Whichever prioritization technique you select, you'll be better off if you consider the factors above in your analysis than if you just listen to the loudest voice in the room. The squeakiest wheel shouldn't necessarily be first in line for the grease.

Lesson 16	Without a documented and agreed-to project scope, how do you know whether your scope is creeping?

When I ask students in my training courses how many of them have worked on a project that suffered from scope creep, nearly everyone raises their hand. Then I ask how many of those projects had a defined scope statement: practically none. What does the idea of scope creep even mean if a project's scope was never clearly defined?

The Specter of Scope Creep

Scope creep—the ongoing and uncontrolled growth of functionality—has plagued software projects since time immemorial. Scope creep often is cited as a reason why a project failed to meet its planned schedule. But you can't even know whether scope creep is taking place unless there's some agreed-upon reference point that states, "Here's what we intend to do in this period of time."

Every planned chunk of work begins with a baseline of functionality that the team intends to implement during that chunk.

We can define *scope* as a set of capabilities that stakeholders agree to be delivered in a specific iteration, build, or product release. Scope prescribes the boundary between what's in and what's out for a body of work. The scope for any portion of the project represents a subset of the product vision, a stepping-stone on the pathway from project initiation to ultimate product delivery. Every planned chunk of work begins with a baseline of functionality that the team intends to implement during that chunk. That baseline is the reference point for scope change.

People traditionally regard scope creep as a bad thing. It suggests that requirements elicitation was incomplete or inaccurate, thereby leading to an ongoing stream of added and amplified requirements. As we've seen, it's impossible to fully define all the requirements for any sizable project up front, and it's unrealistic to expect them to remain static. Every project must anticipate some requirements churn and growth as users try out early releases and get both new ideas and a better understanding of the problem.

Stifling change because of scope creep fear (creepophobia?) can lead to products that achieve their initial vision yet don't meet customer needs. However, continuous scope growth can drive a project off the rails if plans and schedules don't accommodate changes through contingency buffers and ongoing prioritization. (See Lesson 25, "Icebergs are always larger than they first appear.") Incorporating every new requirement that comes along guarantees schedule and budget overruns.

Agile projects deliberately don't attempt to define the scope for an entire project. Instead, they define each iteration's scope based on which items from the product backlog the product owner allocated to it for implementation. New requirements or other work items are added to the backlog. The product owner prioritizes new backlog items against the rest of the remaining work so that they can allocate the items to a future iteration at the right time. This approach helps to target user needs accurately, but it also can cause an uncertain back end on the ultimate delivery schedule.

How to Document Scope

The simplest scope-representation technique lists the requirements, features, or backlog items scheduled for implementation during a particular development cycle, as in an agile release plan (Thomas 2008a). Other useful techniques for representing scope at various levels of detail include these:

- **Context diagram,** which reveals nothing about the system internals but identifies entities outside the system—users, other software systems, hardware devices—that connect to it across the system boundary (Wiegers and Beatty 2013)

- **Use case diagram,** which depicts actors outside the system boundary and the use cases through which they interact with the system (Ambler 2005)

- **Ecosystem diagram,** which shows how multiple systems are interconnected so that you can judge the ripple effect of a change on systems that don't directly interface to yours (Beatty and Chen 2012)

- **Iteration backlog,** which identifies the set of product backlog items that an agile team plans to complete during a single iteration (Scaled Agile 2021a); called a sprint backlog on a Scrum project

- **User story map,** which shows the activities, steps, and details of user stories that define the scope of an entire product, an iteration, or a specific feature or portion of the user experience (Kaley 2021)

- **Feature road map,** in which you define several levels of increasing capability for each feature and then describe the scope of a particular release by listing the specific enrichment levels of the individual features that the release includes (Wiegers 2006a)

- **Feature tree,** which visually decomposes major features into subfeatures that a planner can group to define each development cycle's scope (Beatty and Chen 2012)

- **Event list,** which identifies the external events that each release will handle (Wiegers and Beatty 2013)

In each case, the purpose of defining scope is to define the capabilities that a particular portion of the project is to deliver. That distinction establishes the scope boundary and serves as the reference point for considering scope modifications while development is underway.

Is It in Scope?

Since the scope will be somewhat volatile, every project needs a practical change management process. Simply throwing proposed items into the backlog unfiltered isn't helpful. There should be some well-communicated mechanism by which stakeholders can request changes so that the right people can assess their impact and decide whether to include them. A formal change process doesn't kick in until the team establishes a baseline for a particular body of work. Before that point, we know that requirements are dynamic and the scope is evolving. During each increment of work, change control should become more viscous as time progresses to increase the chance of delivering on the baseline as scheduled.

The question to ask when someone proposes a new requirement is, "Is this in scope?" There are three possible answers.

- **Yes, it's clearly in scope.** The proposed functionality is needed to achieve our objectives for the current development cycle. Therefore, we must add it to our work in progress.

- **No, it's clearly out of scope.** This requirement doesn't contribute to our business objectives for the current body of work, so we need not address it now. We could place it into the backlog of pending work for future consideration, or we might reject it.

- **It's not in scope as the scope is currently defined, but it ought to be.** The project sponsor must make a business decision as to whether to increase the project's scope to accommodate the new capability. If the requested change would add sufficient business value, then increasing scope is the right choice. But it always comes at a price. If scope increases, something else must move to accommodate it: other functionality, schedule, cost, staff, or quality. Change is never free.

Fuzzy Requirements = Fuzzy Scope

How people write requirements can lead to an uncertain understanding of scope. Ambiguity might lead one party to think that a particular function is obviously in scope, whereas someone else disagrees. Vague terms like *support, etc., for example,* and *including* (even worse, *including but not limited to*) are intrinsically uncertain. I don't like to see them in requirements statements. Here are some examples.

- "The system shall process characters A, B, C, etc." Will all readers agree on where that list ends and what all it contains? The open-ended *etc.* makes me nervous.

- "The system shall support Microsoft Word documents." Readers could have very different ideas of exactly what functions *support* refers to. Suppose a project manager or product owner makes plans based on a restricted interpretation of *support*. Later on, you find that the customer who requested this function has a much broader expectation. Is that scope creep? Or is it just a refinement of the original expectation into specifics, thereby revealing the rest of the iceberg? Writing requirements carefully before making commitments helps to avoid such problems.

Ambiguous and incomplete requirements can cause problems when scope debates arise on contracted projects. One project included a requirement that a vendor migrate several sets of data from the client's existing information system into the vendor's new software package (Wiegers 2003). After the project was underway, the client identified several more data sets to be converted. The client considered these to lie within the original project scope and balked at paying extra for the new conversions. The vendor disagreed. Between that and other problems, the eventual outcome was a canceled project and an expensive lawsuit. As another example, a consultant friend was hired as an expert witness for five contracted projects that resulted in lawsuits and multimillion-dollar settlements. Four of the project failures involved poorly defined requirements, and two of those involved scope issues.

Wise contractors will include contingency buffers to accommodate a certain amount of growth and scope fuzziness. However, quoting a price that includes such buffers might be off-putting to a prospective client. Contracts need to explicitly address how to handle scope increases and who will pay for them. The more crisply you can distinguish what's included from what is not, the less painful these debates will be.

I have a friend who makes sure the project's purpose can be stated concisely enough to fit on a T-shirt. He keeps that purpose visible on meeting agendas and notes, documents, and other public locations. I've also known people who wrote their vision and scope statements on a poster board that they brought to requirements discussions. That visibility helps people answer the question, "Is this new requirement necessary to meet that purpose?" That's the core issue behind scope management.

Change happens, although excessive change suggests that nobody understood the problem adequately in the first place. Clearly defining the scope of a planned body of work focuses the team on creating a valuable deliverable within the schedule and budget constraints and permits sensible business decisions when change requests come along.

Next Steps: Requirements

1. Identify which of the lessons described in this chapter are relevant to your experiences with requirements development and management.

2. Can you think of any other requirements-related lessons from your own experience that are worth sharing with your colleagues?

3. Identify any practices described in this chapter that might be solutions to the requirements-related problems you identified in the First Steps at the beginning of the chapter. How could each practice improve how your project teams handle requirements?

4. How could you tell whether each practice from Step 3 was yielding the desired results? What would those results be worth to you?

5. Identify any barriers that might make it difficult to apply the practices from Step 3. How could you break down those barriers or enlist allies to help you implement the practices?

6. Put into place process descriptions, templates, guidance documents, checklists, and other aids to help future project teams apply your local requirements best practices effectively.

Chapter 3

Lessons About Design

Introduction to Design

If the domain of requirements is about defining problems and the characteristics that solutions must have, design is about crafting those solutions. Some people say that requirements are about *what* and design is about *how*. It's not that clear-cut.

As Figure 3.1 illustrates, the boundary between requirements and design is not a crisp black line, but rather a fuzzy gray area (Wiegers 2006a). During requirements exploration, it's valuable to take some tentative steps into design thinking, such as by creating prototypes. Contemplating how the problem knowledge might lead to a solution helps people refine the product's requirements. Users who interact with a prototype find that it clarifies their thinking and triggers new ideas because a prototype is more tangible than an abstract list of requirements.

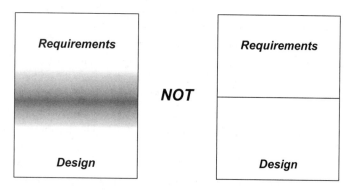

Figure 3.1 *The boundary between requirements and design is a fuzzy gray area, not a crisp black line.*

Transitioning from even excellent requirements into specific bits of a design is neither easy nor obvious.

The essence of software design is relating requirements to pieces of code, but transitioning from even excellent requirements into specific bits of a design is neither easy nor obvious (Davis 1995). Whenever someone asks me how people design software, I'm reminded of an old cartoon by Sidney Harris that shows two scientists standing in front of a blackboard covered with equations. One scientist points to a place on the board that says "Then a miracle occurs" and suggests that that section needs to be a bit more explicit.

Some aspects of software design do appear almost miraculous, somehow crystallizing from the ether based on the designer's experience and intuition. Certain activities, such as database design, are systematic and analytical. Others are more organic, with a design emerging incrementally as designers explore the transition from problem to solution. User experience design involves artistically creative approaches, based on a solid understanding of human factors. Designers often rely on common patterns that recur in software design to reduce the amount of invention required (Gamma et al. 1995). Ken Pugh (2005) provides some insights into the designer's thought process in his book *Prefactoring*.

Different Aspects of Design

Software design encompasses four major aspects: architectural, detailed (or low-level), database, and user experience design (Figure 3.2). All of these design aspects are subject to numerous constraints that restrict the options available to the designer. Constraints might arise from requirements for compatibility with other products, applicable standards, technology limitations, business policies, regulations, cost, and other factors. Physical products that contain embedded software are subject to other constraints, including dimensions, weight, materials, and interfaces. Constraints increase the design challenge by telling designers what they *cannot* do, just as requirements dictate what the design *must* do.

Architectural design refers to the structure of the system and its components, or architectural elements (Rozanski and Woods 2005). These elements consist of code modules for software-only systems, which could be aggregated into multiple interconnected subsystems for a large product. Physical products with embedded software will include mechanical and electrical hardware components. Designing

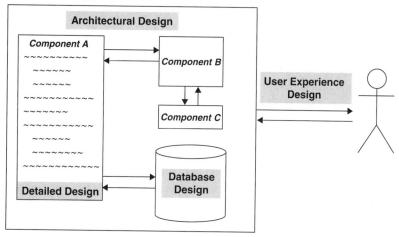

Figure 3.2 *Software systems involve architectural, detailed, database, and user experience design.*

an architecture involves partitioning the system into components, defining each component's responsibilities, and allocating specific requirements to the appropriate components. Specifying the interfaces between components is another aspect of architectural design. (See Lesson 22, "Many system problems take place at interfaces.")

Detailed design focuses on the logical structure of individual program components—code modules, classes and their methods, scripts, and so forth—and the details of interfaces between modules. Algorithm development is a significant aspect of detailed design.

Database design is necessary when an application creates, modifies, or accesses a database. Database design includes identifying data entities or classes and the relationships among them, as well as itemizing each entity's data elements and their data types, properties, and logical connections. Constructing procedures to create, read, update, and delete stored data (sometimes collectively called CRUD) also is part of database design. Designing reporting functionality and report layouts straddles database and user experience (UX) design. After all, the only reason you put data into a computer is so that people can get it out again and access it in some useful form.

Any application that has human users involves *user experience design*, which is a huge discipline of its own. *User interface (UI) design*—also called human-computer interaction or HCI—is a subset of UX design. UI design involves both architectural and detailed aspects. A user interface's architecture depicts dialog elements—places where the user and system can interact—and the navigation pathways between them that describe user task flows. Detailed UI design addresses the specifics of the user's interaction with a product, including screen layouts, cosmetics, input controls, and the properties of individual text blocks, graphics, input fields, and output displays. Both architectural and detailed UI designs drive the user's perception of ease of learning and ease of use or, collectively, usability.

Do You Have a Good Design?

Design involves devising the optimal solution that will fulfill a plethora of requirements over the product's life. The design must enable implementing the correct functionality and achieve the expected characteristics for numerous quality attributes. (See Lesson 20, "You can't optimize all desirable quality attributes.") Further, the design must efficiently accommodate enhancement and modification both during the development process and following release.

Over the years, software engineering pioneers such as Edsger Dijkstra, David Parnas, Barbara Liskov, Larry Constantine, and Glenford Myers have elaborated principles that guide designers toward better results, which others have compiled into useful resources (Davis 1995, Gamma et al. 1995, Pugh 2005). Conforming to principles like the following leads to designs that are less complex, less failure prone, and easier to understand, modify, extend, and reuse than they might be otherwise.

- **Separation of concerns.** The design should be divided into modules that are independent of each other and have well-defined, nonoverlapping responsibilities.

- **Information hiding.** Each module should conceal the internal details of its data and algorithms from the rest of the system. Other modules should access the module's data and services only through the defined module interface. This way, each module's implementation can be modified when necessary, without affecting other modules that invoke it.

- **Low coupling.** Coupling refers to how intertwined two software components are. Nicely modular designs exhibit low coupling between components so that changing one module should require minimal changes in others (TutorialsPoint 2021).

- **High cohesion.** Cohesion refers to the extent to which a module's functions logically belong together, such that each module ideally performs a single, well-defined task (Mancuso 2016).

- **Abstraction.** Abstraction allows developers to write code that doesn't depend on specific implementation details, such as the platform's operating system or the user interface. Abstraction facilitates portability and reuse.

- **Defined and respected interfaces.** A well-defined module interface makes it easy for developers of other code modules to access that module's services. It also facilitates replacing a module when necessary, because the interface it presents to the rest of the system remains unchanged. The same principle applies to external interfaces the system presents to the outside world.

Design discussions sometimes treat design as a straightforward extension of requirements or bundle it in with implementation as "development," but it's better to regard design as a distinct exercise. Someone will design the software on every project, whether or not they treat design as a discrete activity and whether or not they record the designs in some form.

I worked on a project where coding directly from the requirements would have yielded a far more complex program than we devised by exploring design options first. It wasn't apparent from the requirements, but three of the system's eight computational modules used the same algorithm, three more shared a common algorithm, and the last two used a third algorithm. Eventually, we would have noticed that we were writing the same code multiple times, but we were happy to spot the repetition before implementation.

Instead of leaping straight from requirements to code, it's well worth the time to evaluate alternative design approaches and choose the most appropriate one. This chapter describes six valuable lessons I've learned from my software design experiences.

First Steps: Design

I suggest you spend a few minutes on the following activities before reading the design-related lessons in this chapter. As you read the lessons, contemplate to what extent each of them applies to your organization or project team.

1. List design practices that your organization is especially good at. Is information about those practices documented to remind team members about them and make it easy to apply them?

2. Identify any problems—points of pain—that you can attribute to shortcomings in how project teams deal with architectural, detailed, database, user experience, or other design activities.

3. State the impacts that each problem has on your ability to complete projects successfully. How do the problems impede achieving business success for both the development organization and its customers? Design shortcomings can lead to brittle systems that are not easily modified or improved, subpar performance, duplicated code, inconsistencies within a product or across related products, and usability problems.

4. For each problem from Step 2, identify the root causes that trigger the problem or make it worse. Problems, impacts, and root causes can blur together, so try to tease them apart and see their connections. You might find multiple root causes that contribute to the same problem, as well as several problems that arise from a single root cause.

5. As you read this chapter, list any practices that would be useful to your team.

Lesson 17   Design demands iteration.

In his classic book *The Mythical Man-Month,* Frederick P. Brooks, Jr. (1995) advises, "Plan to throw one away; you will, anyhow." Brooks is referring to the idea that, on large projects, it's advisable to create a pilot or preproduction system to figure out how best to build the complete system. That's an expensive prospect, particularly if the system includes hardware components. However, a pilot system is valuable if you have technical feasibility questions or if a suitable design strategy isn't clear initially. A pilot system also reveals the unknown unknowns, factors you hadn't yet realized were significant.

While you're unlikely to build and then discard a preliminary version of most products, you do need to iterate on potential designs before the team gets very far into construction. Creating the simplest possible design sounds attractive, and it does accelerate solution delivery. Rapid delivery might meet a customer's short-term perception of value, but it may not be the best long-term strategy as the product grows over time.

There's always more than one design solution for a software problem and seldom a single best solution (Glass 2003). The first design approach you conceive won't be the best option. Norman Kerth, a highly experienced designer of software, furniture, and other items, explained it to me nicely:

> You haven't done your design job if you haven't thought of at least three solutions, discarded all of them because they weren't good enough, and then combined the best parts of all of them into a superior fourth solution. Sometimes, after considering three options, you realize that you don't really understand the problem. After reflection, you might discover a simple solution when you generalize the problem.

Software design isn't a linear, orderly, systematic, or predictable process. Top designers often focus first on the hard parts where a solution might not be obvious or perhaps even feasible (Glass 2003). Several methods facilitate iteration as a designer moves from an initial concept to an effective solution. One method is to create and refine graphical models—diagrams—of the proposed designs. This technique is addressed in Lesson 18, "It's cheaper to iterate at higher levels of abstraction." Prototyping is another valuable technique for iterating on both technical and UX designs.

The Power of Prototypes

A prototype is a partial, preliminary, or possible solution. You build a piece of the system as an experiment, testing the hypothesis that you understand how to design the system well. If the experiment fails, you redesign it and try again. A prototype is valuable for assessing and reducing risk, particularly if you're employing a novel architectural or design pattern that you want to validate before committing to it.

If you intend a prototype to grow into the product, you must build it with production-level quality from the beginning.

Before you construct a prototype, determine whether you intend to discard it and then develop the real thing, or grow the preliminary solution into the product. A key point is that if you intend a prototype to grow into the product, you must build it with production-level quality from the beginning. That takes more effort than building something temporary that you'll discard after it has served its purpose. The more work you put into a prototype, the more reluctant you become to change it significantly or throw it away, which impedes the iteration mindset. Your prototyping approach should encourage cyclical refinement and even starting over if necessary.

Agile teams sometimes create stories called *spikes* to research technical approaches, resolve uncertainty, and reduce risk before committing to a specific solution (Leffingwell 2011). Unlike other user stories, a spike's prime deliverable is not working code, but rather knowledge. Spikes could involve technical prototypes, UI prototypes, or both, depending on the information sought. A spike should have a clear goal, just like a scientific experiment. The developer has a hypothesis to test. The spike should be designed to provide evidence for or against the hypothesis, test and confirm the validity of some approach, or allow the team to make an informed technical decision quickly.

Proofs of Concept

Proof-of-concept prototypes, also called *vertical prototypes,* are valuable for validating a proposed architecture. I once worked on a project that envisioned an unconventional client–server approach. The architecture made sense in our computing environment, but we wanted to make sure we weren't painting ourselves into a technical corner. We built a proof-of-concept prototype with a vertical slice of functionality from the UI through the communication layers and the computational engine. It worked, so we felt confident this design was workable.

Experimenting on a proof-of-concept prototype is a way to iterate at a relatively low cost, although you do need to build some executable software. Such prototypes are valuable for assessing the proposed design's technical aspects: architecture, algorithms, database structure, system interfaces, and communications. You can evaluate architectures against their needed properties—such as performance, security, safety, and reliability—and then refine them progressively.

Mock-ups

User interface designs always require iteration. Even if you're following established UI conventions, you should perform at least informal usability testing to choose appropriate controls and layouts to meet your ease-of-learning, ease-of-use, and accessibility goals. For instance, A/B testing is an approach in which you present users with two UI alternatives for a given operation so that they can choose which one makes the most sense to them. The people who conduct an A/B test can observe user behaviors with the different approaches to determine which option is more intuitive or leads to more successful outcomes. It's simpler, faster, and cheaper to conduct such experiments while you're still exploring the design than to react to post-delivery customer complaints or lower-than-expected click-through rates on a web page.

As with requirements, UX designs benefit from the progressive refinement of detail through prototyping. You can create *mock-ups,* also called *horizontal prototypes* because they consist of just a thin layer of user interface with no functional substance below it. Mock-ups range from basic screen sketches to executable interfaces that look authentic but don't do real work (Coleman and Goodwin 2017). Even simple paper prototypes are valuable and are quick to create and modify. You can use a word processing document or even index cards to lay out the data elements in boxes representing potential screens, see how the elements relate to each other, and note which elements are user input and which are displayed results. Watch out for these traps with user interface prototyping.

- Spending too much time perfecting the UI's cosmetics ("How about a darker red for this text?") before you've mastered the screen flow and functional layouts. Get the broad strokes right first.

- Customers or managers thinking the software must be nearly done because the UI looks good, even if there's nothing behind it but simulated functions. A less polished prototype shows that it isn't yet finished.

- Coaching prototype evaluators as they attempt to perform a task that isn't obvious to them. You can't judge usability if you're helping the users learn and use the prototype.

If you don't invest in repeatedly exploring both user experience and technical designs before committing to them, you risk delivering products that customers don't like. Thoughtlessly designed products annoy customers, waste their time, erode their goodwill toward your product and company, and generate bad reviews (Wiegers 2021). A few more iteration cycles will get you much closer to useful and enjoyable designs.

> **Lesson 18**   It's cheaper to iterate at higher levels of abstraction.

One way to revise a design is to build the entire product several times, improving it with each cycle. That's not practical. Another way is to implement just small portions of the solution, including the hard parts or the parts you don't understand yet, to determine what design approaches will work best. That's the idea behind prototyping, as we saw in the preceding lesson.

Yet a third strategy is to build an operational portion of the system so that users can work with it and provide feedback that improves the subsequent extensions.

This incremental approach is the thrust of agile software development. It's a good way to solicit user input on something tangible so that you can adjust the work to meet customer needs better. You might discover that your initial design was satisfactory for that first chunk of the product, but it won't support the product's growth through continued development. Or you could find that the team didn't make well-thought-out design decisions in the rush to deliver working software, so they must revisit those decisions later. (See Lesson 50, "Today's 'gotta get it out right away' development project is tomorrow's maintenance nightmare.") Shortcomings in system architecture and database designs often are costly and time consuming to rectify. Therefore, building a hasty implementation in the first few iterations without carefully exploring the technical underpinnings can come back to painfully bite the team.

The common factor for all three of these design strategies is building working software to evaluate your design ideas. Incrementally improving designs in this fashion is relatively slow and expensive. You could find yourself reworking what you've built several times to reach a suitable design.

An alternative approach is to iterate at a higher abstraction level than executable software. As Figure 3.3 illustrates, it's more expensive to iterate on artifacts at low abstraction levels than high. That's because you have to invest more work in creating the artifacts you're assessing and revising. Design modeling provides a cost-effective iteration alternative.

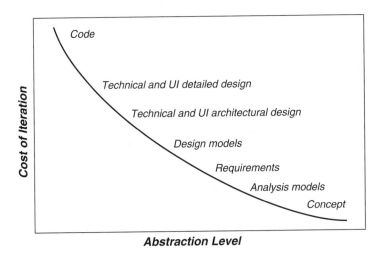

Figure 3.3 *The cost of iteration is lower at higher levels of abstraction.*

Stepping Back from the Details

For both requirements and designs, there's great value in drawing pictures that represent various aspects of the system and then iterating on those pictures. It's far faster to modify a diagram than to rewrite code. Working software is tangible; analysis and design models are abstract in that they represent something other than themselves. Diagrams that depict information at a high level of abstraction let people step back from the trees and study the forest as a whole from particular angles.

Whether you're using simple hand-drawn sketches or high-resolution diagrams drawn in a software modeling tool, you're modifying the design at a conceptual, not physical, level. The models won't show all the nitty-gritty bits of reality in an actual product, but they will help you visualize how the pieces fit together. Because of the value it can bring, I regard modeling as an essential skill for any business analyst (BA) or software designer (Wiegers 2019a).

A consulting client protested when I suggested that his team would benefit from diagramming specific aspects of their project. "Our system's too complex to model," he claimed. But wait—by definition, a model is simpler than the thing it's modeling. If you can't handle the model's complexity, how can you expect to handle the problem's complexity? The diagrams certainly can become intricate and confusing for intricate and confusing systems. That very challenge is a strong argument for using techniques to understand and manage the conceptual complexity.

For both requirements and designs,
there's great value in drawing pictures that
represent various aspects of the system and
then iterating on those pictures.

Rapid Visual Iteration

As we saw earlier, user interfaces have two levels of design: architectural and detailed. When you view a UI screen, you see a piece of the detailed design, with its visual design theme, text layout, images, links, input fields, options, and controls. If you need more precision, you can specify the detailed design of a screen or web page using a tool such as a display-action-response (DAR) model (Beatty and Chen 2012). However, iterating on the detailed UI design requires that you modify the individual display elements. Those revisions can become tedious unless you're using an efficient screen builder tool.

The UI's architectural design reveals itself through the navigation options each screen presents. You can refine an architectural design rapidly by drawing a *dialog map* (Wiegers and Beatty 2013). A dialog map represents a user interface architecture in the form of a state-transition or statechart diagram. Each display that the system presents to the user constitutes a distinct state the system can be in.

Figure 3.4 illustrates a simplified portion of the dialog map for my consulting company's website. Each rectangle represents a dialog element where the user and system can interact. A dialog element could be a web page, workspace, menu, dialog box, message box, even a line prompt. The arrows in the dialog map indicate defined navigation paths from one dialog element to another. You can label the arrows to indicate the conditions and/or actions that trigger the navigation. (I didn't do that here.) Representing a UI at this level of abstraction prevents people from being distracted by the details of each dialog element's appearance. They can focus on the big picture of how a user would interact with the system to accomplish a task by flowing through a sequence of dialog elements.

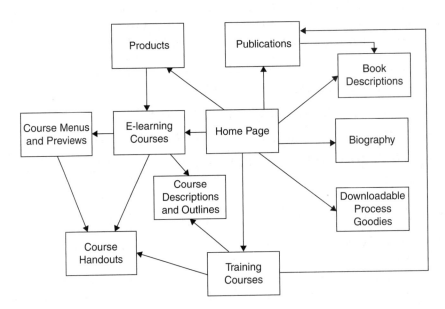

Figure 3.4 *A dialog map shows navigation options between dialog elements, such as web pages.*

I once led a discussion with several users to get our heads around how a particular task sequence could best function in the new system we were specifying. I had a whiteboard marker in one hand and an eraser in the other. I quickly sketched out a possible navigation flow on the whiteboard using the boxes and arrows of a dialog map. We knew—and cared—nothing about what the screens might look like, only their names and a general notion of their purpose. As the group critiqued my drawing and suggested changes, I would erase a piece and draw something different. In this way, we could rapidly adjust until we reached a shared concept of the optimal navigation flow. Along the way, we also found some errors and omissions in our original thoughts. Iterative modeling like this is a powerful thinking aid, a way to refine initial design concepts.

A model like a dialog map is static. You can walk through a series of boxes on the diagram to imagine how the user would perform a task. The next iteration level to refine a UI design is a dynamic simulation. You mock up a set of screens in a suitable tool—possibly as simple as Microsoft PowerPoint—to create a storyboard of the UI that looks more real. That lets you simulate the user experience more precisely by navigating from one such screenshot to another in a task flow. This process moves the iteration from a high-level model down one level of abstraction to a simple UI mock-up. A selective combination of quick design modeling, simulation, and prototyping will take less effort than implementing the entire user interface and then modifying it until your users are happy.

Iteration Made Easy

When I began modeling software systems, I quickly discovered two truths. First, I needed to make multiple cycles because my first attempt never yielded an ideal design. Second, I needed tools that made it easy to revise my diagrams. If I had to completely redraw a picture every time I thought of a change, I wouldn't make more than one revision.

Software modeling tools became popular in the 1980s and 1990s. They make it easy to modify diagrams, such as dragging the arrows attached to an object along with it when you reposition or resize an object. The tools know the symbology and syntax for several standard analysis and design notations. They can validate diagrams and point out possible errors. General-purpose diagramming packages like Microsoft Visio now incorporate some of the standard symbology sets for software models. However, general drawing tools lack the validation capabilities that are valuable in dedicated modeling tools, along with the ability to integrate multiple diagrams and their associated data definitions for a whole system.

Modeling makes it easy to explore multiple approaches quickly and conceive a better design than you could create with just a single attempt. Keep in mind that you need not generate perfect models. Nor must you model the entire system, just the parts that are especially complex or uncertain. Diagramming tools facilitate iteration, but it's easy for users to get caught up in an infinite revision cycle, mousing around endlessly in an attempt to perfect the models. Such analysis paralysis takes iteration to an extreme that's no longer productive.

Visual models are communication aids, ways to represent and exchange knowledge. If we're going to communicate, we need to speak the same language. Therefore, I strongly recommend using established notations when modeling requirements or designs. A proposed system architecture can be modeled as a straightforward block diagram, but lower-level designs demand more specialized symbology. The most popular notation for object-oriented design is the Unified Modeling Language or UML (Page-Jones 2000). If you want to explore, revise, document, and share your design ideas, adopt a standard like UML instead of inventing your own notations that others might not understand. Modeling doesn't fully replace prototyping, but any method that facilitates rapidly reviewing and revising designs at a high level of abstraction will help you build better products.

| Lesson 19 | Make products easy to use correctly and hard to use incorrectly. |

I recently tried out some online life-expectancy calculators to estimate my statistical expiration date. Many such calculators are simplistic, asking for just a few bits of data and then making a fuzzy guess. I was pleased to find a comprehensive calculator that requested no fewer than thirty-five pieces of information about my personal characteristics, family background, medical history, and lifestyle. The website provided drop-down lists so that I could select values for the many data items it requested. However, the website did have one small user interface design problem, as Figure 3.5 illustrates.

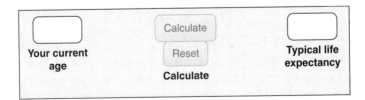

Figure 3.5 *It's too easy to accidentally click on the Reset button in this web form instead of the Calculate button.*

After entering all this data, I went to click on the Calculate button to see how much longer I might be around. However, I accidentally hit the Reset button instead. As Figure 3.5 shows, those two buttons are styled identically, are not easy to read because of a medium-gray-on-light-gray-against-gray-background color scheme, and actually touch each other, something you rarely see in UI designs. Not only that, but the prompt to trigger the calculation appears below the Reset button, not adjacent to the Calculate button, so I instinctively clicked on the button above the "Calculate" prompt. When I accidentally clicked on Reset, all thirty-five of my data entries disappeared immediately. I had to start the process again since I still wondered what my future might hold.

This website makes it too easy for the user to make a mistake. Such design problems are annoying. Maybe I'm the only user who ever accidentally clicked on the Reset button, in which case it's my problem, not the website's. Even informal usability testing might have revealed the button layout risk, though. Three simple changes could improve this design.

1. Move the Calculate and Reset buttons farther apart and position each prompt near the corresponding button so that the user is less likely to hit the wrong one by accident.

2. Style the Calculate and Reset buttons differently, such as making the riskier one—Reset—smaller and red, and making the desired one—Calculate—larger and green.

3. Protect users against error by asking them to confirm destructive actions like discarding all their data. You know, just in case they hit the wrong button by mistake.

A well-designed user interface makes the product both easy to use correctly and hard to use incorrectly. Prompts and menu options are clearly written using terminology the expected users will understand. The designer provides backout options to let the user return to a previous screen or restart a task, preferably without having to reenter information they already provided. Data inputs appear in a logical sequence. The appropriate values to enter into each field are evident because of how the fields are structured: using drop-down lists, or with adjacent guidance text.

Users appreciate systems that they understand, that prevent or correct user errors, and that communicate with them clearly and helpfully.

These properties are characteristic of an effective UI design. They make it easy for users to accomplish what they need to do when using a website or application. As well as designing for efficient usability, designers must also consider what could go wrong and how to prevent or respond to any missteps. Designers can choose to deal with potential errors in four ways (Wiegers 2021).

1. Make it impossible for the user to make a mistake.

2. Make it difficult for the user to make a mistake.

3. Make it easy to recover from an error.

4. Just let it happen. (Please don't.)

Make It Impossible for the User to Make a Mistake

Preventing errors is the preferred strategy. If the user must enter a particular piece of data, a blank input field invites arbitrary entries that the program must validate. Providing a drop-down list (or other control) with the allowable choices constrains the input to legal values. Don't provide invalid selection options. I've seen credit-card expiration date drop-down lists that included years earlier than the current one, which makes no logical sense. Similarly, I've seen controls that let the user enter non-existent dates, like February 30. Accepting invalid input data will result in an error when the app or web page tries to process the information.

Make It Difficult for the User to Make a Mistake

If you can't make user errors impossible, at least make them challenging. In the life-expectancy calculator example mentioned earlier, I proposed three ways to make it less likely that a user will click the wrong button by mistake. Another good practice is to label the options in dialog boxes to avoid ambiguity regarding the system's response to each choice. Don't make the user enter the same information twice, which doubles their opportunities to make a mistake and takes twice the time. For instance, if a form requests both the user's shipping and billing addresses, let the user indicate they're the same by ticking a checkbox.

Make It Easy to Recover from an Error

Despite your best efforts, errors will sometimes still occur, either on the user's part or behind the scenes when the system does its work. Design to make it easy for the user to recover from such situations. Easy recoverability is a characteristic of a robust software system. *Robustness* is a quality attribute that describes how well a product handles unexpected inputs, events, and operating conditions. A multilevel undo/redo function and clear, meaningful feedback messages that help the user correct any errors are particularly helpful. Cryptic numeric error codes about HTML errors, database access problems, or network failures can help with technical diagnosis, but they don't do an average user any good.

Just Let It Happen

The least desirable design option is to let the error occur and force the user to deal with the consequences. Suppose the user asks to initiate some use case that has certain preconditions that must be satisfied for the system to perform the task properly. The software should test those preconditions and help the user satisfy them if necessary, rather than just charging ahead and hoping for the best. It shouldn't even initiate the use case if the preconditions cannot be satisfied. The design should detect potential showstopping conditions as early as possible to avoid wasting the user's time. Users appreciate systems that they understand, that prevent or correct user errors, and that communicate with them clearly and helpfully.

By the way, the life-expectancy calculator that I tried suggested that I'll probably be around for a few more years. That was good news, even if using it did put a double-sized dent in my life expectancy, thanks to the less-than-ideal UI design.

Lesson 20	You can't optimize all desirable quality attributes.

The next software app I use had better not have any bugs in it, no 404 "page not found" errors or help screens that don't match the form with which I'm working. It shouldn't use much memory or slow down my computer, and it ought to free up all the memory it used when it's done. The app should be completely secure: no one can steal my data or impersonate me. It should respond instantaneously to my every command and be completely reliable. I don't want to see any "internal server error" or "application is not responding" messages. The user interface should never let me make a mistake. I should be able to use the app on any device I want, with instantaneous downloads and no timeouts. It should let me import and export any data I need from other sources. Oh, yes, I almost forgot—this app should be free too.

Doesn't that sound like a fabulous app? It sure does! Are my expectations reasonable? Of course not!

It's impossible to get the best of all possible worlds for every aspect of a software system's capabilities and characteristics. There are inevitable trade-offs among various aspects of quality—increasing one often causes an unavoidable decrease in another. Consequently, an essential part of requirements analysis is understanding which characteristics are the most important so that designers can address them appropriately.

Dimensions of Quality

Software project teams must consider a broad set of *quality attributes* as they explore requirements. Quality attributes are also called *quality factors* and *quality of service requirements*. The terms *Design for Excellence* and *DfX* refer to quality attributes as well, where X is a property of interest that designers strive to optimize (Wikipedia 2021a). When people talk about nonfunctional requirements, they're usually referring to quality attributes.

Nonfunctional requirements aren't directly implemented in software or hardware. Instead, they serve as the origin for derived functionality, architectural decisions, or design and implementation approaches. Some nonfunctional requirements impose constraints that limit the choices available to the designer or developer. For instance, an interoperability requirement could constrain a product design to use certain standard interfaces.

I've seen lists of more than fifty software quality attributes, organized in various hierarchies and groupings. Few projects will need to worry about that many. Table 3.1 lists some quality attributes that every software team should consider as they learn what quality means for their product (Wiegers and Beatty 2013). Physical products that contain embedded software have some additional quality attributes, such as those listed in Table 3.2 (Koopman 2010, Sas and Avgeriou 2020).

Table 3.1 *Some important quality attributes for software systems*

Quality Attribute	Key Interest
Availability	Can I use the system when and where I need to?
Conformance to Standards	Does the system comply with all applicable standards for functionality, safety, communication, certification, and interfaces?
Efficiency	Does the system use computer resources economically?
Installability	Can I easily install, uninstall, and reinstall the system and upgrades?
Integrity	Does the system protect against data inaccuracy, corruption, and loss?
Interoperability	Does the system connect well with others to exchange data and services?

Table 3.1 (continued)

Quality Attribute	Key Interest
Maintainability	Can developers easily modify, correct, and enhance the system?
Performance	Does the system respond sufficiently quickly to user actions and external events?
Portability	Can the system be migrated to different platforms easily?
Reliability	Does the system run when it's supposed to without failing?
Reusability	Can developers reuse portions of the system in other products?
Robustness	Does the system respond sensibly to erroneous inputs and unexpected operating conditions?
Safety	Does the system protect users from harm and property from damage?
Scalability	Can the system easily expand to accommodate more users, data, or transactions?
Security	Does the system protect against malware attacks, intruders, unauthorized users, and data theft?
Usability	Can users easily learn how to use the system and efficiently accomplish their tasks with it?
Verifiability	Can testers determine whether the software was implemented correctly?

Table 3.2 *Some additional quality attributes for physical products containing embedded software*

Quality Attribute	Key Interest
Durability	Will the product hold up well under normal usage conditions?
Extensibility	Can new functionality, sensors, or other hardware be added easily to the product without disrupting its functioning?
Fault Handling	Does the product detect, recover from, and log faults that occur?
Manufacturability	Is the product easy and cost-effective to manufacture?
Resource Usage	Does the product retain enough slack capacity in the resources consumed for memory, network bandwidth, power, processor capacity, and so forth?
Serviceability	Can people efficiently perform preventive and corrective maintenance on the product?
Sustainability	Does the product have minimal adverse environmental impacts over its life cycle, from extraction of raw materials to manufacturing, usage, and disposal?
Upgradability	Can the product be enhanced easily by adding or replacing components?

As with functionality, designers must
balance the value of achieving some quality
goal against the cost.

One property that doesn't appear in either of these tables is cost. As with product functionality, designers must balance the value of achieving some desired quality goal against the cost of achieving it. For instance, everyone would like the software they use to be available for use all the time, but achieving that can be expensive.

One of my consulting clients had a manufacturing control computer system with an availability requirement of 24 hours a day, 365 days a year (366 in leap years), with zero downtime acceptable. They met that requirement by having redundant computer systems. They could install software updates on the offline system, test the software, cut over to put that system online, and then update the second system. Having two independent computer systems was expensive, but it was cheaper than not manufacturing their product when the control system was down.

Specifying Quality Attributes

Designers need to know which quality attributes are most important, which aspects of those often-multidimensional attributes are paramount, and the target goals. It's not enough to simply say, "The system shall be reliable" or "The system shall be user friendly." The BA needs to ask questions during requirements elicitation to understand just what stakeholders mean by reliable or user friendly. How would we be able to tell whether the system was reliable or user friendly enough? What are some examples of not being reliable or user friendly?

The more precisely the BA can state the stakeholders' quality expectations, the easier it is for designers to make good choices and assess whether they've reached the goal. Roxanne Miller (2009) provides many examples of clearly written quality attribute requirements in numerous categories. When possible, state quality goals in measurable and verifiable ways to guide design decisions. Consider using Planguage, a keyword language that permits precise, quantitative specification for such vague attributes as availability and performance (Simmons 2001, Gilb 2005). Specifying requirements this carefully takes some time, but that's time well spent compared to restructuring a product after it fails to meet customer expectations.

Designing for Quality

Designers can optimize their solution approach for just about any quality parameter, depending on what they've been told—or think—is most important. Without guidance, one designer might optimize for performance, another usability, and a third portability across delivery platforms. The project's requirements explorations need to identify which attributes are more important than others to guide the designers in the most important direction for business success. That is, you need to prioritize nonfunctional requirements just as you do functionality.

Prioritization is essential because of the trade-offs between certain pairs of quality attributes. Increasing one quality attribute often requires that the designer compromise in some other areas (Wiegers and Beatty 2013). Here are some examples of quality attribute conflicts that demand trade-off decisions.

- Multifactor authentication is more secure than a simple login password, but it reduces usability because of the additional steps and possibly devices involved.

- A product or component that's designed to be reusable might be less efficient than if the code for that functionality were optimized for a single application. Provided the performance penalty is acceptable, it still could be sensible to create a reusable component.

- Optimizing a system for performance could reduce its portability if the developers exploited specific operating system or language properties to squeeze out every bit of performance.

- Optimizing certain aspects of a complex quality attribute could degrade others. For instance, within the broad usability domain, designing for ease of learning by new or occasional users might make the system less efficient for use by an expert.

On the other hand, some pairs of quality attributes exhibit synergies. Designing a system for high reliability will enhance several other attributes:

- Availability (If the system doesn't crash, people can use it.)

- Integrity (The risk of data loss or corruption from a system failure is reduced.)

- Robustness (The product is less likely to fail because of an unexpected user action or environmental condition.)

- Safety (If a product's safety mechanisms work reliably, nobody gets hurt.)

The quality attribute interactions demonstrate why the project team must understand early on what quality means to the key stakeholders and align everyone's work toward those objectives. Stakeholders who don't work with BAs to shape this understanding are at the mercy of designers who will make their best guess. If you don't explore nonfunctional requirements during elicitation and specify them precisely, you're just lucky if designers build in the properties that customers value.

Architecture and Quality Attributes

The development team needs to understand which attributes require close attention early on so that they can make appropriate architectural design choices. A system's architecture affects multiple attributes, including availability, efficiency, interoperability, performance, portability, reliability, safety, scalability, and security. Because compromises are often needed, if architects don't know which attributes are most important, they might make design choices that don't lead to the desired outcomes.

It's costly to go back late in development or after release and reengineer the system's architecture to remedy quality shortcomings. Building systems incrementally without early knowledge of the most significant quality goals can lead to problems that might be hard to rectify, particularly if both hardware and software are involved. As is so common with software projects, spending a little more time up front to better understand the quality goals can lead to less expensive and more durable solutions.

| Lesson 21 | An ounce of design is worth a pound of recoding. |

When I wrote my first book twenty-five years ago, I didn't know what I was doing. I began with a comically skimpy outline; my initial book architecture was severely flawed. With guidance from an exceptionally patient editor (thanks, Wendy!), I restructured the manuscript into something far more readable. That restructuring took a full month of cutting and pasting, dragging and dropping, patching and smoothing. It added no value to the content but much to the delivery.

That painful rework experience delivered a powerful message. Since I've begun investing a lot more effort into designing a book at both the architectural and detailed levels, I've never had to do more than minor sequencing tweaks. I can then concentrate on content, not structure. As we saw in Lesson 18, "It's cheaper to iterate at higher levels of abstraction," moving items around in a book outline is far easier than reorganizing and rewriting sentences.

The same lesson applies to software design. Time invested in thoughtfully considering the design is more than repaid by time *not* spent fixing problems later—up to a point. You can certainly waste time trying to perfect a design in the face of uncertainties, so you need to scale your design efforts to the nature of the problem. Even after doing your best to craft a design, you might discover shortcomings later on and have to tune it up. Nonetheless, time spent considering how to structure various aspects of your program helps you avoid excessive redesign and recoding.

Technical Debt and Refactoring

Designs executed in haste can generate *technical debt*, shortcomings that someone must resolve in the future to maintain the product's proper functioning and expandability. (See Lesson 50, "Today's 'gotta get it out right away' development project is tomorrow's maintenance nightmare," for more about technical debt.) A modest amount of technical debt could be an acceptable trade-off if skimping on design and hacking the code together accelerates achieving a pressing business objective. However, the flaws remain. The longer the team waits to address them, the more extensive, costly, and disruptive the rework will be. As with any loan, technical debt should be viewed as temporary and steadily paid off.

Rework to reduce technical debt often takes the form of refactoring. *Refactoring* is the process of restructuring existing code to improve its design without changing its functioning. You might decide to restructure some code to simplify it, make it more maintainable or extensible, improve its efficiency, remove duplicated and unneeded portions, or make other improvements. Substantial design changes can require significant recoding effort, when the team would prefer to be creating new useful functionality. I get uncomfortable when I see the prefix *re-* used this many times. We are doing something over again that we've already done once.

Design rework consumes effort without adding much immediate value to the customer, but it's necessary to maintain a stable foundation for continued product growth. Good design minimizes creating technical debt, whereas refactoring chips away at accumulated technical debt. A judicious balance of the two will yield the best results. Deficient initial designs can lead to excessive rework; overly prescriptive designs can consume excessive time and may still miss the mark. Two quotations from design experts reveal the dichotomy:

> By continuously improving the design of code, we make it easier and easier to work with. This is in sharp contrast to what typically happens: little refactoring and a great deal of attention paid to expediently adding new features (Kerievsky 2005).

> It is practically impossible to think of everything or know everything in the beginning of a project... However, you can use your experience and the experiences of others to guide you in a certain direction. You can make decisions today that might minimize changes tomorrow (Pugh 2005).

As Ken Pugh indicates in the preceding quote, a design goal is to make sensible decisions now to prevent unnecessary changes in the future. Use your judgment and input from your business stakeholders to guide design choices based on how likely it is that certain portions of the product will have to change.

Accruing technical debt because the team doesn't have time to perform design properly merely pushes the problem into the future.

Architectural Shortcomings

Making small design adjustments as you go along isn't too painful. It steadily and incrementally improves the product. Major architectural restructuring to improve product robustness or the user experience is more disruptive.

As an illustration of how a deficient architectural design affects the user experience, consider the many different ways to delete an item from a smartphone. The user actions, prompts, and icons vary depending on what you're deleting: text message, mail message, saved map location, photo, note, calendar event, alarm, contact, missed phone call, or an entire app. Some deletion actions require confirmation; others do not. The process sometimes varies if you're deleting a single instance of the object or multiple instances. It gets confusing for the user.

Designers could have avoided many of these inconsistencies had they worked from common UI standards and an overarching design architecture. Design thinking at that level might have enabled some code reuse as well. Reuse is an excellent way to improve quality, boost developer productivity, and reduce the user's learning curve. It would take an excessive amount of work to achieve commonality in those delete operations at this late stage of product maturity. And that's just for one operation that appears in some form in nearly every software system.

Software developers always create a design, either on the fly or through careful consideration. Accruing technical debt because the team doesn't have time to perform design and implementation properly merely pushes the problem into the future, where it continues to grow in impact. Investing in design—what Ken Pugh (2005) terms *prefactoring*—can save considerable restructuring and recoding down the road when you'd rather work on something else.

Lesson 22	Many system problems take place at interfaces.

The simplest software system consists of a single code module and an interface to the user. An *interface* describes how two architectural elements intersect, either internally between two components of a multicomponent system or between the system and its external environment. Some interfaces must follow established standards and protocols, such as for communications and hardware connections or to incorporate a module from a reusable library. Other interfaces are specific to a particular application.

Any sizable software system has many modules and numerous internal interfaces between system components, as one component invokes another to provide some service. A system could also present external interfaces to human users, other software systems, hardware devices, networks, and the computer's operating system, as illustrated in Figure 3.6. Products that contain both hardware and software components introduce additional interface complexities.

Internal and external interfaces are common sources of problems. For instance, reusable code libraries with poorly or incorrectly documented interface descriptions can increase coding time as developers struggle to integrate the components into their system. The conscientious designer will ensure that all pieces of a complex system fit together correctly across their mutual interfaces. New components that developers integrate into an existing system must conform to established interface conventions.

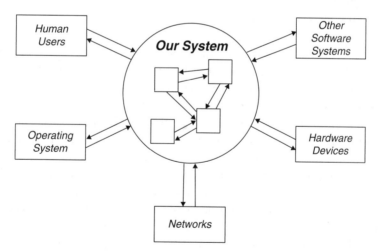

Figure 3.6 *Software systems have internal interfaces between components and external interfaces to other entities.*

Technical Interface Issues

An interface defines a contract or agreement regarding how two architectural elements—one a requestor and the other a provider—connect to exchange data, services, or both. Each of these elements has a clearly defined boundary and a set of responsibilities or services it provides. Defining an interface involves more than just stating how to invoke an operation across it. A complete interface description contains numerous elements (Pugh 2005, Rozanski and Woods 2005):

- The syntax (type and format) and semantics (meaning) of service requests and responses that cross the interface, including both data and control inputs and outputs

- Constraints that restrict the data types or values that may be passed across the interface

- The mechanism or protocols by which the interface functions, such as messaging or a remote procedure call

- Preconditions that state conditions that must be true at the beginning of an interaction across the interface

- Postconditions that state conditions that will be true following the interaction for both success and exception scenarios

Problems can arise if the responsibilities for the requestor and provider components that share an interface aren't clear. Functionality could be duplicated across the components, or functionality could be missing because the people working on the two components each thought the other would handle it. Architectural components should always respect their established interfaces. For instance, a code module should never attempt to access code or data in another module except through their mutual interface.

Each implementation of an interface should conform to what its contract specifies (Pugh 2005). Further, the implementation should do no harm, such as consuming excessive memory or holding locks on data objects unnecessarily. The design also must handle interface errors. If an interface implementation can't perform its responsibilities for some reason, it should provide an appropriate notification to assist in recovery efforts.

I recently began reading an e-book that I borrowed from the library in my iPad's web browser. I repeatedly tried to download the file for offline access, using the button provided for that function. The download would begin, but then I'd see the uninformative error message shown in Figure 3.7. Apparently, there was some repro-ducible failure with the interface between my iPad and the server that hosted the e-book, which the software duly reported to me. But I have no clue from this message where the problem lay or what to do about it. I never could download that e-book or others that I tried to access in the same way.

Designers should thoroughly plan and study the system's internal and exter-nal interfaces to prevent such user annoyances. Complex systems that have many interconnected components are challenging to modify. Changing one of the inter-face definitions can launch a cascade of changes in the other connected compo-nents. Unless the system is architected with clearly defined component interfaces, technical debt can accrue as the team adds new capabilities that require interface changes. Problems can also arise if new functionality doesn't respect the existing interfaces.

When designing an interface, it's common to start with everything the designer thinks a user—whether a human or another system—might need. This approach can result in bloated interfaces loaded with functionality that the interface's users won't ever employ. It's preferable to pursue a requestor-driven design by asking, "What functions will the users of my interface actually need?" Writing tests before

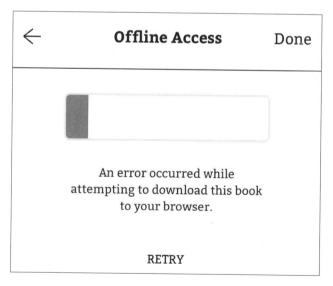

Figure 3.7 *This message didn't help me correct an interface error between my iPad and the e-book server.*

implementation helps designers think through how the interface will be used so that they can incorporate the required interface capabilities without including unnecessary elements. Understanding the tasks that users will want to perform with the software also contributes to building a streamlined UI.

Try to anticipate likely changes developers will make in the system over time and consider how they might affect the interfaces. This anticipation is particularly important when growing an application in iterative and incremental development life cycles. The priority of planned incremental enhancements will inform developers about those portions of the system that are more likely to change and those that should remain more stable. Designing the architecture well from the outset facilitates sustained product growth and frequent releases (Scaled Agile 2021b).

Input Data Validation

Each component involved in an interaction should validate the inputs it receives across the interface before processing them. Many security exploits occur because bad actors inject malicious code across an interface that doesn't reject it as an invalid input. My website's error log occasionally shows messages suggesting that a user attempted to access the site with invalid inputs. Fortunately, my website hosting provider looks for such dangerous inputs and blocks them. Microsoft (2017) recommends some practices for validating user input to thwart these types of malware attacks. Conforming to secure coding standards and using tools to scan for interface risks and other security threats also reduces system security vulnerabilities (SEI 2020).

Figure 3.8 provides a heuristic to guide your assessment of interface behavior. Following a proper design-by-contract interface strategy will ensure that your components lie in the two quadrants within the heavy dashed line.

Each component involved in an interaction should validate the inputs it receives across the interface before processing them.

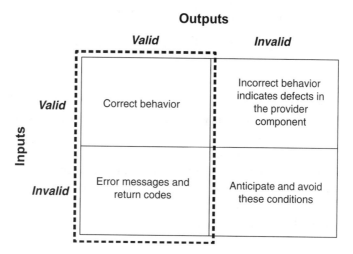

Figure 3.8 *Looking at valid and invalid inputs and outputs lets you assess proper interface behavior (courtesy of Gary K. Evans, personal communication).*

A well-designed system will properly handle exceptions that take place at both internal and external interfaces. I recently tried to print a document from my Windows PC to a printer on my home Wi-Fi network. The printer was powered on and connected to the network, but my PC insisted the printer was offline. I had to restart my PC, which then correctly discovered the printer as being online and sent the print job. Some unhandled interface problem between the PC and the printer apparently had broken the connection between them, with no way for me to repair it other than the drastic action of a computer reboot.

User Interface Issues

Users aren't concerned with a system's internal architecture but with its user interface. User interface shortcomings lead to products that users regard as being thoughtlessly designed. Inconsistent UI behavior confuses and frustrates users, as we saw with the diverse smartphone deletion operations described in the preceding lesson. Poorly designed user interfaces lead to products that aren't easy or obvious to use, waste the user's time, make it too easy to make a mistake, and don't work well in realistic usage scenarios (Wiegers 2021).

Defining UI standards helps provide a consistent user experience both throughout an application and across multiple related applications. When I managed a small software group, we adopted UI guidelines for the applications we developed for internal company use. These guidelines helped all of our applications look and behave similarly. Our users could recognize from the UI that an app they used came out of our group, but they couldn't tell which team member designed the UI because of its style.

Well-designed user interfaces should require little support documentation in the form of help screens, user guides, and tip sheets (Davis 1995). They make it easier for users to get up to speed on a new application, and users will make fewer errors when they use it. There's a vast body of literature on software UX design; a valuable resource is the classic book *About Face* by Alan Cooper et al. (2014). Any designer will benefit from usability expert Jakob Nielsen's usability heuristics for UI design (Nielsen 2020). Keeping the design focused on usage rather than on product features can help avoid many UX problems. (See Lesson 4, "A usage-centric approach to requirements will meet customer needs better than a feature-centric approach.")

Interface Wars

Interface problems sometimes come to light as the team integrates code modules into the product. Integration testing failures when multiple modules are combined can trigger finger-pointing as developers attempt to determine where the problem lies. This conflict isn't healthy. If the architecture is appropriately structured, interfaces are well defined, developers respect the interfaces, and modules pass their unit tests, then integration should progress smoothly—and without rancor.

Next Steps: Design

1. Identify which of the lessons described in this chapter are relevant to your experiences with different aspects of software design.

2. Can you think of any other design-related lessons from your own experience that might be worth sharing with your colleagues?

3. Identify any practices described in this chapter that might be solutions to the design-related problems you identified in the First Steps at the beginning of the chapter. How could each practice improve the way your project teams design their products?

4. How could you tell whether each practice from Step 3 was yielding the desired results? What would those results be worth to you?

5. Identify any barriers that might make it difficult to apply the practices from Step 3. How could you break down those barriers or enlist allies to help you implement the practices?

6. Put into place guidance documents, checklists, or other aids to help future project teams apply your local design best practices effectively.

Chapter 4

Lessons About Project Management

Introduction to Project Management

The Project Management Institute defines a *project* as "a temporary endeavor undertaken to create a unique product, service or result" (PMI n.d.). It defines *project management* as "the application of knowledge, skills, tools, and techniques to project activities to meet the project requirements."

These definitions sound reasonable, but I don't think project management is a discrete discipline. Instead, project management involves managing many activities that—in the aggregate—contribute to project success. These activities could be performed by a single individual, a group or hierarchy of managers on a large project, or collaboratively by partitioning activities among multiple team members. For instance, on a project following Scrum, various project management responsibilities are distributed among the Scrum Master, product owner, and other team members. When I say *project manager* in this book, I refer to whoever is involved with the activities of guiding projects from inception to successful completion, regardless of their job titles or other project responsibilities.

Project management involves managing many activities that—in the aggregate—contribute to project success.

This introduction describes some of the domains included in project management; several of these are addressed in more detail in this chapter's lessons. Even if you aren't a specialist project manager, you manage your own work and have project delivery responsibilities. Much of this chapter's contents therefore applies to individuals as well as to project teams.

People Management

Projects are carried out by people, ranging from a single individual through a small colocated team to a cast of hundreds working on multiple subprojects in numerous locations. Managing a project involves identifying what must be done and when, determining the mix of skills needed to do it, identifying individuals to fill the various project roles, and then bringing them in at the right time. Once people are on board, they need to be managed, led, and perhaps trained appropriately. Occasionally, it might be necessary to replace certain individuals because of their performance or an improper fit to the work.

Requirements Management

As we saw in Chapter 2, all projects have requirements. Most requirements describe the product itself; others describe related project work, such as developing training materials or transitioning to a replacement system. Some projects launch with an already completed baseline set of requirements. On others, developing requirements is an ongoing part of the project work. For the latter, the team must have both people who are skilled in requirements activities and the time needed to do the requirements work. Adjusting project plans to keep the team focused on delivering the necessary system capabilities and characteristics is a core project management activity.

Expectation Management

An essential part of managing a project is to set realistic expectations that stakeholders understand and accept. Those expectations include the properties of the solution that the project team will deliver and the delivery parameters. Delivery parameters include the schedule for interim and final deliveries, cost, quality, resources required, and limitations—things the solution will not include. Frank discussions help ensure that the project participants know what others expect from them, which facilitates negotiating mutually acceptable—and achievable—commitments (Karten 1994).

Some stakeholders might not be happy with particular expectations. However, project managers must deal with reality, not with fantasies of ideal but unachievable outcomes. When project situations change, project managers need to negotiate adjusted expectations with the affected stakeholders.

Task Management

Delivering the expected value from a project requires that many tasks be completed correctly in the right sequence. Some tasks can't begin (or complete) until others are either begun or completed. Participants need to identify tasks at an appropriate level of granularity, allocate resources to each task, and roll up sets of tasks into milestones that show progress to defined checkpoints. The project manager needs to sequence the work to achieve the project's objectives in the shortest time and at the lowest cost, avoiding unnecessary wait states and delays. Task management is a continuous juggling act.

Commitment Management

Project managers make commitments to their customers, their own managers, and their team members. Similarly, those other participants make commitments to the project manager and one another. Commitments often are based on estimates, which have intrinsic uncertainty. As one experienced project manager pointed out, "Estimates are not actuals in advance." Everyone must make commitments in good faith based on the best information available. They should track progress toward those commitments, honestly adjust them as realities change, and take action when a commitment isn't fulfilled.

Risk Management

All projects contain unknowns and risks. A vital success factor is anticipating potential risks, assessing their likely impact on the project, and controlling them to the extent possible. Failure to manage risks actively is an invitation to let the resultant problems surprise—and perhaps derail—the project. The project manager is focused on enabling success, but they also have to keep an eye open for trouble ahead. Risk management is worrying about the what-ifs before they become the what-do-we-do-nows.

Communication Management

Communication is at the core of project management. Projects generate information regarding status, issues, resource expenditures and needs, changes, expectations, and the like. Project management encompasses acquiring this information, storing it appropriately, and sharing it with the right people at the right time. Large projects that involve multiple teams in numerous locations, sometimes speaking different languages and with diverse cultures and communication preferences, pose particular communication challenges.

Change Management

It's safe to assume that a project's final product won't be precisely what people anticipated at the outset. The project manager must cope with changes in requirements, priorities, resources, technologies, processes, and regulations. Each team should establish mechanisms at the beginning to help them anticipate and accommodate change with as little disruption as possible. Agile projects are explicitly structured to accommodate change, welcoming new requirements and dynamically adjusting the backlog of remaining work to ensure that the team is always working on the top-priority activities.

Resource Management

I don't like to hear managers refer to human beings as "resources," but people do constitute the largest—and most costly—resource on most software projects. Besides assembling the right staff, managers need to provide physical facilities, computer systems, communications infrastructures, testing laboratories, and access privileges for contractors. Managing the project's budget is another critical activity.

Dependency Management

Many projects have dependencies on outside factors beyond their control. They might be awaiting delivery of software or hardware components from a third party before they can proceed. One project that built a new printer was delayed because the international standard for the new hardware interface protocol was not yet finalized. Tasks and activities can have internal dependencies within the project, also. A project manager must identify such dependencies, incorporate appropriate lead times into the project schedule, and monitor status to see whether each dependency will be fulfilled. It's also a good idea to create contingency plans in case a dependency fails.

Dependencies can run the other way too. If the current project is itself a dependency for another one, the project manager should communicate status frequently to the other project team so that they know what to expect.

Contract Management

Contracts constitute legally binding agreements among parties. Not all projects involve formal contracts, but someone must attentively manage those that do. Failing to deliver on a contract can have significant consequences. A developing organization might have contracts with customers, vendors of goods, and subcontractors who perform portions of the project work. Contracts should include such details as who will pay for customer-requested scope changes and the consequences of failing to meet contractual commitments.

Even on projects with no formal contracts, agreements reached among the participants imply some level of "contract." These tacit contracts can be more difficult and critical to manage, simply because they're not explicitly negotiated and documented. It would be unwise for a project manager to ignore implicit agreements, expectations, or commitments simply because "we don't have a written contract."

Supplier Management

Software projects often involve outsourcing (and hence contracting). The entire body of development work could be outsourced to a third-party company, possibly offshore. Some projects outsource only certain activities, such as system testing. Building partnerships with these suppliers involves establishing contractual agreements, communication mechanisms, common tools, quality expectations, and dispute resolution processes. Third-party supplier arrangements introduce risks and dependencies over which the project manager might have little influence.

Managing Away the Barriers

Based on this lengthy list of subdisciplines, project management clearly is an extensive and challenging process on any sizable project. The people responsible for each project's success should assess which of these domains apply to their project and ensure that they have the appropriate experience, skills, and time available, either in themselves or in other team members.

The project manager's primary responsibility is to clear out obstacles that impede the team's progress. I like to think of the project manager as working for the team, not the reverse. Someone has to provide resources, resolve conflicts, negotiate outcomes, coordinate activities, run interference, and keep the team running smoothly. By any title, on any project, that's a big responsibility. This chapter presents twelve lessons that can make the project manager's job easier.

First Steps: Project Management

I suggest you spend a few minutes on the following activities before reading the project management-related lessons in this chapter. As you read the lessons, contemplate to what extent each of them applies to your organization or project team.

1. List project management practices that your organization is especially good at. Is information about those practices documented to remind team members about them and make it easy to apply them?

2. Identify any problems—points of pain—that you can attribute to shortcomings in how project teams estimate, plan, coordinate, and track their work.

3. State the impacts that each problem has on your ability to complete projects successfully. How do the problems impede achieving business success for both the development organization and its customers? Common problems include the following:

   • Inadequate visibility into the necessary work and its status

   • Communication gaps

   • Collaboration shortcomings

   • Unrealistic estimates and plans

   • Unfulfilled commitments

   • Unexpected risks that materialize into problems

   • Failed dependencies

4. For each problem from Step 2, identify the root causes that trigger the problem or make it worse. Some root causes are internal to the project team or organization; others arise from sources outside the team that are beyond your control. Problems, impacts, and root causes can blur together, so try to tease them apart and see their connections. You might find multiple root causes that contribute to the same problem, as well as several problems that arise from a single root cause.

5. As you read this chapter, list any practices that would be useful to your team.

Lesson 23 **Work plans must account for friction.**

I overheard this conversation at work one day:

Manager Shannon: "Jamie, I know you're doing the usability assessments on the Canary project right now. Several other projects are also interested in usability assessments. How much time do you spend on that?"

Team Member Jamie: "About eight hours a week."

Manager Shannon: "Okay, so you could work with five projects at a time then."

Do you see any flaws in Shannon's thinking? Five times eight is forty, the nominal hours in a work week, so this discussion seems reasonable on the surface. But Shannon hasn't considered the many factors that reduce the time that individuals have available each day for project work: project friction (as opposed to interpersonal friction, which I'm not discussing here).

There's a difference between elapsed hours on the job and effective available hours. This difference is just one factor that both project planners and individual team members must keep in mind as they translate size or effort estimates into calendar time. If people don't incorporate these friction factors into their planning, they'll forever underestimate how long it will take to get work done.

Task Switching and Flow

People do not multitask—they task switch. When multitasking computers switch from one job to another, there's a period of unproductive time during the switch. The same is true of people, only it's far worse. It takes a little while to gather all the materials you need to work on a different activity, access the right files, and reload your brain with the pertinent information. You need to change your mental context to focus on the new problem and remember where you were the last time you worked on it. That's the slow part.

Some people are better at task switching than others. Maybe I have a short attention span, but I'm pretty good at diverting my focus to something different and then resuming the original activity right where I left off. For many people, though, excessive task switching destroys productivity. Programmers are particularly susceptible to the time-sucking impact of multitasking, as Joel Spolsky (2001) explains:

> When you manage programmers, specifically, task switches take a really, really, really long time. That's because programming is the kind of task where you have to keep a lot of things in your head at once. The more things you remember at once, the more productive you are at programming. A programmer coding at full throttle is keeping zillions of things in their head at once.

People do not multitask—they task switch.

When I was a manager, a developer named Jordan said he was flailing. Jordan didn't understand the priorities of items in his work backlog. He would work on task A for a while, then feel guilty that he was neglecting task B, so he'd switch to that one. He was getting little done as a result. Jordan and I worked out his priorities and a plan for allocating time to tasks in turn. He stopped flailing, his productivity went up, and Jordan felt much better about his progress. Jordan's task-switching overhead and priority confusion affected both his productivity and his state of mind.

When you're deeply immersed in some work, focused on the activity and free from distractions, you enter a mental state called *flow*. Creative knowledge work like software development (or writing a book) requires flow to be productive (DeMarco and Lister 2013). You understand what you're working on, the information you need is in your working memory, and you know where you're headed. You can tell you've been in a state of flow when you lose track of time as you're making great progress and having fun. Then your phone pings with a text message, an e-mail notification pops up, your computer reminds you that a meeting starts in five minutes, or someone stops by to talk. Boom—there goes your flow.

Interruptions are flow killers. It takes several minutes to get your brain back into that highly productive state and pick up where you were before the interruption. Some reports suggest that interruptions and task switching can impose a penalty of at least 15 percent of a knowledge worker's time, amounting to more than one hour per day (DeMarco 2001). A realistic measure of your effective work capacity is based not on how many hours you're at work or even how many hours you're on task, but how many *uninterrupted* hours you're on task (DeMarco and Lister 2013).

To achieve the high productivity and satisfaction that come from an extended state of flow, you need to actively manage your work time. The potential for distractions and interruptions is ever-present unless you take steps to block them out. Jory MacKay (2021) offers several recommendations for reducing context switching and its accompanying productivity destruction.

- **Timeblock your schedule to create clearer focus boundaries.** Planning how you will spend your day, with dedicated blocks of time allocated to specific activities, carves out opportunities for extended deep concentration. If the nature of your work permits, devote certain full days each week to focus on your most important individual tasks, to more actively collaborate with others, or to catch up on busywork.

- **Build a habit of single tasking throughout the day.** One of my talented but less productive team members was able to get more work done when we agreed that he would set aside half-day blocks of time during which he didn't answer the phone, texts, or e-mails—at all.

- **Employ routines to remove attention residue as you migrate from one task to the next.** Physically moving on to the next activity doesn't immediately unplug your brain from the previous one, which can be a distraction. A small transition ritual or distraction—a cup of coffee, an amusing video—can help you make that mental break into a new work mode.

- **Take regular breaks to recharge.** The intense concentration of a state of flow is great—up to a point. You must come up for air occasionally. Stretch your tired neck, arms, and shoulders. To minimize eyestrain, periodically focus your eyes on something in the distance for a few seconds instead of staring at the screen endlessly. Short mental breaks are refreshing before you dive back into that productive flow state.

Effective Hours

At-work hours seep away through many channels. You attend meetings and video chats, respond to e-mails, look things up on the web, participate in retrospectives, and review your teammates' code. Time gets lost to unexpected bug fixes, kicking around ideas with your coworkers, administrative activities, and the usual healthy socializing.

Working from home offers myriad other distractions, many of them more fun than project work. Even if you work forty hours a week, you don't spend anywhere near that many on your project.

One software group of mine measured how we devoted our time on projects for several years (Wiegers 1996). Individuals tracked the time (to half-hour resolution) they spent working on each project in ten activity categories: project planning, requirements, design, implementation, testing, documentation, and four types of maintenance. We didn't try to make the weekly numbers add up to any total. We just wanted to know how we really spent our time, compared to how we thought we spent our time, compared to how we were supposed to spend our time.

The results were eye-opening. In the first year we collected data, we devoted an average of just 26 hours per week to project work. The tracking made us all more conscious of finding ways to focus our time more productively. However, we never exceeded an average of 31 hours of project time per week.

Several of my colleagues have obtained similar results, averaging five to six hours per day on project work. Other sources also suggest that a typical average of ideal work hours—"uninterrupted attentive time for project tasks"—is about five hours per day (Larman 2004). Rather than relying on published figures to estimate your effective project time, collect your own data. Recording how you work for a few typical weeks will provide a good idea of how many hours per week you can expect to devote to project tasks, which affects the team's projected productivity or velocity.

The intent of this time tracking is not so that managers can see who's working hard. Managers shouldn't even see the data for individuals, just aggregated team or organizational data. Knowing the team's average effective weekly work hours helps everyone make more realistic estimates, plans, and commitments.

Other Sources of Project Friction

Besides the daily frittering away of time on myriad activities, project teams lose time to other sources of friction. For instance, most corporate IT organizations are responsible for both new development and enhancing and repairing current production systems. Since you can't predict when something will break or a change request will come along, these sporadic, interruptive maintenance demands usurp team members' time with unplanned work.

Distance between project participants can retard information exchanges and decision-making. (See Lesson 39, "It takes little physical separation to inhibit communication and collaboration.") Even with the many collaboration tools available, projects with people in multiple locations and time zones should expect some slowdown from communication friction. Sometimes you can't reach an individual, such as a key customer representative who has the answer you need. You have to either wait until they're available or make your best guess so that you can proceed. That slows you down, especially when an incorrect guess leads to rework.

The team composition can further impose friction if project participants speak different native languages and work in diverse cultures. Unclear and volatile requirement priorities can chew up hours as people spend time researching, debating, and adjusting priorities. The team might have to temporarily shelve some incomplete work if a new, higher-priority task inserts itself into the schedule. Unplanned rework is yet another time diversion.

I know of a contract project that involved a customer in the eastern United States and a vendor in western Canada (Wiegers 2003). Their project plan included some peer reviews of certain deliverables. However, the long-distance reviews took longer than expected, as did follow-up to verify the corrections made. Slow decision-making across the distance further reduced the project's pace. Sluggish iteration to resolve requirements questions and ambiguity about who the right contact people were for each issue were further impediments. These—and other—factors put the project behind schedule after just the first week and eventually contributed to its failure.

Planning Implications

Project friction has a profound impact on estimation, so both individuals and teams must keep it in mind. I estimate how long individual tasks will take as though I will have no distractions or interruptions, just focused and productive time. Next, I convert that ideal effort estimate into calendar time based on my effective work-hour percentage. I also consider whether any of the other aforementioned sources of friction could affect my estimates. Then I try to arrange my work so that I can focus on a single task at a time until it's complete or I hit a blocking point.

My colleague Dave described what happens on his current project, whose manager doesn't consider the impacts of time lost to excessive multitasking:

> The manager likes to split people up between teams, 50 percent here and 50 percent there, or 50, 25, and 25. But when this happens, it seems like they forget the percentages and think the team has all full-time people. Then they seem surprised at how long things take. Also, being on multiple teams means more overhead in meetings and less coding time.

If people always create estimates without accounting for the many ways that time splitting and project conditions can slow down the work, they're destined to overrun their estimates every time.

Lesson 24	Don't give anyone an estimate off the top of your head.

You're a business analyst (BA) or product owner. As you walk down the hall in your workplace, you bump into Melody, one of your project's customer representatives. "I'd like to add something to that project we're working on," Melody says. You stop and listen to her description of the new feature. "How much work do you think it would take to put that in?" she asks.

You ponder for a moment. "About three days," you reply.

Melody says, "Great, thanks. Let's do it." You both resume your journeys down the hallway.

You return to your desk and think about Melody's new feature some more. The more you look into it, the larger it appears. You realize that there's no way the team can implement it with just three days of effort, as you had told Melody earlier. There's a lot more to it than you thought. As you understand the feature better, you're also concerned that it might conflict with another feature the team has planned for the next development cycle. Is it too late to change your reply to Melody?

Hasty Predictions

The best response to a request for an estimate is, "Let me get back to you on that." An estimate you provide in passing based on limited information and superficial analysis could be terribly inaccurate, yet it sounds a lot like a commitment to the other person. Melody took you at your word, so now you have to explain that her request is larger than you initially appreciated. Some negotiation and replanning will be needed before the team can commit to adding this new feature. That can be an awkward conversation. As Mike Cohn (2010) points out:

> "We estimate this will take seven months" was translated into "We commit to finishing in seven months." Estimating and committing are both important, but they should be viewed as separate activities.

It's tempting to give someone a quick estimate off the top of your head, but try to suppress that temptation until you've studied the request more. Those quick responses aren't analytically derived estimates, but rather guesses pulled out of thin air. Before you provide an estimate, make sure you know just what the request encompasses. Then assess what it realistically would take to deliver on that request.

Quick—and maybe not very accurate—estimates are a common problem when dealing with new requirements and change requests. Impact analysis often reveals that the problem is larger than you appreciated based on your initial information. If you provide a realistic estimate, the requester might elect to drop the whole thing because it's not worth the time or cost required. It's better to know that before you begin implementing the new functionality, instead of getting partway done and then abandoning it when the change turns out to be unjustifiably large. I've seen that happen; it's an expensive waste of effort.

When you study the problem and derive your best estimate for a piece of work, consider the following factors and include the answers when you deliver the estimate.

- What assumptions influenced your estimate? How can you verify their validity?

- Do you know who will be doing the work? Different team members have different skill sets; some are more productive than others. If you don't know who would handle it, you have to assume some average performance level.

- Someone will have to write and execute tests for new functionality. You might need a code review and regression testing to make sure the change didn't break anything else. Make it clear whether your estimate encompasses this full scope of work or just the coding part.

- Have you considered unobvious impacts and extra work that might be required beyond simply implementing the new functionality? It could affect other functionality or negatively impact some quality attribute. It might require design modifications, interface changes, or user documentation updates.

- Can you think of any risks that might affect your sunny-day, everything-goes-fine estimate?

The fuzzier the problem statement and the less certain the assumptions are, the fuzzier the estimate will be.

Fear of Fuzz

Sometimes the people who receive estimates don't realize how much uncertainty even a carefully crafted estimate can have. The fuzzier the problem statement and the less certain the assumptions are, the fuzzier the estimate will be. If customers hear a single number like "three days," that's what they're going to remember and count on. Providing an estimate in the form of a range—best case to worst case—instead of a single-point value is a reminder that an estimate is an approximate prediction of the future, not a guarantee (McConnell 2006). The listener might still choose to focus on the lower number of the range: "So it's *possible* you'll be done in three days, right?" It's important to communicate expectations clearly when you present an estimate.

A significant problem when providing a bald, unsupported estimate is that the people who receive the estimate have little understanding of how you formulated it. You can do a thorough job of analyzing, planning, and allowing for contingencies, yet the response could still be, "That's ridiculous. It can't take you that long to get it done." A superficial guess that lacks careful analysis will be more optimistic and hence better received, but that just sets everyone up for more disappointment when reality sets in.

We all like to provide instant gratification when someone asks something of us. However, if you take the time to reflect on a problem before you offer an estimate for solving it, you'll paint yourself into fewer commitment corners.

| Lesson 25 | Icebergs are always larger than they first appear. |

My manager once called me and asked, "Got an hour?" He'd been approached by a scientist who'd written a simple BASIC program on his PC to calculate formulas for chemical solutions he used in his research. The scientist wanted one of us software people to port his program to our mainframe so that others could use it.

This seemed like a quick job on the surface. My manager's initial request really would have taken only a couple of hours. However, I realized that there was much more to the problem. The program needed to include more calculations than this scientist had addressed, because different researchers worked with different chemicals. The calculations had to be more accurate than his simple homegrown approach considered. We also needed a flexible interface that would work for a large user group and to generate reports suitable for use in the lab.

I explored the full spectrum of requirements and researched how to improve the computational accuracy. Then I designed a solution and UI, coded the software, and tested the application. This project consumed just over 100 hours of my time. It was a good investment, as the application was heavily used for years.

Most software projects don't turn out to be 100 times larger than initially estimated. However, projects do tend to balloon from their initial conception through more thorough problem analysis and change requests during development.

The longer the project takes, the more you can expect it to grow. Software industry analyst Capers Jones (2006) found that the requirements set on large projects typically grows between 1 percent and 3 percent per calendar month during development. If you don't anticipate some growth and plan to accommodate it, you're certain to fall behind plan.

Iterative development approaches acknowledge that the iceberg's size isn't fully understood at the outset.

You've probably heard that a large fraction of an iceberg is hidden below the water's surface. Similarly, a lot of the work needed to execute a software project might not be visible initially. Iterative development approaches acknowledge that the iceberg's size isn't fully understood at the outset. As software is delivered in chunks, stakeholders will think of more functionality to add. That is, the more they see, the more they'll want (Davis 1995). The iceberg is always bigger than you thought it was initially, and it just keeps growing.

Contingency Buffers

One way to deal with requirements growth is to build *contingency buffers* into project schedules. Buffers provide a margin for error, a way to handle uncertainty. When you plan a development cycle, you're basing your estimates on limited information about the project's scope, assumptions that might not be true, and other variables. Because of these unknowns, it's a good idea to add some slack to the schedule in the form of contingency buffers. Otherwise, the first new requirement that comes along, the first estimate that turns out to be low, or the first unanticipated task will wreck the schedule.

A contingency buffer isn't an arbitrary fudge factor pasted into the schedule, nor arbitrary inflation of all the individual estimates. You can calculate sensible buffers based on your previous experience with schedule overruns and requirements growth. Quantitative risk analysis is another method, letting you think through the potential risks facing your project, their likelihood of occurrence, and how they could harm the schedule. Critical chain project management is a technique for incorporating well-thought-out buffers (Goldratt 1997). They can go at the end of a sequence of dependent tasks—*feeding buffers*—and also at the end of the overall project—a *project buffer.* Figure 4.1 illustrates how to position both types of buffers in a Gantt chart schedule representation.

On an agile project, consider incorporating a modest contingency buffer into each iteration to account for project uncertainties. This buffer will help keep your iteration cycle on track and reduce the need to defer uncompleted work to later iterations. You might also plan an extra iteration at the end of the project as a buffer to accommodate deferred and added user stories and other lingering work, as Figure 4.2 illustrates (Thomas 2008b).

Let's see one way to incorporate buffers into an agile project (Cohn 2006). User stories—or, more generally, backlog items—come in different sizes, which many

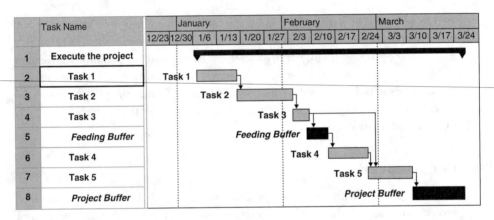

Figure 4.1 *A feeding buffer follows a group of tasks, and a project buffer follows the final task in a project's Gantt chart.*

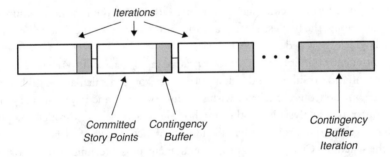

Figure 4.2 *Contingency buffers can be added to an agile project's iteration plan both at the end of each iteration and as an extra iteration at the end of the plan.*

teams estimate in units of *story points* (Cohn 2004). Agile projects measure the team's velocity on each development iteration of a few weeks' duration. *Velocity* is a measure of how many story points the team can deliver per iteration.

Suppose your product backlog contains an estimated 150 story points of work. Your velocity measurements indicate that the team can deliver an average of thirty points per iteration, suggesting a project duration of five iterations. You might base your overall delivery plan on a slightly more conservative velocity of twenty-five points per iteration, for a total of six planned iterations (150 ÷ 25). Your committed delivery plan now includes an average of five points of contingency in each iteration.

The team still plans iterations as though they'll deliver thirty points in each. That is, they work toward an internal goal (30) that's more ambitious than their external commitment (25). The difference constitutes slack that can account for items that turn out to be bigger than estimated, unanticipated work, bug fixes, refactoring, and other activities that consume time. The team's velocity measurements might already include the impact of ongoing bug fixes and refactoring, but surprises can happen at any time on any project (Cohn 2014).

Risky Assumptions

Incorporating contingency buffers does increase the expected delivery schedule, so managers and customers might push back against them. "That's just padding," they protest. "If you take that padding out, you'll be done earlier, right?" Probably not.

A contingency buffer doesn't change the future. It provides a safety margin to account for unknowns, the unexpected, and estimation inaccuracies. Yanking out the buffer doesn't eliminate those variables; it just reduces your ability to cope with them and still meet commitments. A manager who excises contingency buffers is making several assumptions.

- The scope information you have in hand today is well understood, accurate, and stable.

- All estimates are accurate, or at least any inaccuracies will balance each other out.

- You know who will be working on the project, and the team will remain intact throughout the project.

- Team members won't be interrupted by performing support work on a previous product or other diversions.

- No one will fall ill, go on vacation, or leave the company.

- No risks will turn into problems, and no new risks will raise their ugly heads.

- All dependencies the project has on external factors will come through on time.

Those assumptions paint the development team into a corner that's just about guaranteed to cause an overrun. If you encounter resistance to your contingency buffers, point out some unexpected experiences from previous projects. Ask whether there's any reason to believe that the new project will be different, that none of those unpleasant experiences will recur. If not, the buffers should stay.

The best way to justify your contingency buffers is to show how you calculated them based on previous project experience in the organization. Historical data that indicates how much requirements growth your projects typically experience helps you defend a buffer to accommodate such growth.

I once spoke with a senior manager at one of my consulting clients about a huge project they expected to take five years to complete. I told him about the industry data that suggested a requirements growth rate of perhaps 2 percent per month for a project of that size. That growth rate could make the ultimate product of a sixty-month project more than twice as large as initially estimated. "That sounds plausible," he replied.

Then I asked, "Do your project plans include any contingency buffers to accommodate that growth?" His predictable answer was, "No." I suspect that project took a lot longer than five years.

Contracting on Icebergs

The iceberg phenomenon also affects contracting projects. If you're a contractor who wants to land the job, you might be tempted to exclude contingency buffers from your bid to keep the price low. But what happens when you discover the true size of the iceberg? Or what if the customer requests a scope increase and won't agree to postpone any of the other committed requirements?

If your plans included contingency buffers, you could accommodate some modest growth without trashing the budget or schedule. When the customer asks, "Can you add this one little requirement or make this one extra change? You'll still be done on time, right?" the buffer might let you answer in the affirmative. The customer would view your "yes" answer as a sign of your flexibility and desire to satisfy. Without some planned slack capacity, though, a growing project could force you to eat the cost overrun and perhaps miss a schedule commitment.

I've heard the practice of presenting an unrealistically low bid to land the contract described as "the best liar wins" syndrome. You'll have to decide whether you want to do business based on your best assessment of the future or on fantasies that might come back to bite you. Incremental development approaches help to cope with size uncertainty, acknowledging up front that there's much you don't know yet that could affect the project's outcome. Some customers will balk at an open-ended project, though.

The Beauty of Buffers

Planning for possible future occurrences doesn't change what will happen in the future. It does improve your ability to roll with reality without wrecking your plans. If you don't know the iceberg's full size, expect it to be larger than it appears and plan accordingly. Building some flexibility into any commitment helps to keep deliveries on schedule.

Suppose all goes well on the project and you don't fully consume the allocated contingency buffers. You might deliver ahead of time—everybody wins.

Lesson 26	You're in a stronger negotiating position when you have data to build your case.

When you meet with a salesperson at a car dealership to negotiate the price, you're at a disadvantage. Salespeople have a lot of data at their fingertips, including the following:

- The manufacturer's suggested retail price for the vehicle you want
- What the dealer paid for the car (invoice price)
- The minimum profit the dealer will accept
- The dealer cost and markup on any accessories or options
- Any special promotions or incentives available to either the dealer or the customer
- What your trade-in is worth
- What the last people who bought the same car paid

You probably have only one piece of data available: the sticker price on the window. If you've done some homework, you might have inside price information from a source like Consumer Reports. That preparation has worked well for me. Otherwise, though, the salesperson is in a far stronger negotiating position than you because of the extra information they have at hand.

Where Did You Get That Number?

A software project doesn't come with a preset sticker price to use as a starting point, but an analogous data imbalance can influence negotiations among key stakeholders. Suppose I'm a project manager. The project sponsor—some senior manager, marketing, or my primary customer—asks me how long it will take to complete a new project and what it will cost. Based on my understanding of the project and my experience, I develop and present an estimate. If the sponsor doesn't like the estimate, two possible outcomes can ensue. In one, I try to defend my estimate—without data—while the sponsor insists on a more aggressive target. That's not so much a negotiation as a debate that I'm likely to lose.

An alternative outcome is based on data, not on emotion, pressure, or political power. I describe to the sponsor how I came up with my estimate, perhaps something like this.

- I worked with knowledgeable and experienced team members who understand the kind of work the new project involves.

- We estimated the project's size based on the information we had about it at the time, including a factor for uncertainties and anticipated growth based on our previous experiences. We used a group estimation technique like Wideband Delphi (Wiegers 2007) or one of several agile estimation methods (Sliger 2012).

- We made certain assumptions that influenced our estimate.

- We referred to our previous experience on similar projects, from which we had recorded data regarding the project size, our estimates, the actual results, risks and surprises we encountered, and so forth.

- We assessed the extent to which the reference projects were good models for the new one to judge how different characteristics of the new project would affect our estimates.

- Based on our previous productivity measurements, we calculated most likely, pessimistic, and optimistic estimates of duration and cost.

If the sponsor still dislikes the estimate after I've explained it like this, we can have a fact-based discussion about it. Maybe the project is unlike anything we've done before, and our reference data isn't relevant. That would increase the risks and the estimation uncertainty. Maybe we don't understand the project well enough to generate a meaningful estimate. We'll have to approach it incrementally, estimating each chunk as we go along. That brings an associated uncertainty about when the project will be completed and what it will ultimately cost. Our foundational data and analytical estimation process serve as the basis for a balanced discussion about reality; whether we all like that reality is an entirely separate matter.

Data is your ally. A manager once pushed back on an estimate I presented. I explained how I generated the estimate based on our records from previous projects and why I thought her assumption of greatly increased productivity wasn't realistic. I asked about her basis for assuming that this project would suddenly go more quickly and more smoothly than the projects we'd worked on previously. She didn't have a good explanation. It was more a matter of hopeful aspiration than realistic expectation. Hope is not a strategy.

No one can predict the future accurately. The best you can do is extrapolate from previous experience, make adjustments where warranted, and acknowledge the uncertainties.

Principled Negotiation

Anytime there's a gap between a stakeholder's expectations—or demands—and your prediction of the future in the form of an estimate, you'll need to negotiate. *Principled negotiation* is a method to arrive at mutually acceptable agreements (Fisher et al. 2011). Principled negotiation involves four precepts.

- **Separate the people from the problem.** If the discussion comes down to a personal struggle between you and someone with more organizational power, you'll lose unless you can build a compelling case to sway their position.

- **Focus on interests, not positions.** Don't dig in your heels and defend your estimate to the death. Instead, seek first to understand the other party's interests—a more empathetic approach. What are their goals, needs, concerns, pressures, and constraints? Perhaps there's a way to satisfy both their interests and yours by modifying the problem statement or the proposed solution.

- **Invent options for mutual gain.** If you're being pressured to make a promise you know the team can't fulfill, look for alternative mutually acceptable outcomes with feasible objectives to which you can commit. See whether there's some way to meet in the middle. Neither party gets everything they want in most successful negotiations, but both can live with the outcome—a compromise.

- **Insist on using objective criteria.** Here's where your data comes in. Facts and analysis are more powerful persuaders than loudly stated opinions, arguments, and anecdotes. Use your data to build the case to support your estimates, and respect the data your negotiating counterpart presents.

No one can predict the future accurately. The best you can do is extrapolate from previous experience, make adjustments where warranted, and acknowledge the uncertainties. Let your data do the talking, and invite those with whom you're negotiating to share theirs. There's a possible meeting of the minds and acceptable outcome in there somewhere.

Lesson 27	Unless you record estimates and compare them to what actually happened, you will forever be guessing, not estimating.

When you face a new piece of work, someone wants to know how long it's going to take. That person might be a customer, manager, teammate, or yourself. Unless the work is an exact duplicate of something you've done before, you need to estimate based on previous analogous experience. Memories are faulty, though. Even if you remember how long some earlier activity took, you probably don't remember how long you *thought* it was going to take. To create reasonably accurate estimates, you need data, not vague recollections. Data constitutes a set of facts we can analyze to understand, predict, and improve.

Someone once asked me, "If we should base our estimates on historical data, where do we get historical data?" The simplest answer is that if you record what you did today, that becomes historical data tomorrow. Individuals, teams, and organizations should get in the habit of recording their estimates and keeping records of actual outcomes. This is the only way to get better at estimating upcoming activities.

If there's a big discrepancy between a forecast and the ultimate reality, explore why and consider how you could create more realistic estimates for similar work in the future. Did you have to perform more tasks than you expected? Did they take longer than you thought? Were your productivity assumptions overly generous? Did unexpected factors impede the work? As you accumulate data over time, you can calculate some averages to help you generate more meaningful estimates for future work. Without the data, you're just making guesses.

Multiple Sources of Historical Data

There are four potential sources of historical data. First is your personal experience. Individual performance varies significantly depending on the skills and experience of the person who performs the work. I've been self-employed in a one-person consulting and training company for more than twenty years. Knowing how long it takes another consultant to, say, develop a training course doesn't help me predict how long it would take me to do something similar. I must rely on my personal history, so I keep records of my plans, estimates, and actual task durations for work that I might encounter again.

Some years ago, I decided to create e-learning versions of six of my training courses. Having never done anything like that previously, I had no idea how long it might take. I created a task list with all the steps I could think of. As it was a novel experience and I faced several learning curves, I had overlooked some tasks, which I added to my planning list for subsequent projects. I recorded how long it took me to perform each item on the first course I developed.

From that data, I estimated how long the next course would take. I adjusted the estimate based on the learning curves I had now mastered, new tasks I had discovered, and differences between the two courses. After completing that second course, I compared my estimates to how long each step actually took so that I could derive still better estimates for the remaining courses. Having that data available helped me prepare a decent estimate when a client hired me several years later to develop some customized e-learning courseware on a fixed-price contract.

I find planning worksheets helpful for thinking of all the work I might have to perform for a particular project and how long each activity might take. They remind me of tasks that I might otherwise overlook. For instance, people often forget to plan time for performing rework following quality control activities like testing and peer review. However, some rework is virtually always needed. I include rework tasks in my estimates, even if I don't know exactly how much time it might take in a particular situation.

Three other historical data sources are your current project, your organization's collective experience, and industry averages for projects similar to yours. The most meaningful data comes from recently completed portions of your current project. That data reflects the influences of the current team, environment, culture, process, and tools on the team's performance. Agile projects are well suited for this data collection. The most accurate forecasts of future performance are based on the average velocity from recent iterations, assuming that the team's composition and the nature and quality of the delivered work remain constant.

Data from previously completed projects in your organization and industry averages are less reliable predictors of your future, as the variations across projects, teams, and organizations increase the uncertainties. Nonetheless, relying on this kind of historical data is still better than estimating based solely on memory or guesswork.

Software Metrics

What's past may be prologue, but memories are fallible and perceptions are subjective. If you want to understand what happened on previous projects and make more meaningful plans, you need to collect some metrics. People can measure various aspects of software projects at three levels: individual contributor, project team, and development organization. Measurements in the categories of size, effort, time, and quality can provide considerable insight into your project work (Wiegers 2007).

- **Size.** Choose some measure of size—the quantity of work—that's meaningful for the kind of work you're doing. Possibilities include requirements, function points, user stories, story points, classes, and—more dubiously—source lines of code. For my e-learning courses, I counted the numbers of course modules and slides.

- **Effort.** Track the labor hours of effort needed to create each deliverable or complete each piece of work. Combining size with effort lets you calculate your productivity.

- **Time.** Record the estimated and actual durations of work done in units of calendar time. Numerous factors influence how work effort translates into calendar time, as we saw in Lesson 23, "Work plans must account for friction."

- **Quality.** Counting defects found by various means shows which quality practices work best to find errors and where the quality improvement opportunities lie. Recording the time spent on rework to correct defects also helps with planning. If you know where the faulty work originated—a specific iteration, requirement, or activity—you'll have a clearer idea of where to focus extra quality effort in the future.

In his book *Software Estimation* (2006), Steve McConnell points out numerous issues associated with measures in each of these categories. McConnell stresses the importance of clearly defining each metric you collect so that people can record data in consistent ways. Unless you're benchmarking against an external reference, internal measurement consistency is more important than absolute truth. For instance, all team members should track their effort and count defects in the same way. Suppose that some team members include debugging and rework effort as part of development, others lump it in with testing, and still others don't record it at all. That apples-and-oranges variability doesn't yield meaningful data for predicting the future.

The golden rule of metrics is to use data to understand and improve, not to punish or reward anyone.

The idea of software metrics makes some people nervous. Software measurement is indeed a delicate area, with many potential pitfalls (Wiegers 2007). The golden rule of metrics is to use data to understand what's happened and improve results, not to punish or reward anyone. People are also concerned about how much time it will take to collect and analyze the data, but I've found that recording some basic information about project activities requires little effort. It's a habit you get into as just part of your work process.

It's impossible to reconstruct metrics data accurately long after the work was done. Therefore, establish mechanisms to collect and store data as you go along. A retrospective at the end of a development cycle offers a good opportunity to aggregate data to evaluate the past and plan the future. If you invest a little time writing down what happened today, then tomorrow you'll have historical data to help you estimate the next piece of work.

Lesson 28	Don't change an estimate based on what the recipient wants to hear.

Suppose your customer asks how long it will take you to complete the next portion of your project. Based on your analysis of the work, you reply, "About two months."

"Two months?" sneers the customer. "My twelve-year-old daughter could do that job in three weeks!" You resist the temptation to suggest he hire his daughter then.

You try again. "Okay, how about one month?"

Now, what changed in those few seconds? The task didn't get any smaller. You didn't instantly become more productive. Nobody else suddenly appeared to help with the work. The customer just didn't like your first answer, so you offered an alternative that might go over better. If your estimate and the requester's expectation are too far apart, you'll need to negotiate to reach some agreement. However, there's no justification for altering a thoughtfully crafted estimate just because someone wasn't pleased with it (Wiegers 2006b).

An estimate is a prediction of the future. We base estimates on what we know about the problem at the time, our previous experiences with similar work, and the assumptions we make. If we're thorough, we'll also consider any dependencies on factors outside our control, possible risks, potential changes in the problem statement, and uncertainties that could affect our plans. The less we know about all these factors, the less likely it is that the estimate will match the ultimate reality. Someone else whose thought process involves different parameters could generate quite a different estimate for the same work.

Goals versus Estimates

It's important to distinguish an estimate from a goal. I once observed a discussion between a senior manager and a developer regarding a new project. The developer's expectation for the project's duration was four times longer than the manager's expectation. The developer simply agreed to the manager's demand for the much shorter schedule, which had zero probability of being achieved (and wasn't).

A more rational approach would have been for the developer to say, "Here's how I came up with my estimate. How did you come up with yours?" In this case, though, the manager didn't have an estimate; he had a goal. The developer didn't have an estimate, either; he had a guess. The goal and the guess were miles apart. Had either of the two parties developed a true estimate, they might have been closer together. Instead, it became an adversarial debate, with the individual who had more power gaining a lip-service commitment from the other one.

It's important to distinguish an estimate from a goal.

When to Adjust

Your estimate should be independent of what you think the requester wants to hear. Having said that, there are times when it does make sense to change an estimate or—stated more properly—to reestimate, including these:

- If you discover that an assumption or piece of information was wrong
- Once you get into the work and understand the task better
- When the scope of the work changes
- If you find that you're making progress faster than you expected (it happens)
- When conditions change, such as the people working on the project
- When a risk materializes or a dependency fails

Unless some change like this takes place, it's not appropriate to alter your prediction of the future.

If your estimate doesn't align with someone else's goals, expectations, or constraints, the parties should collaboratively investigate the gap. It doesn't help anyone to bury the conflict unresolved. You can question assumptions, discuss risks, and try alternative estimation methods to validate—or reject—the estimate. Perhaps the historical data that you relied on wasn't an appropriate model for estimating the work under consideration. You can negotiate scope, resources, or quality to see whether there's a knob to turn to reach a more acceptable estimate. But if you've prepared an estimate analytically, don't cave just to make someone else smile. They won't trust your future estimates, because they know they can override them if they apply enough pressure.

Lesson 29	Stay off the critical path.

Identifying the many tasks that must be performed is the core of project planning. Many of those tasks must be carried out in a particular sequence, and some tasks are linked to others, so the planner must also identify timing dependencies between tasks. It gets complicated.

Critical Path Defined

Project planners often draw an *activity network diagram* (also called a PERT chart) to show these timing relationships between tasks. Figure 4.3 shows an activity

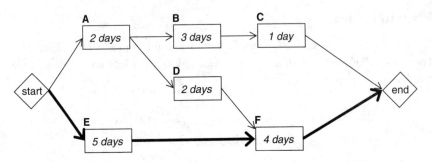

Figure 4.3 *The critical path (heavy arrows) is the longest sequence of task dependencies between project start and end.*

network diagram for a project with just six tasks, labeled A through F. The estimated duration is shown for each task. Actual activity network diagrams include a lot more information, such as the earliest and latest start and finish dates for each task. For simplicity, let's assume that no task can begin until all of its predecessor tasks are completed. That is, Task F can't begin until Tasks A, D, and E are finished.

If you add up the estimated durations of the tasks in the various pathways that lead from start to end, you'll see that path EF is the longest, at 5 + 4 = 9 days (heavy arrows). That task sequence is the *critical path*. It defines the shortest estimated duration needed to complete the project (Cohen 2018). If any task on the critical path overruns its schedule, the project's overall completion date gets pushed out by the duration of that delay. New tasks that are added to the critical path will similarly delay project completion.

Tasks that don't lie on the critical path have some slack time, also called *float*. They can run long without delaying the overall project—up to a point. For instance, Tasks A and D combined have one day of slack: 2 + 2 = 4 days, which is one day shorter than Task E that's on the critical path.

The critical path can change, though. Suppose Task A consumes four days, double the original estimate. The critical path now would become ADF at ten days (4 + 2 + 4), thereby pushing the project to a one-day overrun of the nine-day EF path.

Added tasks that aren't on the critical path will consume effort but won't delay the project's completion, provided there's enough slack to accommodate them. However, if those people were otherwise going to be working on critical-path tasks that now will be delayed, then those additional tasks could indeed extend the critical path's duration.

To shorten a project, you need to find ways to accelerate the critical-path tasks.

Tasks on the critical path have no slack time. If you want to shorten a project, you need to find ways to accelerate the critical-path tasks, perhaps by performing some of them in parallel. Astute project managers will keep a close eye on the critical path and try to ensure that those tasks complete on time or early.

Keeping Out of the Way

My philosophy is to keep my work off the project's critical path as much as possible. I don't want to be the bottleneck who's holding up someone else's progress. I prioritize my daily work by considering the two dimensions of importance and urgency (Covey 2020). A task that lies on the critical path is more urgent than one that does not. If a task could force other people to wait until I complete it before they can continue with their part of the work, that task jumps to the front of my priority queue. I strive to avoid being the cause of dead time and wait states that could impede the whole project.

I apply this thinking when writing books. The process of conceiving, planning, proposing, writing, reviewing, editing, and publishing a book is about a yearlong project with many activities, particularly if more than one author is involved. Much of the work can be done in parallel or in an arbitrary sequence. Sometimes, though, one participant must complete a particular activity before someone else can take their next step. For example, I can't finalize a manuscript chapter until all of my beta readers (manuscript reviewers) have returned their comments. Unless I built in some slack time—which I do—to stay on schedule, I must ignore late-arriving review input, thereby wasting the reviewer's time and possibly reducing the book's quality.

To get off the critical path quickly, when the publisher sends me the typeset pages for final proofreading, I drop everything else and start reading. The publisher can't make corrections or finalize the index until they receive my review feedback. Delays in proofreading could potentially delay publication, depending on how much slack time we included in the schedule and whether we're ahead of plan overall.

Frequent communication is essential to staying on a schedule. Sometimes two parties are waiting for the other to respond because of confusion over whose turn it is. You don't get an answer to an e-mailed question, so you call, text, or e-mail the other person again: "Did you understand my request in the e-mail I sent you three days ago? Or did you already reply, and either I didn't receive your e-mail or I over-looked it?" One person is holding up the other one unnecessarily. There are many ways a project can slip when people are juggling multiple activities that they must finish in a particular sequence.

I always feel good when I promptly complete an activity that I know could other-wise slow down someone else and perhaps the entire project. I leap off that critical path as quickly as I can.

Lesson 30	A task is either entirely done or it is not done: no partial credit.

"Hey, Phil, how are you coming on implementing that subsystem?"

"Pretty good. I'm about 90 percent done."

"Wait—weren't you 90 percent done a couple of weeks ago?"

"Yes, but now I'm *really* 90 percent done!"

The notion that software projects and tasks are reported to be 90 percent done for a long time is something of an industry joke (Wiegers 2019b). (A related joke states that the first half of a software project consumes 90 percent of the resources; the second half consumes the other 90 percent of the resources.) This optimistic but misleading status tracking makes it difficult to judge when you'll truly complete a body of work. We all need to resist the temptation to cross items off our to-do task list until they're entirely finished. If you tell yourself or someone else, "I'm all done except...," you're not done.

What Does "Done" Mean?

A fundamental question is what exactly we mean when we say some piece of work is done. You might have finished all the tasks you initially thought were needed, only to discover that the job involves more work than you realized. This sometimes happens when implementing a change in an existing system, as you keep encountering addi-tional components to modify. We often don't think of all the necessary activities when we plan some chunk of work. The larger the chunk, the more likely we are to overlook some tasks.

If you tell yourself or someone else, "I'm all done except...," you're not done.

The agile community has tackled this question head-on by incorporating the *definition of done,* or DoD, into activity planning (Datt 2020b, Agile Alliance 2021a). Early in the project, the team should itemize the criteria they'll use to determine whether they've completed a specific backlog item, task, or iteration. Checklists are helpful to specify the minimum work that must be completed to consider a particular task or product increment to be finished.

The definition of done provides objective criteria for judging how a project or iteration is progressing toward successful completion. Done means *entirely* done, such as an increment of software that has been fully coded, tested, integrated into the product, and documented and hence is potentially releasable to customers. Individual units of work, such as implementing user stories, are either 100 percent done or they're not done; there's nothing in between (Gray 2020).

I often create planning worksheets that itemize the steps involved when I perform recurrent activities. These worksheets reduce the chance that I'll overlook anything and help me estimate how much time to plan for each instance of the activity. The worksheets also let me track progress. Figure 4.4 shows a portion of such a worksheet for converting my PowerPoint training courses into e-learning courses, as I described in Lesson 27. I use the Status column to track the tasks I've started, those I've completed, and those I've not yet begun.

Status	Task
	1. Split course slides into modules in separate PowerPoint files.
	2. Tune up slides for each module. Add background and footers.
	3. Complete instructor notes for all slides.
	4. Create scripts for all slides, with animation timing markers.
	5. Record audio scripts for all modules.
	6. Import audio scripts and synchronize animations.
	7. Publish all slide modules in e-learning format.
	8. Create an HTML shell with module menu and other links.
	9. Create course handout PDF.
	10. Test the entire presentation.
	11. Correct errors found during testing.
	12. Establish pricing.
	13. Develop description and marketing materials.

Figure 4.4 *A planning checklist shows some of the tasks involved with creating an e-learning course from a PowerPoint presentation.*

The tasks in the list vary considerably in size. Establishing pricing (Task 12) takes just a few minutes; recording the audio scripts for all the course modules (Task 5) will consume many hours. My courses vary considerably in size, from just four modules up to eighteen. I wanted finer granularity than the form in Figure 4.4 provides for tracking both status and the time I spent on module-level tasks. Therefore, I created a spreadsheet to monitor how I'm progressing on each of the activities needed to implement each course module. But the only status values I use are: pending, underway, and done.

No Partial Credit

One problem when assessing doneness is that we give ourselves too much partial credit for tasks that we've begun but haven't completed, which can make us feel happy and overly optimistic. You might contemplate the algorithm for a complex module one morning and conclude that you're about 30 percent done because the algorithm was the hard part. Maybe it was, but writing the code, reviewing it, testing it, and integrating it with other work could still consume a lot of time. It's difficult to assess the percent completion of a large task accurately. It might be larger than first thought, unidentified activities could remain to be discovered, and we're not sure how the remaining work will go.

The first step to address this doneness problem is to break large tasks—milestones—into multiple small tasks, whimsically called *inch-pebbles* (Page-Jones 1988, Rothman 1999). Each inch-pebble might be about four to six labor hours. This size permits good insight into everything you'll need to do to complete the task. A useful heuristic is to identify inch-pebbles that can't be subdivided logically into smaller parts. If you have previous experience performing an activity, you can probably estimate it accurately at a milestone level of granularity. For less familiar, more uncertain, or more complex activities, the finer granularity of inch-pebbles will be more illuminating.

Monitor your progress on these granular inch-pebbles in a binary fashion: done or not. You get no partial credit for incomplete tasks. None. Zero. Progress on a large task is then determined by what fraction of the inch-pebbles for that big task are entirely completed. This tracking is more insightful than trying to guess what percentage of a large and perhaps vaguely defined body of work is finished (Rothman 2004).

By "large task," I mean some unit of work that delivers value to a customer. With my e-learning project, the ultimate goal was to have a completed course that I could sell. Decomposing that large task into the myriad smaller activities involved, as we saw in Figure 4.4, provided visibility into how I was approaching my final goal. Within that major target were multiple course modules, each with its own set of subtasks. Rather than estimating percent completion of the entire project or individual subtasks, I used binary done/not done tracking at the lowest granularity level.

Some project tracking tools include a control that lets you indicate what percentage of a task is complete. Figure 4.5 shows a sample Gantt chart view with a few project tasks. The gray bars labeled Task 1 through Task 4 in the aggregate make up the large objective called "Create a Module." The control to which I'm referring appears as the narrow black bars within the gray taskbars. The black bars indicate how much of each task has been completed. I advise against using those partial-completion indicators. They can mislead you into thinking that you're further along than you really are. I find that the approach of tallying completed, smallish inch-pebbles indicates progress more meaningfully.

Tracking by Requirements Status

Another option for monitoring project progress is tracking requirements status rather than estimating the fractional completion of each requirement's implementation (Wiegers and Beatty 2013). Each requirement—be it a functional requirement, use case flow, user story, feature, or subfeature—that's allocated to a body of work has a specific status at a given time. Possible status values include proposed, approved, implemented, verified, deferred, and deleted. In this approach, a planned body of work is complete when the status of each requirement allocated to it has one of three statuses:

- Verified (the requirement is fully implemented and tested)
- Deferred (the requirement was delayed for later implementation)
- Deleted (the requirement is no longer planned for implementation at all)

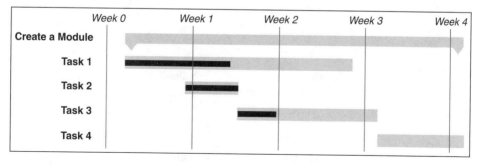

Figure 4.5 *I advise against using the function to show the percent completion of individual tasks (black bars inside gray bars).*

Doneness Leads to Value

The point of project tracking is not simply to make sure you've done all of the planned work. It's to complete chunks of work that will provide value to customers when they're delivered. The best way to gain visibility in your progress toward that value is to flip a task's status to done only when it's truly finished.

Lesson 31	The project team needs flexibility around at least one of the five dimensions of scope, schedule, budget, staff, and quality.

"What do you want: good, fast, or cheap? Pick two." This colloquial notion of a triple constraint or iron triangle appears throughout the project management literature. I've seen several representations of the triangle with different parameters on the triangle's vertices or edges and various assumptions about what's being held constant. In my view, the traditional iron triangle is overly simplistic, although the concept of constraints and trade-offs is certainly valid (Wiegers 2019c).

Five Project Dimensions

I think in terms of five dimensions that a project team must manage, as illustrated in Figure 4.6 (Wiegers 1996). First, there's the scope or features, which describes the product's functional capabilities. But it's important to separate quality from scope. I can write software very quickly if it doesn't have to work correctly. So, unlike the most common iron triangle representations, I show quality as a distinct dimension. The other three dimensions are the time needed to deliver (schedule), the budget (cost), and the staff available to work on the project. Some people add risk as a sixth dimension, but risk is less of an adjustable parameter than the other five.

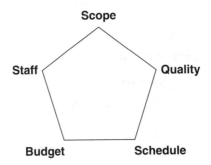

Figure 4.6 *The five dimensions of a software project are scope, quality, schedule, budget, and staff.*

People often combine staff and budget as "resources." I prefer to separate them. Most of the project cost is indeed staff salaries. Sometimes, though, a team has adequate funding but is constrained by a headcount limit. In that case, perhaps the project manager can tap the budget to buy a package solution, license some software components, outsource part of the work, or engage contractors.

Each project must decide which dimensions are most critical and balance the others to achieve the essential project objectives. The trade-offs among these five dimensions are not simple or linear. For example, if you add staff, the cost could well increase, and the schedule might be shortened—although not necessarily, as Frederick Brooks (1995) pointed out in Brooks's Law: "Adding manpower to a late software project makes it later." A common trade-off is to shorten the schedule or add features at the expense of quality. Anyone who's been victimized by buggy software questions such trade-off decisions, but development organizations do make that choice—sometimes deliberately, sometimes by default.

Each dimension can take one of three properties on a project:

- A constraint

- A driver

- A degree of freedom

Constraints define restrictions within which the project must operate. The project has no flexibility around a constrained dimension. If a team of immutably fixed size is available for a project, then staff is constrained. Cost is a constraint on a project being done under a fixed-price contract, at least from the client's perspective. Quality will be a constraint for a project that develops a safety- or life-critical product. Projects tied to fixed-date contracts or events—think Y2K, elections, Brexit—are schedule constrained.

A *driver* is a key objective or success criterion for the project. For a product with a desired marketing window of opportunity, schedule is a driver. Commercial applications often have features as a driver for competitive purposes. The drivers provide a little flexibility around certain of the dimensions. A specified feature set might be the primary driver of the project, but scope becomes a constraint if the features aren't negotiable at all.

Any project dimension that is neither a driver nor a constraint is a *degree of freedom*. The project manager can adjust degrees of freedom within certain bounds. The challenge is to adjust the degrees of freedom to achieve the project's success drivers within the limits that the constraints impose. For instance, projects following agile methods treat scope as a degree of freedom, adjusting the scope of what each iteration delivers to fit within the time constraint of their iteration schedule.

I have bad news: a project with zero degrees of freedom is likely to fail. All five dimensions can't be constraints, and they can't all be drivers. An added feature, a team member who departs, a risk that becomes a problem, an estimate that's too low—all will trash the schedule because the overconstrained project manager has no flexibility to respond to those events.

A student in a project management class I taught told me, "Our project has a fixed budget, we can't get more people, all the features are critical, there can't be any defects, and we have to finish on time." I wasn't optimistic about that super-constrained project's chances of success.

A project with zero degrees of freedom is likely to fail.

Negotiating Priorities

A significant aspect of this model is that the team, customers, and management should agree upon the dimensions' relative priorities at the project's outset. For instance, schedule is often presented as a constraint when it's actually a driver. The way to tell the difference is to ask a question like, "I understand that you want this delivered by June 30. What happens if it's not done until the end of July?" If the answer is to forget the whole thing because it won't be useful to us or we'll be socked with contractual penalties, then schedule truly is a constraint. But if the answer is, "Well, we'd like it by June 30, but we can live with July 31 if we have to," then schedule is a driver.

The Flexibility Diagram

A *Kiviat diagram*—also called a radar chart, star chart, or spider chart—provides a visual way to depict the amount of flexibility for all five dimensions; Figure 4.7 shows an example. Readily generated in Microsoft Excel, a Kiviat diagram has multiple axes radiating from a common origin point. All the axes are the same length and normalized to the same scale. In this case, each axis represents how much flexibility the project manager has in the corresponding dimension, so I call these pictures *flexibility diagrams* (Wiegers 1996).

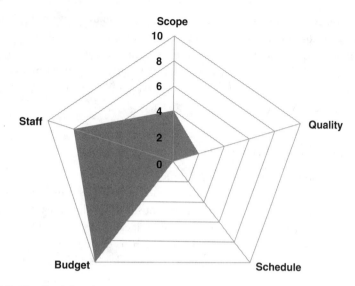

Figure 4.7 *The flexibility diagram for a reusable software component shows that schedule is a constraint, quality and scope are drivers, and staff and budget are degrees of freedom.*

I use a relative scale from zero to ten to indicate flexibility. Plotting a point at zero—the origin—indicates that the dimension for that axis is a constraint with no flexibility. A point fairly low on the axis, between zero and about four represents a driver. The project has a small amount of flexibility in that dimension. Any dimension plotted at a higher value on its axis represents a degree of freedom that offers more latitude for adjustment. Connecting the plotted points for the five dimensions outlines an irregularly shaped pentagon. Different types of projects will lead to flexibility diagrams having distinct shapes.

Figure 4.7 shows the flexibility diagram for a reusable software component my team once developed. The schedule was constrained because this component had to be delivered before several other applications being developed concurrently could use it. Therefore, the schedule dimension had zero flexibility. The component's reliability and correctness were very important, so quality was an important success driver. I've plotted quality with a flexibility value of two in the figure. We needed to deliver a core set of capabilities initially but could grow the functionality over time. Hence, the project scope has a flexibility of four. We had considerable latitude regarding budget and staff: it had to get done on time. Therefore, the values for these degrees of freedom are plotted high on their respective axes.

The flexibility diagram is not a high-resolution or quantitative tool. The pentagon's shape visually indicates the project's important aspects, but we don't try to calculate the area of the pentagon or anything like that. However, the pentagon's size does provide a rough indication of how much flexibility the project manager has to work with. A small pentagon means that you have multiple constraints and drivers, making it more challenging to steer a path to success.

Applying the Five Dimensions

This five-dimensional analysis can help a project manager decide how best to respond to changing project conditions or realities to meet a project's prime objectives. Suppose staff is a constraint. If new requirements must be included, the only parameters that can potentially change are scope, quality, budget and schedule. Nothing is free. The flexibility diagram can facilitate a discussion to decide how to proceed. Can some other features be cut or deferred? Can we add a development iteration and extend the schedule to accommodate the new functionality? Must the product work perfectly on Day 1? Contemplating these five dimensions is a more rational way to understand your project priorities than assuming that every aspect of the project is vital and nonnegotiable.

> **Lesson 32**   If you don't control your project's risks, they will control you.

A company once engaged me to determine why a recent international contracting project had failed. As I studied the project records, I discovered that the team had maintained a list of project risks—a solid project management practice. However, their monthly status reports showed only the same two minor risks each time, with a minimal estimated threat from each of them. Since the project failed, some additional risks apparently sneaked up and attacked it when no one was looking. The project managers failed to consider some common risks on complex, distributed projects: slow decision-making, communication issues, scope changes, requirements ambiguity, overly optimistic commitments, and so forth. We can take several messages from this experience.

- If you've identified just two risks for a multimillion-dollar project, you haven't looked closely enough.

- If you underestimate the potential threat a risk could pose, you might not pay enough attention to it.

- If the same items remain on your list of top risks month after month, either you're not actively managing them or your mitigation efforts aren't working.

A risk is a potential problem that hasn't happened yet.

What Is Risk Management?

A *risk* is a condition or event that has the possibility of harming your project (Wiegers 1998a). It's a potential problem that hasn't happened yet. The goal of risk management is to ensure that the project will succeed despite the potential negative consequences of the risks it faces. Risk management is an essential component of effective project management. It's been said that project management *is* risk management, particularly for large-scale projects (Charette 1996). Put more whimsically, risk management is project management for adults (DeMarco and Lister 2003).

Risk management involves identifying scary conditions and events, assessing their possible impact on the project if they were to materialize into problems, prioritizing them, and trying to control them. Formal risk management focuses your energy on the greatest looming threats. There's no point in worrying about something that wouldn't do much harm even if it happened or a highly unlikely occurrence. No one can predict the future, but you don't want to be blindsided by something that you perhaps could have seen coming and evaded.

Identifying Software Risks

An amazing number of things can go wrong on a software project. Each project team should devote both early and ongoing effort to confronting its fear factors. If risk management isn't someone's responsibility, it won't get done. Large projects often appoint a risk officer who has the lead responsibility for coordinating risk-related activities. Following are several techniques for identifying potential risks to your project.

Brainstorming
Group sessions let all team members participate in risk identification. They'll each bring different perspectives and experiences to the table and have complementary thoughts about concerns that keep them up at night. A good place to start is to

examine any assumptions the team is making, including those that feed into esti-mates, as tenuous assumptions might contain risk.

I've found that many of the proposed risks that come out of such sessions actually state current project realities. Those aren't risks: they're problems. You need to deal with existing problems more energetically than potential problems.

Published Compilations

Another strategy is to start with an extensive list of risks drawn from software books. Books by Capers Jones (1994) and Steve McConnell (1996) include lengthy lists of software risks that are largely as relevant today as when the books were published. Lists of various project risks also can be found online, such as one from Bright Hub PM (2009).

Reviewing a long catalog of potential risks is a little frightening, like reading all the potential side effects of some medication. Not all items will apply to your project, but the lists can alert you to possibilities you wouldn't have imagined had you started from scratch. Software risks are grouped into categories such as these:

- Requirements and scope
- Design and implementation
- Organization and personnel
- Management and planning
- Customer
- Outsourcing and contractors
- Development environment and process
- Technology
- Legal and regulatory

Local History

A third risk identification strategy is to examine accumulated information from your organization's previous projects. These risks will be more relevant to you than those found in a generic risk list. Project retrospectives are opportunities to collect and record both good and bad project experiences. Project events that surprised the team often reflect risks that they didn't anticipate. It's tempting to conclude that some unpleasant event was a one-off, but add it to the master list anyway so that future projects can consider whether it might be a concern for them.

Your organization's risk collection also should include information about mitigation strategies that previous teams had tried for specific risks and how well they worked. Future projects will benefit from relying on previous experience to assess their risks quickly and decide how to control them. Studying previous experience is a way to avoid having to climb every painful learning curve on every project.

Risk Management Activities

Risk management is not a one-time project action, something you do at the beginning of the project and then set aside. Figure 4.8 shows a flowchart of the various activities involved.

Identify Risks. Sift through the software risk compilations you have available and note any that could pertain to your project. Risk lists generally state a condition that might pose a problem, such as "Inadequate reporting requirements from

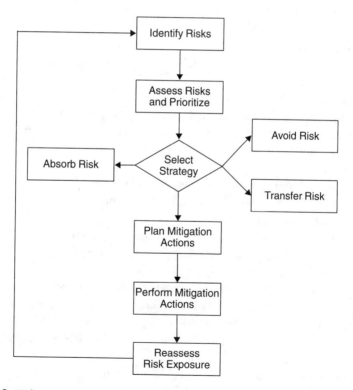

Figure 4.8 *Risk management involves multiple activities.*

internal regulators." Yeah? So what? I like to write risk statements in the form of the condition followed by a possible consequence: "Inadequate reporting requirements from internal regulators could lead to audit failure post-deployment."

Writing risks in this pattern might reveal that a single condition could give rise to multiple consequences, thereby making that a high-leverage condition to control. Alternatively, the same consequence could result from multiple risk conditions. In that case, it might be hard to avoid the consequence entirely, so consider developing a contingency plan to deal with the consequence if it becomes necessary.

Assess Risks and Prioritize. Once you've built a list of conditions and their possible consequences, think about how much damage each one could do to your project. Risk assessment considers two dimensions:

1. What's the probability of the risk becoming an actual problem? Some risks are unlikely to materialize, but others pose a clear and present danger.

2. How much impact could the problem have on the project if it did materialize? Some impacts are too minor to worry about; others could be devastating.

I like to estimate probability on a scale from 0 to 1 and impact on a relative scale from 0 to 10. Multiplying the probability by the impact yields an estimate of the exposure from each risk item.

After estimating the risk exposures, sort your list by descending exposure to float the highest-threat items to the top. That prioritization step will focus your attention where it's needed most. Start your risk control planning at the top of the prioritized list and work your way down. Savvy project managers keep their top-10 (or so) risk list front and center for continuous monitoring.

Select Strategy. You have four choices of how to respond to each risk. The first option is simply to absorb the risk. Yes, it could happen, and it could have some negative impact, but you decide not to take any action—you'll just wait and see what happens. Sometimes you have no choice. If you identified a potential change in a government regulation as a risk, for instance, you can't do anything about that. If you must absorb a risk, consider devising a contingency plan, just in case.

A second strategy is to avoid the risk entirely by changing direction, such as choosing different technologies or business partners who pose less danger. As a third possibility, perhaps you can transfer the risk to some other party so that it's no longer your concern. Most frequently, though, you'll need to go with option four: try to mitigate the risk to reduce your exposure.

Plan Mitigation Actions. Mitigation planning involves selecting actions to reduce the likelihood of the risk becoming a problem or to reduce the impact if it does. Mitigation actions become project tasks, someone must own each one. Also, try to identify any triggering conditions or events that would alert you to the risk becoming a looming threat, not just a possibility.

Perform Mitigation Actions. Even great plans are useless unless they're executed. Monitor implementation of the mitigation actions just as you would any other project task to ensure that they're carried out as intended.

Reassess Risk Exposure. If your mitigation actions are successful, the exposure from those risk factors should decrease. (If they aren't successful, try something different.) As Figure 4.8 indicates, risk management is a cycle, not a sequence of one-time activities. A good practice is to reevaluate your top-10 risk list weekly (McConnell 1996). The risks you're actively addressing should drift down your prioritized risk list as their estimated risk exposure decreases. Monitor items farther down the list to see whether their status has changed. Risks can drop off the list entirely if their window of opportunity for doing damage has passed. Alternatively, project conditions might change such that a risk that initially wasn't too threatening becomes either more likely or more impactful. New risks can pop up at any time, so everyone on the project should keep their eyes open.

There's Always Something to Worry About

The risks are out there whether you choose to look for them or not. Failing to manage your risks is tantamount to accepting them and absorbing the consequences. My preference is to confront project threats early and often. It comforts me to see the active risk list dwindle as the team's mitigation actions succeed.

Alternatively, you could ignore the risks and just hope nothing surprising and unpleasant happens. Good luck with that.

Lesson 33	The customer is not always right.

It's fashionable in our society to say, "The customer's always right." This statement implies that if a customer asks for something, you're obligated to deliver. You may have seen a sign at a business that said, "We have only two rules. Rule #1: The customer is always right. Rule #2: If the customer is wrong, see Rule #1."

The customer is not always right, but the customer always has a point.

The reality, of course, is that the customer is *not* always right. Sometimes the customer is misinformed, unreasonable, confused, in a bad mood, or didn't do their part. I prefer to say that the customer is not always right, but the customer always has a point, and we need to understand and respect that point. That's not the same thing as always doing what any customer says they want.

Being "Not Right"

I remember being irritated at the interminable road construction going on near my house. I had to pass through a torn-up intersection every day for months. "Why is it taking so long to finish this road?" I would think every time I drove through the mess. Then I realized an important fact: I don't know anything about road construction! I had no basis for assessing how long it ought to take to rebuild that intersection. The construction was annoying, but it wasn't reasonable for me to demand that it be finished earlier if that wasn't realistically achievable. I could be a dissatisfied "customer" of the new road, but that didn't mean my expectations were right. Let's see some examples of how a software customer might not always be right.

Conflicting Requests

Suppose two customers demand conflicting solutions to a problem, such as different ideas regarding how some part of a system should function. They clearly can't both be right. Nevertheless, some thought process on each of their parts led to their respective requests. We must understand the rationale behind the requests to assess which one is more closely aligned with achieving the project's business objectives. That's the requirement we should address.

Solutions versus Needs

During an elicitation discussion, a customer representative might present not their requirements, but rather some proposed solutions they have in mind. A skilled BA can detect when a stated need is actually a solution idea and ask questions to reveal the underlying problem. Sometimes the customers don't fully grasp the point of this dialogue. Their reaction might be, "I told you what I need. Haven't you heard that the customer's always right? Call me when you're done." This attitude doesn't reflect a nicely collaborative approach to solving the real problem.

A Surrogate Representative

A customer might offer to provide requirements on behalf of some user class to which they do not belong. This happened to me when I was the lead BA on a project. Our two most important user classes were a large community of chemists and a few people who worked in the chemical stockroom. The woman who managed the chemical stockroom told me, "I was a lab chemist until a few years ago. I can give you all of the chemists' requirements for this system." Unfortunately, she was wrong. Her understanding of what today's chemists expected from the system was out of date and incomplete. It would have been a mistake for us to rely solely on her input. Instead, we found several actual chemists to help us understand their requirements, which worked out much better.

The same problem can occur if a manager in the user community offers to serve as the representative for requirements discussions. The manager might not know all the day-to-day details about how users perform their work. Maybe the manager's experience is obsolete. In either case, the manager can't do as good a job of presenting user requirements as perhaps they think they can.

In Through the Back Door

Someone might try to bypass established processes to gain an advantage for themselves. I once asked a group at a consulting client site how requirement changes and enhancements got made on their system. An awkward silence ensued. The people in the group exchanged knowing glances. Someone finally said, "If the customer wants to make a change, they always tell Philippe or Debbie. They know Philippe and Debbie will work the change in, but the rest of us will give them a hard time about it."

The company had a mechanism for evaluating change requests, but that customer tried to slip changes in through the back door instead of following the process. People definitely will try to bypass ineffective and unresponsive processes, and perhaps they should. In this case, though, the customer just didn't want to bother going through the process and possibly have the decision makers reject their change request.

Jumping the Gun

My colleague Tanya, a skilled BA and software engineer, was hired by a company to specify the requirements for—and perhaps implement—a new information system to automate some of their activities. This was a brand-new, major transition. Tanya began by understanding and documenting the potential users' current manual business processes. From there, she planned to develop a proper set of solution requirements. The users, who had been leery of switching to an automated system, were delighted with Tanya's work and receptive to the project.

Unfortunately, the users' manager took Tanya's impressive binder of preliminary current-state work, erroneously claimed that the requirements had been completed, and decided to buy an existing software package that a friend of his just happened to sell. That new package was woefully inadequate and failed to meet the user needs. Had the manager waited until Tanya had specified the real solution requirements, he could have made a more appropriate build-or-buy decision that would have achieved the desired business objectives.

Positional Power

Customers sometimes demand that their requirements should get top priority because of their organizational status or other influential position over the project. (See Lesson 15, "Avoid decibel prioritization when deciding which features to include.") Those demands can be a problem if people request functionality that won't be used frequently enough to justify putting it ahead of other capabilities. Just because certain individuals have power doesn't mean they're right.

That said, high-level people who have far more visibility into the company's strategic plans than the development team has could legitimately prioritize requirements in a way that might not seem logical to the team. Understanding the reasoning behind their request will help to align everyone toward the proper business objectives.

Change Isn't Free

A common example of the customer not always being right is when they ask for new functionality or other changes but expect the price and delivery date to stay the same. Their attitude seems to be, "Change is free; just do it." It sounds like a Dilbert comic, but it happens in real life.

Respecting the Point

We're all customers in our daily lives. We buy products from stores and services from assorted providers. We aren't always right, even though we'd like to think we are. I might see my doctor, convinced from an Internet search about my diagnosis of some medical symptoms, only to learn that I'm completely off-base. One time I took my car to a service shop to get the brakes replaced. When I picked up the car, the mechanic told me the brakes didn't need replacement, just adjustment—no charge. In that instance, it was to my advantage to be wrong as the customer.

Remember, though: the customer always has a point. There's a reason behind what they're requesting—or demanding. As software providers, we can't say we're providing the best solution unless we respect the customer's point, seek to understand it, and satisfy the request if it's the right thing to do. When the customer's wrong, we have to explain that with all due respect and resist the pressure to do something inappropriate just because some customer demanded it.

| Lesson 34 | We do too much pretending in software. |

Because reality isn't always the ideal they have in mind, people sometimes pretend that things are different from how they are. Pretending could involve alternative facts or even outright fabrication, but the pretending I'm talking about here is more a matter of self-delusion or unwarranted optimism. Sometimes it's sticking one's head in the sand and hoping reality isn't still there. Other times it's wishful thinking.

Living in Fantasyland

As an example, we might pretend that we've identified all of the relevant project stakeholders. We imagine that they and we understand their objectives and that we've accumulated all the necessary requirements and other project information. There's a chance that's not correct, though. What if we didn't conduct a thorough stakeholder analysis, starting with a long list of potential stakeholders and considering which of them pertain to our project? What if we weren't able to identify or work with people who can accurately communicate each group's needs and constraints? Those situations could all cause problems.

Even if we did interact with suitable stakeholders, we pretend—perhaps *hope* is a better word—that we got the right requirements and recorded them accurately so that others can work with them. Former U.S. president Ronald Reagan adopted the Russian proverb "Trust, but verify" when discussing arms treaties with the former Soviet Union. That concept applies to software projects as well. We trust the people we work with, but we must also verify their information and confirm that work done based on that information was performed correctly.

Software people sometimes do some pretending regarding project management. We pretend that we've thought of all the necessary work and that our estimates are accurate. It's comforting to imagine that a project's scope is well understood and won't grow out of control, but that's not always the case. We pretend that none of the risks or surprising events that clobbered our previous projects will be a problem this time. Maybe not, but we're likely to encounter new disruptions, so we need to anticipate that possibility and consider how to respond. All project participants need honest, accurate information to keep the project on track. Managers should encourage their team members to deliver good news quickly—and bad news even sooner.

Irrational Exuberance

People who expect their next project to go more quickly and smoothly than the last one might be confident that the team's enhanced experience will pay big dividends. Or they could just have great faith in the team. I've heard managers espouse the grand productivity increases their teams will reap from new tools and methods. However, they didn't factor in the learning curve that will slow the team down for a while. Nor did they consider whether vendor marketing hype influenced their expectations. They just pretended the productivity miracle would happen.

We might pretend that we have top-flight talent on our team, although it's not possible for every team to have 90th-percentile staff. Some companies genuinely have built software organizations populated with superb talent. That implies that more people from the lower part of the capability distribution are clustered in other places. I've observed a broad spectrum of organizational capabilities in my consulting work, with some standing out at both ends of the scale.

Another form of pretending is to imagine that team members can devote 100 percent of their time to project work and still find time to learn, innovate, and grow the team's capability (Rothman 2012). That doesn't work at all. As we saw in Lesson 23, "Work plans must account for friction," many factors erode the time spent on the job down to a reduced level of effective work time. A manager who pretends that full utilization of staff time on project work is feasible and desirable is denying reality. Not having time to learn, explore, and improve sentences the team to always work in the ways it always has. That's a meager foundation for expecting better results the next time.

Games People Play

Teams and organizations sometimes claim they're following a particular process or methodology either because they know they're supposed to or because it sounds good in some context to say that they are. In reality, though, they're doing something different. Maybe they conform to certain parts of the process but skip others that they find inconvenient, time consuming, or hard to follow.

I consulted to a government agency that had an interesting pretending behavior. Their projects were funded on a biennial schedule that ran from July 1 of one year through June 30 two years later. They always completed their projects on schedule, by June 30. If the system wasn't completely shippable by then, they'd deliver an incomplete and buggy version so that they could still claim schedule success. Then they would pay for the completion and fixes in the next funding cycle. They pretended they never missed a delivery schedule in this way, but I don't think the strategy fooled anyone.

Sometimes I'm not that crazy about reality, but it's all I've got. I must live with it.

Does any pretending go on in your organization? If so, what are the impacts? Is there anything you can do about it?

I'm not a big fan of pretending. Hoping that the world is different from how it really is can be comforting, but it's not constructive. Sometimes I'm not that crazy about reality, but it's all I've got. I must live with it. So must we all.

Next Steps: Project Management

1. Identify which of the lessons described in this chapter are relevant to your experiences with project management.

2. Can you think of any other project management-related lessons from your own experience that are worth sharing with your colleagues?

3. Identify any practices described in this chapter that might be solutions to the project management-related problems you identified in the First Steps at the beginning of the chapter. How could each practice improve the way your project teams plan and track their projects?

4. How could you tell whether each practice from Step 3 was giving you the desired results? What would those results be worth to you?

5. Identify any barriers that might make it difficult to apply the practices from Step 3. How could you break down those barriers or enlist allies to help you implement the practices?

6. Put into place process descriptions, templates, guidance documents, and other aids to help future project teams apply your local project management best practices effectively.

Chapter 5

Lessons About Culture and Teamwork

Introduction to Culture and Teamwork

Every organization, company, department, and team has its own culture. In brief, the culture describes "how we do things around here." A healthy software culture is characterized by a set of common values and technical practices that drive the behaviors and decisions of people in the organization (Wiegers 1996, McMenamin et al. 2021). A healthy culture includes commitments at the individual, project team, and organizational levels to build high-quality products through the sensible application of appropriate processes and practices. If all goes well, the team members have a good time along the way too.

My first book, published in 1996, is titled *Creating a Software Engineering Culture*. It itemizes fourteen shared values—cultural principles—that my software development group had adopted. Looking back at that list, I believe they're still relevant to successful software development. Indeed, several of them appear as lessons in this book.

- Lesson 44: High quality naturally leads to higher productivity.

- Lesson 47: Never let your boss or your customer talk you into doing a bad job.

- Lesson 48: Strive to have a peer, rather than a customer, find a defect.

- Lesson 60: You can't change everything at once.

An organization's culture grows organically unless leaders actively steer it in a particular direction. A random collection of behaviors aggregated from everyone's past experiences is unlikely to jell spontaneously into a healthy culture. Young companies for which software is the principal product often establish powerful cultural imperatives that best serve their teams and the work they perform (Pronschinske 2017). Conversely, an IT department within a nontechnology corporation inherits the company's general cultural characteristics. Steering the IT culture to one more suitable for contemporary knowledge work can be an upstream swim. IT people's work differs from some other types of corporate work, so it makes sense that their culture should evolve in a different—preferably compatible and complementary—direction.

As an illustration, I used to work in a large consumer products company with a glacial decision-making process. It seemed that no one could make a decision unless everyone who was affected in any way by any part of the decision was 100 percent okay with the entire decision. Everyone involved in making a decision seemed to hold a veto. Unanimity is great, but business must move forward—you can't make decisions that way on a fast-moving software project. Certain aspects of the corporate culture clashed with the demands of today's nimble and responsive IT work.

Keeping the Faith

Managers influence an organization's culture through their vision, words, and behaviors. By taking various culture-building actions, managers foster collaborative teamwork and consistent alignment with positive cultural values. But culture is a fragile thing. Culture-killing actions can easily undermine the quality-oriented foundations the group has gradually built up (Wiegers 1996, McMenamin et al. 2021).

The best sign that an organization has firmly established an improved culture is that the new attitudes, practices, and behaviors persist even after key leaders depart. A small software group that I managed for several years made substantial improvements in how we worked together, and we saw the benefits in the systems we delivered. In three years, we grew from a group of five up to eighteen. As new people joined the team, they absorbed our cultural values and helped us sustain the behaviors and practices we believed were important. Eventually, we hired a new manager to replace me, as I didn't enjoy being a manager. Several other new people joined the group at the same time.

Disappointingly, the new manager didn't fully share our commitment to continuously enhancing our software development process, nor my improvement philosophy of "gentle pressure, relentlessly applied" (see Lesson 54). Unless leaders sustain their steering toward continuous improvement, some team members might backslide into their comfort zone of familiar practices. Sure enough, some of the process changes we had made gradually decayed. Others, however, were still practiced by those team members who had internalized them as the best way to work.

Cultural Congruence

Congruence is a crucial element of a healthy culture. *Congruence* means that the managers and team members behave in the ways the organization claims to value, not according to unspoken rules that might conflict with the official value statements (McMenamin et al. 2021). Incongruent actions infect the culture, undermining the declared focus on high quality standards and ethical behaviors. Questions like the following can reveal whether the culture is congruent or not.

- Do managers practice what they preach, or do they fold under outside pressure, such as delivering products that haven't yet satisfied their release criteria?
- Do technical practitioners follow established processes, or do they cut quality corners and do what's expedient in the face of looming deadlines?
- Do team members make and keep realistically achievable commitments, or do they make overly ambitious promises that too often go unfulfilled?

If your organization has a different set of values than this list implies, you might select different questions to test the culture for congruent behaviors. Regardless of what principles the team values, people should act in ways that are consistent with them.

The behaviors that an organization's managers reward provide a clear sign of their true values. One company conducted two major legacy-system replacement projects concurrently (see Lesson 44, "High quality naturally leads to higher productivity," for more about this case). Team A skimped on design and concentrated on coding; their system failed or misbehaved daily. The "commando squad" that Team A formed to get their system up and running again after each failure received a public award for outstanding customer service. In contrast, Team B built their system according to solid software engineering principles; it worked well, despite coming in a few months late. That team received no award or recognition.

Management clearly favored the Team A heroes who put out the fires over the Team B practitioners who quietly prevented fires by following high-quality development practices. Morale on Team B initially suffered when management treated them as losers for being late while lauding the first team's heroic efforts. But when Team A's system collapsed, Team B's morale improved as they took pride in their solid achievements. Which group would you prefer to work with? I'll take Team B.

Crystallizing the Culture

An organization's culture is usually intangible, an unspoken understanding of how people work together and what's important to them. Some companies codify significant elements of their culture in employee handbooks (Pronschinske 2017). Public communication like that keeps the cultural values visible and facilitates sharing them with new team members.

Making cultural factors explicit helps all team members buy into shared values, which leads to improved collaboration.

In his book *Software Teamwork,* Jim Brosseau (2008) recommends that teams adopt a team contract, an agreement that identifies common values, rules of engagement, and norms of behavior they can all live by. Each team should craft its own contract, rather than adopting one imposed by management, inherited from another team, or discovered online. The team contract should reflect each team's specific nature, but it also needs to mesh with other teams and the company as a whole. The team contract should be a working, living document to which people refer periodically and update as needed. It might contain statements such as these (Resologics 2021).

- We use a respectful debate system for consensus decision-making.
- We arrive on time for meetings and other scheduled activities and respect the agenda.
- Team members are expected to complete by their due dates all tasks to which they have committed.
- We can disagree among ourselves, but we present a unified position outside the team.
- We welcome multiple perspectives and contrary opinions to maximize our collective creativity.

Making cultural factors explicit helps all team members buy into shared values, which leads to improved collaboration. Writing an explicit team contract lets team members refine and sustain it over time. The contract helps new team members fit in and understand how they can contribute to the existing culture. Software teams are most productive and team members are happiest when the following essential needs are satisfied (Hilliard 2018):

- A safe and comfortable physical environment
- A collaborative environment of integrity and openness
- Team emotional cohesion and mutual support
- Challenging and purposeful—but feasible—work
- The right tools
- Self-determination and autonomy in the work they perform
- Opportunities to contribute technically and grow professionally

IT is an unusual technical discipline in that it attracts—and benefits from the presence of—people with a broad range of backgrounds, characteristics, and perspectives. Beyond the obvious value of ethnic, racial, gender, age, and ability diversities, people having experience in mathematics, engineering, science, creative design, psychology, business, and other fields all bring something to the project and the culture (Mathieson 2019). A development group full of hardcore technology experts will be enriched by the presence of people with strong soft skills and application domain knowledge.

Growing the Group

Effective teamwork requires alignment toward common goals and the mechanisms to achieve those goals. New team members bring their own cultural baggage, both positive and negative. As you interview candidates to join the group, try to judge how well they would merge with your culture.

I once interviewed a developer named Danielle, who was technically solid but balked at our longstanding practice of recording daily metrics on how we spent our time on projects. I explained that we used the data only to understand our project work and help us plan better. Danielle said she simply wouldn't do that; she wouldn't explain why. Maybe she'd had a previous bad experience with a manager who misused metrics data to reward or punish individuals. I appreciated her honesty, but Danielle didn't get an offer. I wasn't willing to take the risk of hiring someone who I knew right away would have a cultural clash with the group. I hired three other developers at that time who fit in quickly and contributed constructively to our continued cultural evolution.

It's worth understanding why a person objects to certain aspects of your current culture or the direction it's heading. They might have a valid point that you haven't yet noticed. Perhaps they've seen a better approach used elsewhere, or maybe they've encountered some long-term downsides of a particular practice or value that you haven't hit yet. That perspective alone can help enhance the team's culture.

You can quickly tell whether some people will mesh well with the rest of the team. Shortly after a developer named Gautam joined my group, we held a group lunch. Another team member, Angie, was always careful about her diet. She would never order a dessert at our occasional lunches, but she enjoyed sampling a bite of other people's desserts. When Gautam's dessert arrived, he handed his plate to Angie without a word. I knew then that Gautam would fit in just fine, and he did.

A few years later, I transferred to a different corporate division where Gautam had grown into a skillful manager. He understood how to lead teams effectively, and I was perfectly comfortable reporting to him. In this chapter, I describe seven lessons that I—and Gautam—learned about culture and teamwork.

First Steps: Culture and Teamwork

I suggest you spend a few minutes on the following activities before reading the lessons related to culture and teamwork in this chapter. As you read the lessons, contemplate to what extent each of them applies to your organization or project team.

1. Would you say your organization has a healthy software engineering culture? Why or why not?

2. Can you identify behaviors and actions that managers or team members take that reinforce a focus on a quality-oriented culture?

3. Have you observed any culture-killing behaviors that negatively influence team members' attitudes, morale, behaviors, or results? Reversing recurrent culture killers is an obvious place to start improving your work environment.

4. How well do you understand your company's culture? Does your software team's culture fit into the company's culture appropriately? If not, what can you do to adjust the fit?

5. Identify any problems—points of pain—that you can attribute to shortcomings in your culture and how people interact both within and across teams. What are the tangible and intangible costs of those shortcomings?

6. State the impacts that each problem has on your ability to complete projects successfully. How do the problems impede achieving business success for both the development organization and its customers? Cultural deficiencies can lead to people who won't exchange information with others, don't accept or fulfill commitments, or bypass established processes inappropriately. Morale problems and staff turnover indicate that the culture has some problems.

7. For each problem from Step 5, identify the root causes that trigger the problem or make it worse. Problems, impacts, and root causes can blur together, so try to tease them apart and see their connections. You might find multiple root causes that contribute to the same problem, as well as several problems that arise from a single root cause.

8. As you read this chapter, list any practices that would be useful to your team.

Lesson 35   Knowledge is not zero-sum.

I used to work with a software developer named Stephan. Stephan was territorial about his knowledge. If I asked him a question, I could almost see the wheels turning in his head: "If I give Karl the full answer to his question, he'll know as much as I do about that topic. That's not acceptable, so I'll give him half of the answer and see if he goes away." If I came back later seeking a more complete response, I might get half of the remaining answer. In this way, I asymptotically approached getting the complete answer to my question.

Extracting information bit by bit from Stephan was annoying. The information I sought was never confidential. We both worked at the same company, so we should have been aligned toward our joint success. Stephan apparently didn't agree with me that freely sharing knowledge with your colleagues is a characteristic of a healthy software culture.

Knowledge isn't like other commodities. If I have $3 and give you one of them, now I have only $2. Money is zero-sum in the sense that I must lose some of it for you to gain something in this transaction. In contrast, if I give you some of my knowledge, I still possess all the knowledge myself. I can share it with other people, as can you. Everyone touched by this expanding circle of knowledge benefits.

A healthy organization fosters a culture of free knowledge exchange and continuous learning.

The Knowledge Hog

Some people hoard information out of insecurity. They fear that if they share some of their precious hard-won knowledge with others, those other people become more competitive with them. Perhaps that's true, but it's flattering for someone to ask for your help. The requester is acknowledging your superior experience and insights. Rarely, someone might ask you for information because they don't want to take the time to figure it out themselves. You don't have to do someone else's work for them, but you should remember that you and your teammates are all working toward the same ends.

Other people carefully protect their knowledge as a form of job security. If no one else knows what they know, the company can't possibly fire them, because too much institutional knowledge would go out the door. Maybe they think they should get a raise because they're the sole holder of so much important information.

People who conceal organizational knowledge pose a risk. They create an informational bottleneck that can impede other people's work. My colleague Jim Brosseau aptly refers to knowledge hoarding as *technical ransom* (Brosseau 2008). Information hiding is an excellent practice for software design; for software teams, not so much.

Rectifying Ignorance

A healthy organization fosters a culture of knowledge exchange and continuous learning. Sharing knowledge enhances everyone's performance, so management rewards people who freely pass along what they know, not those who keep it to themselves. In a learning organization, team members feel that it's psychologically safe to ask questions (Winters et al. 2020). We're all ignorant about most of the knowledge in the universe, so let's learn from our colleagues when the opportunity arises.

Experienced members of an organization can share their expertise in many ways. The most obvious method is simply to answer questions. But more than just answering questions, experts should invite the questions. They should appear approachable to fellow employees, particularly novices, and be thoughtful and patient when someone picks their brains. Beyond simply transferring information, experts can convey insights about how to apply the knowledge to specific situations.

Some organizations use formal mentoring programs to get new team members up to speed quickly (Winters et al. 2020). Pairing new employees with experienced colleagues greatly accelerates learning. When I began my professional career as a research chemist, I was the first guinea pig for a new mentoring program. My mentor, Seth, was a scientist in the group I had joined, but he wasn't in my reporting chain. I felt comfortable asking Seth questions that otherwise might have awkwardly revealed my ignorance to my manager. Seth helped me get rolling in an unfamiliar technology area. A mentoring or "buddy" program reduces the learning curve for new team members and starts building relationships with them immediately.

Scaling Up Knowledge Transfer

One-on-one communications are effective, but they don't scale well. Experienced, talented people are much in demand, both for their project work and for the expertise they can share. To cultivate a knowledge-sharing culture, consider techniques to leverage information more efficiently than one-on-one time spent together. Here are several possibilities.

Technical Talks

My software development team once decided to work through the many excellent programming examples in Steve McConnell's classic book *Code Complete* (McConnell 2004). We took turns studying a particular section and then describing it to the group in a lunch-and-learn session. These informal group learning experiences efficiently disseminated good programming practices across the group. They facilitated a shared understanding of techniques and a common vocabulary.

Presentations and Training

Formal technical presentations and training courses are good ways to communicate institutional knowledge across an organization. I developed several training courses when I worked at Kodak and delivered them many times. If you set up an internal training program, line up enough qualified instructors so that one individual doesn't have to teach the same courses all the time.

Documentation

Written knowledge spans the spectrum from specific project or application documentation to broadly applicable technical guides, tutorials, FAQs, wikis, and tip sheets. Someone must write this documentation, which means they aren't spending that time creating other project deliverables. Written documentation is a highly leverageable organizational asset, provided that team members turn to it as a useful resource.

I've known people who preferred to rediscover knowledge on their own rather than seek it from existing documentation. Those people didn't heed Lesson 7, "The cost of recording knowledge is small compared to the cost of acquiring knowledge." Once someone has invested the time to create relevant and useful documentation, it's a lot quicker to read it than to reconstruct the same information. All organization members should be able to update such documents to keep them valuable as current sources of pooled experience.

Deliverable Templates and Examples

When I worked in a large product development organization, our process improvement group built an extensive online catalog containing high-quality templates and examples of many project deliverables (Wiegers 1998b). We scoured company software departments for good requirements specifications, design documents, project plans, process descriptions, and other items. This "good practices" collection provided a valuable jump-start whenever any software practitioner in the company needed to create some new project artifact.

Technical Peer Reviews

Peer reviews of software work products serve as an informal mechanism for exchanging technical knowledge. They're a great way to look over other people's shoulders and to let them peek over yours. I've learned something from every review I've participated in, whether as a reviewer or as the author of the item being reviewed. The technique of pair programming, in which two people write code together, provides a form of instantaneous peer review, as well as exchanging knowledge between the programmers. See Lesson 48, "Strive to have a peer, rather than a customer, find a defect," for more about reviews.

Discussion Groups

Rather than trying to locate exactly the right person when you have a question, you might post the question to a discussion group or group chat tool within your company. Exposing your lack of knowledge to a large community can be awkward. That's why it's valuable to grow a culture that invites questioning and rewards those who assist. Ignorance is not a tragedy, but an unwillingness to solicit help is.

Discussion participants can offer multiple perspectives on your question quickly. The posted responses are available to everyone in the discussion, which further disseminates the knowledge. You probably weren't the only person who didn't know the answer to that specific question, so good for you for asking. I have a friend who's the most curious person I know. He's willing to ask anyone he encounters in daily life about things he sees them do that are unfamiliar to him. He's learned a lot that way, and the people he asks are always happy to share what they know.

A Healthy Information Culture

Everyone has something to teach—and to learn. When I managed a software development group, I hired a graduate student in computer science as a temporary summer employee. I confess that at first I was skeptical about his understanding of practical software engineering. Similarly, he had some disdain for the process-driven approach our group advocated. After just a few weeks, though, I gained respect for his contemporary programming knowledge, which far exceeded mine. And he acquired an appreciation for how sensible processes can help teams be more effective. We both grew by being open to what the other had to share.

You don't need to be the world's expert on some topic to be helpful. You just need some useful block of knowledge and the willingness to share it. In the world of technology, if you're one week ahead of the next person in some area, you're a wizard. Someone else will doubtless be ahead of you in other areas, so take advantage of their trailblazing. People in a healthy learning culture share what they know and also acknowledge that someone else might know a better way.

Lesson 36	No matter how much pressure others exert, never make a commitment you know you can't fulfill.

In the mid-1990s, I led a formal software process improvement initiative in a product development division of 450 engineers that made digital imaging products full of embedded software. Like many big organizations back then, we used the Capability Maturity Model for Software (CMM) to guide our process improvement efforts (Paulk et al. 1995). The CMM was a five-level framework to help organizations systematically improve their software engineering and management practices. My manager and I had a meeting with the division director, Martin, to discuss our process improvement status, goals, and plans.

Martin balked at my proposed timeline. By carefully assessing our large organization's current status and the gaps we needed to close to achieve the goal, our team had concluded that eighteen months was a realistically achievable target. Martin, who I fear didn't fully understand the challenges, demanded six months. He wanted to be the first director among his peers to achieve the next process milestone. I explained why we believed that was unrealistic. Like the aggressive manager he was, Martin replied, "Don't tell me you can't do it. Tell me what I must do to enable you to do it." That sounds like a nicely supportive posture, but it wouldn't magically solve the problem. Martin reluctantly offered twelve months, but I was positive that goal still was not achievable under any conditions.

As he continued to pressure me to promise results that I knew I couldn't deliver, I finally said, "I'm sorry, Martin, but I can't commit to that." He stared at me.

"You can't commit," Martin said flatly. "Hmmm." It was as though no one had ever resisted his pressures before, and he wasn't sure how to respond. Martin reluctantly accepted our proposed target goal after I assured him that we would work as hard as we could to get there as quickly as possible and would enlist his assistance whenever he could help. Later, back at the office, I heard that my manager—who was a good guy—was telling people, "Karl told Martin he wouldn't commit!" But my manager trusted my judgment.

My pulse rate had shot up as Martin leaned on me. However, it would have been unethical and unprofessional to make a commitment I knew I could not fulfill. It also would have been wrong for me to make a promise that put excessive pressure on my team members by overriding our analysis.

People rarely take commitments they make under duress seriously. Nor do they take seriously commitments that someone else makes on their behalf without consultation and negotiation. Imposing an impossible commitment increases the victim's stress level, but it rarely achieves a miracle. People might even relax their effort if they know they can't make the unachievable goal. Why kill yourself if you're doomed to fail regardless?

Commitments accumulate in dependency chains. Each commitment recipient depends on those who made the commitments to deliver.

Promises, Promises

A *commitment* is a promise that someone makes to perform an action or deliver some body of work in a certain quality state at a specific time. Commitment management is a component of project management, as I described in the introduction to Chapter 4. The concept of not making commitments that you know you can't keep is a personal ethic. It also reflects sound project and people management.

Commitments accumulate in dependency chains, like the one shown in Figure 5.1. Each commitment recipient depends on those who made the commitments to

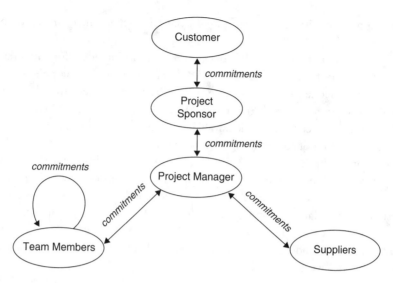

Figure 5.1 *A sequence of commitments leads to a multilevel dependency chain.*

deliver. If everyone negotiates achievable commitments in good faith, they can rely on one another with confidence (Wiegers 2019d). Otherwise, the commitment chain is a house of cards. Any unfulfilled lower-level commitments will undermine the foundation.

As a consultant and author, my practice is to undercommit and overdeliver; I did the same when I was a corporate software developer. Maybe that makes me look overly cautious at times, but it also makes me reliable. One way I stay on schedule is to build contingency buffers into my commitments to account for estimation uncertainties, changing requirements, and other surprises. These buffers provide a safety net in case things don't go as I had planned. I set myself personal targets that are more aggressive than the commitments I make to others. Then I work diligently toward the internal goal, knowing that if I don't quite make that target, I'll still be on track for the external commitment. More often than not, I deliver early. Everyone likes that outcome.

Life Happens

People make commitments with the best of intentions. Then life happens, and sometimes things change. A new assignment or opportunity might arise that diverts time, or the work could be larger than anticipated. Maybe the individual just loses interest in the original commitment and lets it fall by the wayside, hoping no one will notice. But they do notice.

If you discover that you can't fulfill a commitment as intended, for whatever reason, tell those affected as soon as possible so that they can adjust their plans accordingly. When someone makes a promise to me, I count on them to deliver. If my original expectation isn't realistic or something changes, let's talk. Maybe we can reach a mutually acceptable and achievable agreement. But I also recognize that the other person might not come through for various reasons.

I encounter a broken-commitment situation with every book I write. I always line up several volunteer manuscript reviewers to help improve my writing. I need my reviewers' input on specific chapters by particular dates. No reviewer has ever protested that my dates are unrealistic, and yet with every book, some people provide zero feedback. On a recent book, nine of the twenty-six reviewers (volunteers, remember) provided no input, nor an explanation. It's as though they took a vow of silence right after we got started.

If I say I'm going to do something, either I do it, or I explain that I cannot do it after all, with apologies. We all know that situations and priorities can change. If a manuscript reviewer can't contribute to the project after all, I just wish they'd let me know as soon as they can so that I can make adjustments. It's a simple courtesy.

I also never received a cover blurb for one of my books from another author who spontaneously offered to contribute one. Since the book was published twenty-five years ago, it looks pretty doubtful that I'll see that blurb. But he never told me he *wouldn't* do it after he committed. That's all I ask.

Lesson 37   Without training and better practices, don't expect higher productivity to happen by magic.

Several of my consulting clients complained to me that their management told them to do more with less, to be more productive with fewer people. When I asked, "What's being done to enable you to do more with less?" I always got the same answer: "Nothing."

Those demands don't seem reasonable to me. The senior managers appeared to think the software people had idle time on their hands. Were they working at less than full speed with some reserve capacity to exploit if only they were pressed? I doubt that's the case. Cracking the whip and demanding that the horse run faster doesn't work if the horse is already going as fast as it can. At the risk of overstretching the metaphor, you need to understand why the horse isn't running as fast as you want and then search for acceleration opportunities.

Teams can be motivated (or pressured) into working extra hard for a short-term goal, but not indefinitely. Tired people make more mistakes—which leads to time-sapping rework—and they get burned out. If the pressure goes on for too long, people will leave or revert to a normal pace despite management's rantings. Heroic efforts are not a sustainable productivity strategy.

"Doing more with less" means delivering more functionality sooner with a smaller team. If you can't have as many people as you believe you need to achieve compressed schedules, what variables can you manipulate? The options include better processes, better practices, better tools, and better people. Hiring a few top performers is better than staffing a larger team with average performers (Davis 1995). However, you can't just swap out your team for a new set of more capable people. You need to make the people you have more productive.

What's the Problem?

If you need greater productivity, the first question to ask is, "Why isn't our productivity already as high as we'd like?" Answering this question requires reflection and analysis. Begin any solution hunt by identifying the problem's origins. (See Lesson 51, "Watch out for 'Management by Businessweek,'" for a discussion of root cause analysis.) Examine previous projects to see where there might have been opportunities to work more efficiently and effectively. Once you understand the root causes of insufficient productivity, you can search for solutions. Questions to consider include the following.

- What are your teams doing that they don't need to do?
- What are people currently doing that adds value and could perhaps be leveraged further?
- What are your teams *not* doing that would accelerate their work if they did do it?
- What else slows us down?

Some Possible Solutions

One way to improve productivity is to stop doing work that doesn't add proportionate value to the project, the product, or the customer. Is there any unnecessary process overhead? Be careful, though: process steps that don't provide immediate value often pay off later, so consider the consequences before dropping some activity. Do pointless, overly long, or overcrowded meetings waste time? I have a friend who worked for a meeting-crazy technology company. Some meetings simply prepared reports to feed into the next meeting with another group of people just one hour later. She had a hard time getting any work done in that environment.

A second productivity-boosting strategy is to improve the quality of the team's products. Unplanned, excessive rework kills productivity. Instead of moving on to build the next component, team members must redo completed work to repair defects. (See Lesson 44, "High quality naturally leads to higher productivity.") Reducing defects could mean incorporating additional quality-related practices. Adding proven practices like static code analysis and peer reviews consumes time, but they more than pay for themselves by reducing downstream rework. Emphasizing design over refactoring reduces technical debt that the team must repay later. It's a matter of going slow to go fast, a lesson that every craftsperson quickly learns. A related saying that applies to many disciplines is, "Slow is smooth, smooth is fast."

Third, removing barriers to productivity means understanding where time gets wasted. Must people often wait on others before they can proceed with their next step? You can improve throughput by accelerating activities that lie on the critical path to completing a piece of work. Are some team members losing productivity

through excessive multitasking? Revisit Lesson 23, "Work plans must account for friction," to see whether any of the sources of project friction described there are impeding progress.

Your fourth productivity improvement lever is to enhance individual team members' capabilities. I always assume that people do the best job they can, given what they know at the time and the environment in which they work. Both the physical and cultural working environments affect a software developer's productivity and quality performance (Glass 2003, DeMarco and Lister 2013). Selecting more appropriate processes and technical practices can yield significant quality improvements, further boosting productivity. Growing a healthy software engineering culture that motivates and rewards preferred behaviors contributes to efficient work from a happy team.

A manager who wants higher productivity will provide team members with office space that permits their best work, with sufficient square footage, facilities, privacy, and freedom from distractions. When I was at a consulting client's site once, I was appalled at my main contact's workspace in cubical hell. His desk sat inches from his neighbor's. There was barely room around his desk to bring in a chair for me. He had to twist awkwardly to lay out some papers for me to view on a corner of his desk. No one could work efficiently in that cramped, zero-privacy environment. Unfortunately, a software manager informed me recently that, "A manager generally can't affect office space nowadays, and a huge number of cube farms are indeed that bad." That's a discouraging commentary.

Training is a powerful performance enhancement lever, provided that people apply what they learn back on the job.

Tools and Training

The right tools can enhance productivity. The software tools industry has a long history of touting impressive, even order-of-magnitude improvements in productivity if you'll only buy their latest version. In reality, the productivity gain from a single new tool rarely exceeds 35 percent (Glass 2003). Software developer productivity has increased impressively over the years through the accumulated benefits of multiple tools, new languages and development practices, reuse of open-source software and common libraries, and other factors, but there is no single silver-bullet tool or method (Brooks 1995). Remember to account for the learning curve as people figure out how to make a new tool work effectively for them. Look for tools that can automate—and document—repetitive tasks, like testing.

Training is a powerful performance enhancement lever, provided that the people who get trained apply what they learn back on the job. Overwhelmed managers trying to do more with less might hesitate to pull team members away from their keyboards for training, and training courses are expensive. When I managed a small software group, I routinely overran my training budget, with solid upper-management support. I had friends in another department that had no budget for books. That struck me as ridiculous. Suppose you spend $40 on a technical book and read it mostly on your own time. If you save even one hour on your work—any time during the rest of your life—from something you learned in the book, you more than paid for it. The investment in learning pays for itself every time you apply a new practice that yields better, faster results.

Individual Developer Variation

Everyone likes to think that their team has top-flight talent; they want to hire only the best developers. However, the fact is that half of all software developers lie below the median of the performance distribution. Those people all work somewhere, and not everyone can hire from the pool's top echelon. It's not easy to quantify software developer performance, but who does the work significantly affects a team's productivity and quality.

Numerous software literature reports have indicated a tenfold or greater range between the top and bottom performers among software developers (Construx 2010, McConnell 2010). And it's not just developers. People in other project roles—business analyst, tester, product owner—also can vary widely in their performance. However, a recent report by Bill Nichols of the Software Engineering Institute (2020) avers that the 10x ratio of programmer performance is a myth. Nichols's data indicates that an individual's own day-to-day variation accounts for about half of the performance difference observed between developers in any given activity.

My personal experience suggests that the 10x ratio is not implausible. I used to work with a developer who did high-quality, creative work. But he did it less than half as quickly as I could do the same job. I also worked with a senior developer who was at least three times as productive as I was. His dual master's degrees in computer science and computer engineering gave him the skills to efficiently tackle complex problems I simply couldn't handle. Also, he had accumulated an extensive library of reusable components over his career that saved him a lot of time. The three of us thus spanned at least a sixfold performance range, in my view.

There's no question that skilled and talented individuals and teams are more productive than others. Not surprisingly, The Standish Group (2015) reported that projects staffed with "gifted" agile project teams were substantially more successful than those with unskilled teams. As an interesting corollary, small projects had a higher success rate than larger projects, perhaps partly because it's easier to selectively staff a small team with highly capable individuals. Not everyone gets to be, work with, or hire the top technical staff. As Bill Nichols (2020) points out, "Finding a consistently superior programmer is hard, finding a capable programmer is not."

If you can't assemble an all-star team (avoiding arrogant prima donnas in the process), focus on creating a productive environment to get the best results from the people you have. Enhance everyone's talent by sharing local best practices. Observe what makes your most outstanding performers—everyone knows who they are—so good, and encourage everyone to learn from them (Bakker 2020). Technical skills are important, but so are communication, collaboration, mentoring, lack of territoriality, and an attitude of shared product ownership. The best developers I've known had a strong focus on quality. They were nondogmatic and intellectually curious with a breadth of experience, a focus on continuous learning, and a willingness to share.

If you must do more with less, you're not going to get there by decreeing it, putting more pressure on your team, or hiring only at the 90th percentile of talent. The path to increased productivity inevitably involves training, better practices, and improved processes.

| Lesson 38 | People talk a lot about their rights, but the flip side of every right is a responsibility. |

Life brings us many freedoms, along with corresponding obligations. You have the right to own a car, but you also must register and insure it. Along with the right to buy real estate comes a requirement to pay property taxes. As a citizen, you have the right to vote, but you also have a responsibility to make your voice heard at the ballot box.

The combination of rights and responsibilities defines how people fit into society. The United States has a Bill of Rights, the first ten amendments to the United States Constitution. However, there's no corresponding Bill of Responsibilities. Citizens' responsibilities are embodied in thousands of statutes and regulations in countless jurisdictions. We also have social responsibilities to our fellow residents of Planet Earth, just because we're all here together.

People on software projects also have rights and responsibilities. We can organize these two sides of the coin by considering the people we interact with, the rights we expect from them, and our responsibilities to them. Individuals have these rights–responsibilities connections with their fellow team members, customers, managers, suppliers, and the general public. As we work with our collaborators, we should hold conversations along these lines: "Here's what I need from you for us to jointly be successful on this project. What do you need from me?"

Beyond the specific responsibilities of individual commitments we make to others, all software practitioners are responsible for conforming to professional ethics. The two major computing organizations, the Association for Computing Machinery and the IEEE Computer Society, jointly established The Software Engineering Code of Ethics and Professional Practice (ACM 1999). This code addresses a practitioner's responsibilities to act in ways that are consistent with the public interests, maintain confidentiality, respect intellectual property ownership, strive for high quality, and so forth. All software professionals should become familiar with this guide and adopt a personal code of ethics for responsible software development (Löwe 2015).

There's a symmetry between software professionals' rights and responsibilities. Suppose the people in group A have a right to some service or behavior from people in group B. Members of group A, in turn, have some responsibilities to those in group B. You can imagine crafting a bill of responsibilities to accompany each bill of rights for these pairwise relationships. Alternatively, you could devise complementary bills of rights for both parties involved in a relationship, with the corresponding mutual responsibilities implied.

Following are a few examples of rights and responsibilities for some groups involved in software development, drawn from several sources; there are many other suggestions about these topics out there (Atwood 2006, StackExchange n.d.). Consider reading the full source of each example for more ideas about professional rights and responsibilities that apply in your context. You might find it helpful to itemize your local views of rights and responsibilities to help your project stakeholders collaborate more smoothly. If you're uncomfortable with the formalism of writing down rights and responsibilities, consider phrasing these ideas in the form: "It's generally reasonable for me to expect X from you, and it's reasonable for you to expect Y from me."

Some Customer Rights and Responsibilities

As a customer, you have a *right* to expect a business analyst (BA) to learn about your business and your objectives. You have a *responsibility* to educate BAs and developers about your business (Wiegers and Beatty 2013).

As a customer, you have a *right* to receive a system that meets your functional needs and quality expectations. You have a *responsibility* to dedicate the time it takes to provide and clarify requirements.

As a customer, you have a *right* to change your requirements. You have a *responsibility* to communicate requirement changes to the development team promptly.

Some Developer Rights and Responsibilities

As a developer, you have a *right* to have your intellectual property acknowledged and respected by others. You have a *responsibility* to respect others' intellectual property rights by reusing their work only with permission (St. Augustine's College, n.d.).

As a developer, you have a *right* to know the priority of every requirement. You have a *responsibility* to inform the customer of the schedule impact of new and reprioritized requirements.

As a developer, you have a *right* to make and update estimates for your work. You have a *responsibility* to make your estimates as accurate as possible and to adjust schedules to reflect reality as quickly as possible (Wikic2 2006, Wikic2 2008).

Some Project Manager or Sponsor Rights and Responsibilities

As a project manager or sponsor, you have a *right* to expect developers to produce high-quality software. You have a *responsibility* to provide the environment, resources, and time to enable developers to produce high-quality software.

As a project manager or sponsor, you have a *right* to set project goals and establish schedules. You have a *responsibility* to respect developers' estimates and to avoid pressuring developers to accomplish work in unrealistic time frames.

Some Autonomous Team Rights and Responsibilities

As a member of a self-managing, autonomous Scrum team, you have a *right* to manage your capacity, control how you execute a sprint, and establish when a piece of work is done. You have a *responsibility* to determine a sprint goal, create a sprint backlog, assess daily progress toward the sprint goal, and participate in a retrospective to assess how the sprint went and create an improvement plan (Ageling 2020).

Our greatest responsibility is to treat all of our professional counterparts fairly and with respect.

Concerns before Crises

You might think you're entitled to a certain right from some other community, but maybe they're not able or willing to meet your expectation. Whenever you encounter a mismatch like that, the parties must learn how to work together constructively and without rancor. It's worth the time for collaborators to discuss their mutual rights and responsibilities, perhaps recording them to avoid misunderstandings. This dialog is a form of expectation management, which was explained in the introduction to Chapter 4.

I've long had a philosophy in my close personal relationships to deal with a concern before it becomes a crisis. That's a good practice with our professional interactions as well. Most people mean well, even if sometimes it isn't obvious at first glance. Reaching shared understandings regarding rights and responsibilities helps avoid unpleasant interpersonal crises.

Our greatest responsibility is to treat all of our professional counterparts fairly and with respect. We should all be able to do that.

Lesson 39	It takes little physical separation to inhibit communication and collaboration.

In Lesson 12, "Requirements elicitation must bring the customer's voice close to the developer's ear," I described my experience of writing software for a scientist named Sean, who sat close to me. I was highly productive because of the quick feedback I could get from him when necessary. In the middle of our project, Sean moved to an office on the other side of the building. My productivity promptly took a hit. Now I couldn't catch Sean's attention at a moment's notice to answer a question, decide on a user interface option, or refresh my memory. The separation increased the cycle time on resolving even simple issues. The realization that such a modest distance could impair my development productivity was a powerful insight.

Barriers of Space and Time

Out-of-sight separation makes it harder for people to interact informally. As Figure 5.2 shows, when I was working on Sean's project, I could glance up from my desk and see whether he was in his office. If he wasn't there, I'd work on something for which I didn't need his input. That visibility let me optimize my productive time without having to wait for an answer to proceed.

After he moved, I had to try to reach Sean by phone, send an e-mail, wait for our regularly scheduled meeting, or walk to his new office and see whether he was in. The separation problem gets far worse when collaborators are strewn across multiple time zones. The same issue affects daily life too. I have a friend who frequently calls me after he's eaten supper, but since he lives one time zone to the east of me, I'm always sitting down to eat right about then. His calls come at a time that's convenient for him but inconvenient for me. Asynchronous communication works across time and space, but it's slower than talking to someone in real time.

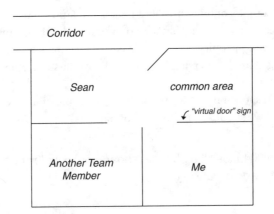

Figure 5.2 *My office layout made it easy for me to see whether my customer, Sean, was in his office.*

The more time zones that are involved, the bigger the connection problem is, and the less overlap time you have during regular work hours. One project had people in several countries that spanned twelve time zones—halfway around the world. Any time they chose for their videoconferences would be awkward for some of the team members. The group rotated their meeting times to inconvenience everyone about equally. This courtesy demonstrated respect for everyone's time and conveyed an important cultural signal: it indicated that the people in all locations were equally significant to the project. No one location should feel subordinate to another.

Designing office spaces to promote collaboration while retaining privacy for focused work is a delicate balance. Ideally, the manager can accommodate each team member's preferences while still providing good interaction opportunities. As we saw in Lesson 23, "Work plans must account for friction," knowledge workers are most productive when they enter a state of flow, deeply immersed in a task. Flow requires freedom from distractions and interruptions. So while people should be close enough to interact readily, they also need private space for concentrated focus.

Proximity is valuable, but we must also be sensitive to everyone's need to get their work done with minimal interruption.

Having a customer nearby is excellent for the development team because they can get questions answered quickly. But think about it from the customer's perspective. Sean wasn't just a chatbot patiently awaiting my next inquiry. He was a research scientist trying to get his own work done. Every question I posed, every request to review a display screen or report, interrupted Sean's state of flow. Proximity is valuable, but we must also be sensitive to everyone's need to get their work done with minimal interruption.

Virtual Teams: The Ultimate in Separation

More and more software professionals work remotely, either by choice or because of the COVID-19 pandemic, thereby possibly rendering moot the debates over how best to design shared office spaces. Virtual teams pose their own massive set of cultural and collaborative challenges, though. It's hard to get to know and understand coworkers you've never met in person, let alone to build—or integrate into—a shared culture of values and practices. My colleague Holly, a BA, described her recent experience:

> Until I had to do it myself, I didn't fully comprehend the challenges involved in creating strong virtual teams. I recently took a new position that is 100 percent remote. The activities I'm performing aren't new to me, but they're different now. The expected startup aspects—meeting my new teammates, learning my new organization's language and communication styles, locating relevant documentation, identifying the technology critical to supporting my role—are all familiar and yet vastly new. Meeting culture has taken on new levels of agony in this new remote world too. People don't walk to meetings any longer; we click out of one meeting and into the next one. Where have our bio breaks gone??

A web search for "challenges of virtual software teams" yields numerous articles that address the many issues involved. If you're in a remote-working environment, it's worth the time to understand the major challenges and consider how best to succeed in the world of virtual teamwork.

A Door, a Door, My Kingdom for a Door!

A closed door is a communication barrier. It can be either a benefit or a nuisance, depending on which side of the door you're on. I've worked in private offices with and without doors, in shared offices, and in landscaped areas with a vast sea of cubicles. The office cluster shown in Figure 5.2 had a door to the corridor, but our three individual offices lacked doors. A visitor coming to see any one of us in the cluster distracted the others.

Fellow employees dropped by my office frequently with computer questions. Eventually, I posted a sign outside my doorway that said "The Virtual Door Is Open" on one side and "The Virtual Door Is Closed" on the other. I hoped that people would recognize when I didn't want to be disturbed. Boy, was I naïve. Most visitors would read the sign and then say, "'The Virtual Door Is Closed,' that's pretty funny. Hey, I've got a question." So that strategy failed. I've heard of people who used an orange traffic safety cone or a velvet rope like those seen in movie theaters across a doorway as a signal to indicate that they were working intently and would prefer not to be interrupted.

I did eventually get an office with a real door, which let me get more work done. Frequently-consulted experts in some companies set up office hours, during which they invite colleagues to come by for discussions (Winters et al. 2020). Maybe it's not as timely for the person with the question, but it does reduce the expert's interruption frequency.

Several years later, I moved to a different building with a completely different culture and environment. I was in cubicle land to an extreme degree. We all had five-foot partitions around our desks, except for the managers, who had private offices (of course). My cube was one of the noisiest spaces in this entire quarter-mile-long building. I sat adjacent to the main corridor running down the building's length, by the top of the escalator, near the bathrooms, and near the meeting and training rooms. Four feet from my desk was the coffee machine, where students would congregate and chat during breaks in training classes. The one good thing about my location was that leftover cake from celebrations was dropped off on the coffee machine's table. I don't drink coffee, but I do enjoy cake.

I'm easily distracted by irritating noises that many other people don't even notice. It took at least two months for me to tune out the distractions in that open space and concentrate on my work. While the open areas facilitated interaction with the people around me, I was highly stressed until I finally adapted to the noisy environment.

There's no perfect solution to designing workspaces to satisfy the conflicting needs of privacy, freedom from distraction, proximity to colleagues for quick interactions, and shared space for project meetings. Geographical separation is problem enough; overlaying cultural differences greatly increases the challenges for effective collaboration. Collaboration tools help geographically separated people work together, but they aren't a complete substitute for real-time, face-to-face interactions. To the extent possible, managers should let the team members design their workspaces to best balance these conflicting goals (DeMarco and Lister 2013). If that doesn't work, I recommend headphones or earplugs.

Lesson 40	Informal approaches that work for a small colocated team don't scale up well.

Bill Gates and Paul Allen, Steve Jobs and Steve Wozniak, Bill Hewlett and David Packard—I'm guessing that none of them had written specifications or procedure books for their early projects. A mind meld between pairs of super-talented wizards who work side by side obviates the need for most documentation. But it's hard to scale a mind meld across time, space, and hundreds of brains thinking in different languages and immersed in different cultures.

Figure 5.3 shows a qualitative scale of project complexity. Projects span the extremes between a pair of geniuses working in a garage and a cast of thousands building the International Space Station (the largest project I could think of). As organizations grow, they take on larger and more complex projects. The two geniuses move out of the garage, hire some other people, and tackle projects with a dozen or two technical people in one location. If you build a product with software

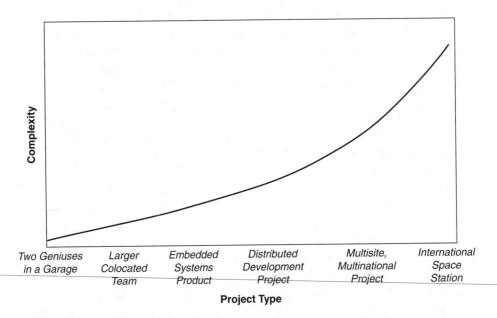

Figure 5.3 *As organizations take on bigger and more complex projects, they must scale up their processes and methods accordingly.*

embedded in a hardware device, your team will include mechanical and electrical engineers. At some point, you might acquire another company in a different city or otherwise partner with people over the horizon in a distributed development project. Companies that build huge, complex products—think airplanes—can have software engineers, hardware engineers, and many other specialists working on dozens of subprojects in multiple countries. Big challenges demand appropriate approaches.

Processes and Tools

As teams, projects, and organizations grow, the need to beef up their processes sneaks up on them. They might recognize the need only after they encounter a problem. Maybe two teams overwrote each other's work, or a task was overlooked because everyone thought someone else was going to do it. Those issues call for better planning, coordination, and communication between team members and groups. Sources of friction and delays creep in as more people are involved, particularly when they're in different locations.

The farther apart team members are, the more process structure they need.

Larger projects call for writing down more information so that others know what's going on and what lies ahead. A persistent group memory of requirements, decisions, business rules, estimates, and metrics begins to look useful. The farther apart team members are, the more process structure they need, and the more they must rely on remote collaboration tools.

For compatibility and facile information exchange, teams in multiple locations need common tools for task management and tracking, modeling, testing, continuous integration, and particularly, code management (Senycia 2020). Open-source software is an extreme example of distributed software development. Contributors to an open-source project can live anywhere in the world. A mass of people who participate in ever-evolving projects need to follow some consistent processes to ensure that all the pieces will fit together. As Andrew Leonard (2020) points out, "No single innovation was more critical to the facilitation of successful remote collaborative software development than the all-important job of version control."

The Need for Specialization

I started out in software writing programs for college classes, for my personal use, and for amusement. Then I began writing programs for other people to use and some small commercial apps. Later, I joined forces with other software developers to take on larger projects. While working on a project by myself, I wore all the project role hats in turn. Depending on what I was doing at any particular moment, I might be functioning as a BA, designer, programmer, tester, documentation writer, project manager, or maintainer.

It's not realistic to expect every team member to be fully proficient in all of those technical domains. As projects and teams get larger, some skills specialization is both natural and beneficial. At some point, even Bill Gates and Paul Allen decided they needed to hire people with skills besides coding to keep their fledgling company growing: technical writer, mathematician, project manager, and so on (Weinberger 2019). I hear it worked out for them.

Communication Clashes

As we saw in Lesson 14, the number of communication links grows exponentially with a group's size. Project participants need mechanisms for exchanging information quickly and accurately. Communication preferences vary also. People instinctively communicate with others in the ways that are most comfortable for themselves, but that's not always what the other parties prefer.

I once facilitated a retrospective for a project that involved a web development team and a human factors team. During the retrospective, a member of the human factors team said that she felt she wasn't included in project communications and didn't always know what was going on. A surprised member of the software team protested, "I copied you in on all of our e-mails." We discovered that the two groups had very different communication preferences and wanted to receive important communications differently.

In this case, the teams were not located far apart, but they definitely had some stylewise separation. As you move to projects involving multiple groups of people, it's important to lay the foundation early on to communicate in ways that work for everyone. Similarly, the groups might make decisions differently. To avoid hard feelings and speed up decision-making, they should discuss how the teams will jointly make decisions—before they confront their first big one.

Successful organizations grow and take on ever-greater challenges. They shouldn't expect the techniques that worked for a few people in a garage to scale up and span large distances. They can dodge some growth pains by anticipating the processes and tools they'll need to integrate the various team efforts. It's less disruptive to build as much infrastructure as possible in advance than it is to introduce it to project participants in the heat of battle. Having the participants get to know and understand their remote counterparts early in the project can help avoid culture clashes. The time spent laying these foundations can prevent a lot of grief down the road.

> **Lesson 41**   Don't underestimate the challenge of changing an organization's culture as it moves toward new ways of working.

In Lesson 36, "No matter how much pressure others exert, never make a commitment you know you can't fulfill," I mentioned that I once led a process improvement program in a large corporate division. The senior manager of that division—three steps above me on the organization chart—enthusiastically supported the effort. But Martin didn't fully appreciate everything involved with moving several hundred software and systems engineers into a new paradigm.

Martin seemed to think we could simply write new software development procedures and everyone would get on board. He rubber-stamped the management policies that we wrote as part of the change framework we were following, but that was it. He didn't announce or explain the policies, set expectations for how they should be applied, define a migration path to the new ways of working, or hold anyone accountable for following the policies. Hence, the policies were broadly ignored, and the new procedures had limited impact initially.

This experience revealed that installing a new process is easier than instilling a new culture. A successful change initiative requires both. You can't just send everyone off to a training class and give them a big honkin' binder of new procedures (or a thin guide, whichever represents the direction you're going) and then expect them to start working effectively in new ways right away. That approach just perplexes and stresses people. It damages management's credibility, even in strong cultures.

Values, Behaviors, and Practices

As I described earlier, a healthy software engineering culture encompasses shared values, behaviors, and technical practices. Engaging team members in the change process increases their buy-in—crafty leaders can make people believe ideas were their own. Members of an organization undergoing a change initiative need to know a lot more than the new practices they're expected to follow. The change leaders will need to explain

- Why change is necessary
- What problems it will address
- What outcomes the organization hopes to achieve as a result
- The impact on the organizational chart
- Any new roles, job titles, or responsibilities
- The expectations of team members as individuals
- The implementation timeline
- Accountability for constructively contributing to the change initiative

For successful culture change, the change leaders must persuade everyone affected to embrace the merits of both the goal and the approach. Persuasion is easier when everyone is well aware of the pain points. A colleague once told me she had never worked on a successful software project. That frustration strongly motivated her to lead process improvement activities to enhance project outcomes and the company's business success.

Change is hard. Not everyone wants to get on board, and you can't evolve a culture if people are kicking and screaming, reluctant to leave their comfort zone. However, those individuals who are most uneasy about the change must not be permitted to hold back the entire initiative. Strive for a sensible balance point between imposing a new way of life by fiat at one extreme and trying to make everyone happy at the other.

Martin said he supported the change initiative in his division, but I'm not sure he was truly committed to it. To me, *support* is a vague and ambiguous word. When someone says, "I support that," often what they mean is, "It's okay with me if that happens" or "That sounds like a good idea." The notion of support as tolerance or approval is very different from a commitment. Committed leaders take action and lead by example. They set concrete goals, provide resources, and demonstrate behaviors that are aligned with the intended outcome. They put something of themselves at risk and are accountable for their organizations' results. Managers who are committed to lasting change know to frame the change in a way that stirs emotions and stimulates actions (Walker and Soule 2017). Platitudes, mandates, and directives don't cut it.

Effective change leaders know that it takes persuasion and time to steer team members toward new values and behaviors. People in the organization have three options: they can help lead the initiative, follow along with the program and do their part, or get out of the way. If the magnitude or nature of the change makes some people too uncomfortable, they'll probably leave; it's better for everyone concerned if they do. I've seen too many cases where people who were unhappy with their organization's new direction took a passive-aggressive approach. They paid lip service to the evolution but ignored or undermined it whenever they could.

Agile and Culture Change

Changing to agile is a major shift in how a software organization operates. I used to say that you can't buy a culture in shrink-wrap and install it like you can a new tool or technical practice, but that's not entirely true with agile. Migrating to, say, Scrum does involve absorbing a prepackaged culture with a set of values, behaviors, and technical practices. Many aspects of the culture must change when transitioning to agile, including these (Hatch 2019):

- Organizational structure and team composition
- Terminology
- Values and principles
- New project roles, such as Scrum Master and product owner
- Scheduling and planning practices
- The nature of collaboration and communication
- How progress is measured
- Accountability for results

That's a lot of disruption to absorb all at once. Traditional software process improvement strategies are incremental: new procedures and practices are incorporated into project activities in digestible bites. Switching to agile involves a more abrupt shift of thinking and practice. Simply training everyone isn't sufficient to gain commitment to the new values, change individual behaviors, and adopt new practices. It takes time for practitioners to unlearn what they've done before and to become comfortable and proficient with new ways of working.

I know of two companies that carried out large-scale agile training for hundreds of their software developers. One company promptly dove into a massive strategic project involving more than 150 people in multiple locations, mandated by senior management to be done using agile. After an investment of several years and a huge amount of money, the project was suspended without delivering anything usable.

The second company adopted an enterprise-level agile framework and decreed it for all projects, regardless of how well it fit the project situation. As a friend at that company explained it:

This was a huge transformation. As it affected all of our development practices, procedures, and audit requirements, the aggressive conversion schedule caused problems in areas where insufficient time or training was provided for smooth transitions. The conversion to agile was presented as a finalized decision. Upper management didn't frame it in terms of solving specific problems within the company, and they didn't try to talk us into wanting it. There were varying amounts of pushback across the organization. A lot of developers were very unhappy because they were hired as waterfall developers, not agile ones.

In an ideal world, everybody responds to profound change by thinking, "What's in it for us?" but most people actually think, "Why are you making me do this?" Some people got over this response; some didn't.

Had management paid more attention to the substantial cultural impacts of these radical, all-at-once transformations, the changes might have been more readily accepted and the results more satisfactory. Time will tell how well these kinds of large-scale transformation attempts succeed.

Internalization

To achieve the desired business outcomes, a process-oriented and cultural change initiative has two objectives. One is *institutionalization*. Institutionalization means that new practices, behaviors, and values have been established across the organization and are now part of the routine ways that projects operate. The second objective is *internalization*. Internalization means that new ways of working have become ingrained in how individual team members think and function.

When team members have internalized new methods and behaviors, they don't perform them because the manager, procedures book, or agile coach told them to. They work that way simply because it's the best way they know to get the job done. Internalization is more difficult and takes longer than institutionalization, but it's also a stronger indication of a successful culture change. Once you've internalized a better way to work, it stays with you forever.

Making fundamental transitions from established ways of working to something very different requires many flavors of change: organizational, managerial, project leadership, rewards, technical practice, individual habits, and team behaviors. It's not something that you can buy or mandate. Senior management must be committed to the change and make a compelling case for it with all those who are affected (Agile Alliance et al. 2021). The cultural transition poses a greater challenge than installing a set of new practices and methods, but you're likely to fail without it.

When team members have internalized new methods and behaviors, they work that way simply because it's the best way they know to get the job done.

Lesson 42	No engineering or management technique will work if you're dealing with unreasonable people.

From time to time, you might encounter someone at work who strikes you as being unreasonable. It could be a fellow team member, manager, customer, or some other collaborator. We've met several such people in previous lessons, including the following:

- A team leader who expected a team member to handle five 8-hour activities per week on different projects (Lesson 23)

- A customer who insisted that she could provide requirements on behalf of a user class to which she didn't belong (Lesson 33)

- A coworker who hoarded knowledge instead of sharing it with his colleagues (Lesson 35)

- A senior manager who hoped to alter the culture in a large organization by decreeing a set of new processes (Lesson 41)

When you encounter someone who doesn't seem to be reasonable, that's not a technical problem—it's a people problem. There are several ways you can respond. One is to defend your position in the form of a debate. Another is to succumb to pressure from the unreasonable person and do whatever they say, even if you don't think it's the right approach. A third option is to pretend to comply but do something else or nothing at all.

A better strategy is to understand what makes such a person appear unreasonable to you and then consider how to respond. They might be defending an entrenched position rather than protecting their legitimate interests. Often, people who seem unreasonable are simply uninformed. Unfamiliar practices, jargon, and cocky software developers can intimidate customers who have little experience working with a software team and lack technical knowledge. People who were disappointed by an earlier project experience could be leery of getting involved again.

When I was the lead BA on one project, I worked with a customer who'd been burned twice on previous projects that failed. He was wary of working with yet another software team. When I learned about his history, I could understand why he didn't trust me—someone he had just met—from the outset. We worked through it, though, with a little patience and explanation, and the project was a solid success.

Try a Little Teaching

If the unreasonable reaction is due to a lack of knowledge, try educating the person. They need to understand the terminology you use, the practices you perform, why those practices contribute to project success, and what happens if you don't do them. The people you work with must understand what input and actions you need from them and what they can expect from you. If a BA begins a conversation with a new customer with, "Let's talk about your user stories," that's intimidating and invites a negative response. The customer has no idea what a user story is or what their role is in the process. Sometimes all it takes is transmitting a little information to resolve what came across as an unreasonable reaction.

I ran into this lack-of-knowledge scenario shortly after becoming the manager of a software group that supported the research laboratories in a large company. I described my group's work at an annual meeting of the senior research management and technical staff. I stated that, from now on, our group would write no software without written specifications. A senior manager named Scott protested, "Wait a minute—I'm not sure your definition of specifications is the same as mine." My first response was, "Then let's use mine." Lest that appear too flippant (which, of course, it was), I then explained what I meant by specifications. Once he understood that I wasn't asking for anything outrageous, Scott agreed that this was a fair expectation.

Who's Out of Line Here?

My conversation with Scott illustrated an important point: make sure *you* aren't the one who's being unreasonable. Business analysts, project managers, or developers might seem to be difficult if they don't agree to do everything that someone asks of them. A business analyst who asks that a user or manager spend time working with the software team could appear unreasonable to someone who didn't expect to invest much effort in the project.

Sometimes people think they have more knowledge than they actually do and exert pressure to take an unsound approach. My friend Andrea, a highly experienced developer and database designer, contracted to a company for which she had previously built several successful systems. A senior developer at the client insisted that their new system's database use a data model that he had developed. Andrea pointed out the serious flaws in the data model, but the client developer threatened, "Use my data model, or I'm canceling the project." Andrea reluctantly agreed. Sure enough, the product suffered many problems, which took great effort to resolve. When Andrea correctly noted that those problems derived from the flawed data model, the client developer accused her of messing up the implementation of his great data model. That client's behavior was unreasonable by any measure; everyone suffered the consequences.

> To make sure that no one comes across as unreasonable, let's try to understand each other's goals, priorities, pressures, drivers, fears, and constraints.

In Favor of Flexibility

Being dogmatic is another way to appear unreasonable. When I worked in a group leading a software process improvement program based on the Capability Maturity Model for Software, I once got pulled into a debate with a less-experienced colleague. Silvia maintained, "The CMM is a *model*. We're supposed to do what it says!" That struck me as an overly constraining misinterpretation. My response was, "The CMM is a *model*. We're supposed to adapt it to our situation!" I thought Silvia was dogmatic and inflexible; she thought I was violating the intent of the CMM by not applying it prescriptively. Through the ensuing discussion, our group reached a shared understanding about how to use the CMM in our environment. Still, I was struck by the big difference in how Silvia and I interpreted what a "model" is for.

   To make sure that no one comes across as unreasonable, let's try to understand each other's goals, priorities, pressures, drivers, fears, and constraints. Let's find out which behaviors and outcomes generate rewards in both of our worlds and which ones generate retribution. Let's craft agreements so that we all know what others expect from us and what we can expect from them. We'll all get along better if we appreciate—and respect—each other's point of view.

Next Steps: Culture and Teamwork

1. Identify which of the lessons described in this chapter are relevant to your experiences with organizational culture and teamwork.

2. Can you think of any other lessons related to culture and teamwork from your own experience that are worth sharing with your colleagues?

3. Identify any practices described in this chapter that might be solutions to the culture- and teamwork-related problems you identified in the First Steps at the beginning of the chapter. How could each practice improve

how your project team members work together? How might you rectify any culture-killing actions and reinforce culture-building actions?

4. How could you tell whether each practice from Step 3 was yielding the desired results? What would those results be worth to you?

5. Identify any barriers that might make it difficult to apply the practices from Step 3. How could you break down those barriers or enlist allies to help you implement the practices effectively?

6. Think of ways to take the best aspects of how your teams collaborate and spread that wisdom to other project teams. How can you instill cultural practices and attitudes that will persist over time to help future teams succeed?

Chapter 6

Lessons About Quality

Introduction to Quality

I wrote a perfect software application once, in assembly language, no less. It wasn't large—an educational chemistry game—but it had zero defects and did everything it was supposed to do correctly. I've also written a lot more code that, despite my best efforts, contained errors that I had to correct later. High-quality software is important to me, as it should be to everyone who creates or uses software systems. We should all strive for quality in the work we do—but what does *quality* mean?

Definitions of Quality

People have tried to define *quality* for ages, but it's elusive. I've seen many attempts at it, but I'm aware of no all-inclusive yet succinct definition that applies to software. The American Society for Quality (2021a) acknowledges this reality with the first part of its definition of quality: "A subjective term for which each person or sector has its own definition." That's true, if not terribly helpful. Different observers will indeed have varying conceptions of what constitutes quality—or the lack thereof—in a given product or service. Here are some other definitions of *quality*; all have merit, but none is complete:

- "1) The characteristics of a product or service that bear on its ability to satisfy stated or implied needs; 2) a product or service free of deficiencies," from the American Society for Quality (2021a)

- The "degree to which a software product satisfies stated and implied needs when used under specified conditions," from the International Organization for Standardization and the International Electrotechnical Commission (ISO/IEC 2011)

- Fitness for use, meaning that a product should satisfy a customer's real needs and lead to customer satisfaction, from quality pioneer Joseph M. Juran (American Society for Quality 2021b)

- Conformance to requirements, from Philip B. Crosby (1979)

- Zero defects, also from Crosby (1979)

- Value to some person, from Gerald Weinberg (2012)

We can draw two conclusions from these diverse definitions: quality has multiple aspects, and quality is situational. We can probably all agree that, in the context of delivered software, quality describes how well the product does whatever it's supposed to do; a more rigorous definition is likely to remain elusive. Nonetheless, each project team needs to explore what quality means to its customers, how to assess it, and how to achieve it, and then communicate that knowledge clearly to all project participants (Davis 1995).

In an ideal world, each project would deliver a product that contains all the features that any user would ever need, with zero defects and perfect usability, produced in record time at minimal cost. But that's a fantasy; quality expectations must be realistic. The decision makers on each project need to determine which aspects of project success are most important and what trade-offs they can appropriately make in pursuit of their business objectives.

Planning for Quality

The aggregated impacts of software quality shortcomings across an organization, a nation, or the planet as a whole are staggering. A detailed analysis estimated the total costs of poor software quality in the United States in 2018 at approximately *$2.26 trillion* if technical debt is not included and $2.84 trillion if it is (Krasner 2018). Just imagine the economic benefits—at every level—that higher-quality software could yield.

As Figure 6.1 illustrates, the classic project management iron triangle or triple constraint usually doesn't explicitly show quality as an adjustable parameter along with scope, cost, and time. You could interpret that absence to mean either that high quality is a nonnegotiable expectation or—more likely—that you get whatever level

Figure 6.1 *The classic project management iron triangle doesn't show quality explicitly.*

of quality the team can achieve within the constraints the other parameters impose. That is, quality is a dependent, not independent, variable (Nagappan 2020b).

However, development teams and managers sometimes decide to compromise on quality to meet a delivery date or include a richer—if imperfect—feature set that makes their product more attractive to its customers. That's why my enhanced five-dimensional model from Lesson 31 in Chapter 4, includes quality as an explicit project parameter, along with scope, schedule, staff, and budget. The people who make release decisions might tolerate the existence of some known defects if they conclude that those defects will have little customer or business impact. The affected users might not agree that the development team made a sensible trade-off decision, though (Weinberg 2012). If a user's favorite feature is the one with a defect, the user is likely to see the entire product as flawed—and tell everyone they know about it.

A software system doesn't need to have many problems to give an impression of low quality. I like to write and record songs, just for fun. I bought an application I can use to write musical scores. Scoring music is a complex problem; the app I use is correspondingly—and unavoidably—complex. It has some usability deficiencies; entering notes is tedious at best. Worse, I've encountered numerous software failures as I tried to create or modify scores. It's highly frustrating to try to enter some ordinary bit of musical data and have the program go nuts, displaying something completely wrong. This application contains an excessively rich set of features, many of which I will never use and some that don't work well at all. I'd rather have fewer features that all work correctly and that satisfy most users' needs.

Software teams will benefit from creating a quality management plan at the beginning of the project. The plan should establish realistic quality expectations for the product, including defining defect severity classifications (severe, moderate, minor, cosmetic). That will help all project participants to think of quality issues in a consistent way. Establishing common terminology and expectations regarding the various types of software testing required further helps to align stakeholders toward a shared objective of building a high-quality solution.

Multiple Views of Quality

Software quality encompasses many dimensions. It's more than simply meeting specified requirements (assuming that those requirements are correct), and it's more than being free of defects. We must consider numerous characteristics to fully understand what quality means for a given product and its users: features, aesthetics, performance, reliability, usability, cost, timeliness of delivery, and so on (Juran 2019).

As we saw in Lesson 20, "You can't optimize all desirable quality attributes," software project teams need to explore a broad set of quality attribute requirements. Because they can't create a product that exhibits ideal quality for every attribute, quality compromises often are necessary. Designers must make decisions that favor certain attributes over others. The various quality attributes have to be specified precisely and prioritized so that decision makers can make appropriate trade-off choices.

Also, how one stakeholder group perceives quality could conflict with another's expectations. A developer might consider high-quality code to be written elegantly and to execute efficiently and correctly. However, a maintainer might more highly value code that's easy to understand and modify. A user could consider high-quality code—to the extent that they think about code at all—as being whatever's necessary to let them use the product easily and without failures. In this example, the developer and maintainer are focused on the product's internal quality, whereas the user cares about its external quality.

Building Quality In

Other than cosmetic and aesthetic improvements, quality isn't something you simply add to the system when you get around to it. You can't just write several availability goals in a user story and add the story to the product backlog for some future development iteration. You must deliberately build in quality from the beginning through the processes you follow, the objectives you set, and your team members' attitudes. Some quality attributes impose constraints that affect aspects of the entire development process, not just specific bits of functionality (Scaled Agile 2021c). Satisfying certain quality attributes presents architectural implications that the team should address from the project's outset.

Quality isn't something you simply add to the system when you get around to it.

It's hard to retrofit quality into a product built on a shaky foundation. If developers take shortcuts in their haste to implement features, they'll accrue technical debt that makes it increasingly difficult to modify and extend the codebase. *Technical debt* refers to accumulated quality shortcomings in implemented software. It has many causes and is a major contributor to missed project deadlines (Pearls of Wisdom 2014a). That debt comes due eventually. (See Lesson 50, "Today's 'gotta get it out right away' development project is tomorrow's maintenance nightmare.")

Customers who suffer because of product quality problems aren't happy about it. Just about every day I encounter some website or other product that's thoughtlessly designed, hard to figure out, wastes my time, or simply doesn't work right (Wiegers 2021). That's annoying because I know that often it's not much harder to build a better product. A software colleague who periodically relates low-quality experiences to me ends his reports with "NWNC," his shorthand for "Nothing works and nobody cares." Sadly, he's right far too often.

The total cost of quality encompasses everything you do to prevent, detect, and correct product defects. (For more on the cost of quality, see Lesson 44, "High quality naturally leads to higher productivity.") Business analysts (BAs), developers, and other project contributors will make mistakes—we're all human. You need to establish technical practices that minimize the number of defects created. You also need to develop a personal ethic and an organizational culture that value defect prevention and early detection. Strive to find defects early before they do too much damage—that is, before they generate too much rework.

Not every product must be perfect, but every product must exhibit *good enough quality,* as judged by users and other stakeholders. The early adopters of highly innovative products have a high tolerance for defects, so long as the product lets them do some cool new things. Other domains—such as medical devices, aircraft systems, and reusable software components—demand far more stringent quality standards. The first step is for each project team to decide what quality, in all its many forms, means for their product. After that, they might find the eight lessons about software quality in this chapter helpful.

First Steps: Quality

I suggest you spend a few minutes on the following activities before reading the quality-related lessons in this chapter. As you read the lessons, contemplate to what extent each of them applies to your organization or project team.

1. How does your organization define quality for its products, both internal aspects of quality for developers and maintainers and external quality for end users?

2. Do your project teams document what quality means specifically for each of their projects? Do they set measurable quality goals?

3. How does your organization judge whether each product conforms to its team's and its customers' quality expectations?

4. List software quality practices that your organization is especially good at. Is information about those practices documented to remind team members about them and make it easy to apply them?

5. Identify any problems—points of pain—that you can attribute to short-comings in how your project teams approach software quality.

6. State the impacts that each problem has on your ability to complete projects successfully. How do the problems impede achieving business success for both the development organization and its customers? Quality problems lead to both tangible and intangible costs, such as unplanned rework, schedule delays, support and maintenance costs, customer dissatisfaction, and uncomplimentary product reviews.

7. For each problem from Step 5, identify the root causes that trigger the problem or make it worse. Problems, impacts, and root causes can blur together, so try to tease them apart and see their connections. You might find multiple root causes that contribute to the same problem, as well as several problems that arise from a single root cause.

8. As you read this chapter, list any practices that would be useful to your team.

Lesson 43 When it comes to software quality, you can pay now or pay more later.

Suppose I'm a BA and I have a conversation with a customer to flesh out some requirements details. I go back to my office and write up what I learned in whatever form my project uses for requirements. The customer e-mails me the next day and says, "I just talked to one of my coworkers and learned that I had something wrong in that requirement we talked about yesterday." How much work must I do to correct that error? Very little; I simply update the requirement to match the customer's current request. Let's say that making that correction cost ten dollars' worth of company time.

Alternatively, suppose the customer contacts me a month or six after we had the conversation to point out the same problem. Now how much does it cost to correct that error? It depends on how much work the team has done based on the original, incorrect requirement. Not only does my company still have to pay ten dollars to fix the requirement, but a developer might have to redo some portion of the design. Maybe that costs another thirty or forty dollars. If the developers already implemented the original requirement, they'll have to modify or recode it. They'll need to update tests, verify the newly implemented requirement, and run regression tests to see whether the code changes broke anything. All that could cost perhaps a hundred dollars more. Maybe someone must revise a web page or a help screen as well. The bill keeps increasing.

Software's malleability lets us make changes and corrections whenever warranted. But every change has a price. Even discussing the possibility of adding some functionality or fixing a bug and then deciding not to do it takes time. The longer a requirement defect lingers undetected and the more rework you have to do to correct it, the higher the price tag.

The Cost-of-Repair Growth Curve

The cost of correcting a defect depends on when it was introduced into the product and when someone fixed it. The curve in Figure 6.2 shows that the cost increases significantly for late-discovered requirements errors. I omitted a numeric scale on the y-axis because various sources cite different data, and software people debate the exact numbers. The cost ratio and steepness of the curve depend on the product type, the development life cycle being followed, and other factors.

For instance, data from Hewlett-Packard indicated that the cost ratio could be as high as 110:1 if a customer discovered a requirement defect in production versus someone finding it during requirements development (Grady 1999). Another analysis

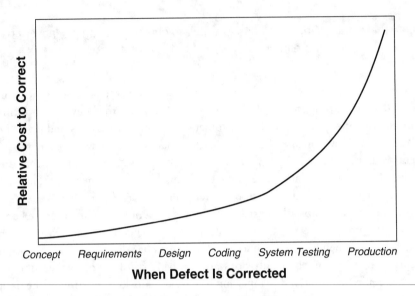

Figure 6.2 *The cost to correct a defect increases rapidly with time.*

suggested a relative cost factor of 30:1 to correct errors introduced during requirements development or architectural design that were discovered post-release (NIST 2002). For highly complex hardware/software systems, the cost amplification factor from discovery in the requirements stage versus the operational stage can range from 29x to more than 1,500x (Haskins et al. 2004).

The cost of correcting a defect depends on when it was introduced into the product and when someone fixed it.

Regardless of the exact numbers, there's broad agreement that early defect correction is far cheaper than fixing defects following release (Sanket 2019, Winters et al. 2020). It's a bit like paying your credit card bill. You can pay the balance due on time, or you can pay a smaller amount now plus the remaining balance along with substantial interest charges and late fees in the future. Johanna Rothman (2000) compared how three hypothetical companies could employ different strategies to deal with defects and consequently experience different relative defect-repair costs. However, in all three scenarios, the later in the project the team fixes a defect, the more it costs.

Some people have argued that agile development greatly flattens the cost-of-change curve (Beck and Andres 2005). I haven't yet located any actual project data to support this contention. However, this lesson isn't about the cost of making a change like adding new functionality—it's about the price you pay to correct defects. A requirements defect that is discovered before a user story is coded is still less expensive to repair than the same defect identified during acceptance testing. Scott Ambler (2006) suggests that the relative defect-correction cost is lower on agile projects because of agile's quick feedback cycles that shorten the time between when some work is done and when its quality is assessed. That sounds plausible, but it only partially addresses the fundamental issue with defect-repair costs.

The issue with cost-to-repair is not only the days, weeks, or months between when the defect was injected into the product and when someone discovers it. The amplification factor depends heavily on how much work was done based on the defective bit that now must be redone. It costs very little to fix a coding error if your pair-programming partner finds it moments after you typed the wrong thing, when knowledge about the defective work is fresh in your brain. However, if the customer calls to report the same type of error when the software is in production, it certainly will be far more difficult to rectify. As an example, a developer friend of mine related this recent experience:

> This week I missed one comma (literally) in a ColdFusion script on a custom website for a client. It caused a crash, which caused him a delay and hassle. Plus, then there were the back-and-forth e-mails, and then me opening up all the tools and source code and finding the bug, adding the comma, retesting, and so on. One darn comma.

Besides the cost-to-repair issue, my friend alluded to another important aspect of late defect detection we should keep in mind: the negative impact on the users.

Harder to Find

Diagnosing a system failure takes longer if the underlying fault was introduced long ago. If you review some requirements and spot an error, you know exactly where the problem lies. However, if a customer reports a malfunction—whether that's one month or five years after someone wrote the requirement—the detective work is more challenging. Is the failure due to an erroneous requirement, a design problem, a coding bug, or an error in a third-party component? Therein lies Ambler's argument for lower defect-correction costs on agile projects: when defects are revealed shortly after they're introduced, it's easier to locate the fault that caused a failure.

After you uncover the root cause—the fault—for a customer-reported system failure, you have to recognize all of the affected work products, repair them, retest the system, write release notes, redeploy the corrected product, and reassure the customer that the problem is fixed. That's a lot of expensive *re-* stuff to do. Plus, at that point, the problem has affected many more stakeholders than if someone had found it much earlier.

Early Quality Actions

Serious defects discovered during system testing can lead to a lot of repair work. Those found after release can disrupt user operations and trigger emergency fixes that divert team members from new development work. This reality leads us to several thoughts about how to pay less for high-quality software.

Prevent Defects Instead of Correcting Them

Quality *control* activities, such as testing, code static analysis, and code reviews, look for defects. Quality *assurance* activities seek to prevent defects in the first place. Improved processes, better technical practices, more proficient practitioners, and taking a little more time to do our work carefully are all ways to prevent errors and avoid their associated correction costs.

Push Quality Practices to the Left

Regardless of the project's development life cycle, the earlier you find a defect, the cheaper it is to resolve. Each piece of software work involves a micro-sequence of requirements, design, and coding, moving from left to right on a timescale axis. We've seen that eradicating requirement errors provides the greatest leverage for time savings down the road. Therefore, we should use all the tools at our disposal to find errors in requirements and designs before they're translated into erroneous code.

Peer reviews and prototyping are effective ways to detect requirement errors. Pushing testing from its traditional position late in the development sequence—on the right side of the timeline—far to the left is particularly powerful. Strategy options include following a test-driven development process (Beck 2003), writing acceptance tests to flesh out requirements details (Agile Alliance 2021b), and—my preference— concurrently writing functional requirements and their corresponding tests (Wiegers and Beatty 2013).

Every time I write tests shortly after writing requirements, I discover errors in both the requirements and the tests. The thought processes involved with writing requirements and tests are complementary, which is why I find that doing both yields the highest-quality outcome. Writing tests through a collaboration between the BA and the tester leverages both the idea of doing it earlier in the process and having multiple sets of eyes looking at the same thing from different perspectives. Writing tests early in the development cycle doesn't add time to the project; it just reallocates time to a point where it provides greater quality leverage. Those conceptual tests can be elaborated into detailed test scenarios and procedures as development progresses.

During implementation, developers can use static and dynamic code analysis tools to reveal many problems far faster than humans can review code manually. These tools can find run-time errors that code reviewers struggle to spot, such as memory corruption bugs and memory leaks (Briski et al. 2008). On the other hand, human reviewers can spot code logic errors and omissions that automated tools won't detect.

The timing of quality control activities is important. I once worked with a developer who wouldn't let anyone review her code until it was fully implemented, tested, formatted, and documented—that is, clear on the right side of her development timescale. At that point, she was psychologically resistant to hearing that she wasn't done after all. Each issue that someone raised in a code review triggered a defensive response and rationalization about why it was fine the way it was. You're much better off starting with preliminary reviews on just a portion of a work item—be it requirements, design, code, or tests—to get input from others on how to craft the rest of the item better. Push quality to the left by reviewing early and often.

Track Defects to Understand Them

The most efficient way to control defects is to contain them to the life cycle activity—requirements, design, coding—in which they originated. Record some information about your bugs instead of simply swatting them and moving on. Ask yourself questions to identify the origin of each defect so that you can learn what types of errors are the most common. Did this problem happen because I didn't understand what the customer wants? Did I understand the need accurately but make an incorrect assumption about other system components or interfaces? Did I simply make a mistake while coding? Was a customer change request not communicated to everyone who needed to know about it?

Note the life cycle activity (not necessarily a discrete project phase) in which each defect originated and how it was discovered. You can calculate your defect containment percentage from that data to see how many problems are leaking from their creation stage into later development activities, thereby amplifying their cost-to-repair factors. That information will show you which practices are the best quality filters and where your improvement opportunities lie.

Minimizing defect creation and finding them early reduces your overall development costs. Strive to bring your full arsenal of quality weapons to bear from the earliest project stages.

| Lesson 44 | High quality naturally leads to higher productivity. |

Organizations and individuals who develop software would love to be more productive. Quality problems pose one of the greatest barriers to high productivity. Teams plan to get a certain amount of work done in a specified time, but then they have to fix problems found in completed work or reallocate effort to repair a production system. That rework saps time and lowers morale. A way to boost productivity is to create high-quality software from the outset so that teams can spend less time on rework both during development and following deployment (Wiegers 1996).

I hate rework, doing over something that I've already completed. I learned this in my ninth-grade shop class. Our first project was to take a short piece of 2×4 lumber, shape it to specific dimensions, and practice using various tools on it. If we drilled a hole in the wrong spot or planed the wood down below the specified dimensions, we had to start over. It took me nine attempts to get it right.

I noticed that a classmate worked more slowly than I did but finished his project in just two tries. He had to do far less rework because of mistakes, and he didn't have to buy nine pieces of 2×4. Both his work quality and his productivity exceeded mine. I learned a vital lesson: go slow to go fast. Ever since then, I've tried to avoid having to do something more than once. Building in quality from the beginning frees up time to devote to new, value-added work. That was true in the woodshop, and it's even truer in software development.

A Tale of Two Projects

To illustrate how poor quality lowers productivity, let's compare two real projects from the same company, as related by consultant Meilir Page-Jones, who worked on Team B. This company's IT department concurrently developed two new core, high-availability applications to replace twenty-year-old legacy systems. We have two projects, two teams, two approaches, and two very different outcomes. (See the introduction to Chapter 5 for more about this case.)

The Approaches

The managers of Teams A and B created time and budget estimates, all of which got slashed by upper management. Team A created a fairly lengthy and boring textual requirements specification, obtained sign-off, and began coding soon afterward. Their attitude was, "If we don't start coding now, we'll never meet the deadline." Team A developed their database design somehow from the procedural code.

Team B's project manager firmly believed in software engineering. Team B created their requirements largely in the form of visual models, supplemented with textual descriptions of use cases, data and their relationships, page layouts, and so forth. They developed their database design from a class-association diagram and created test cases early in development from the software models.

The Results

Team A started large and grew even larger. They met their deadline by adding several developers and testers and working a lot of overtime. They ran 50 percent over budget, much of which they spent on debugging in the months before delivery. Following delivery, Team A received at least one message daily from users that their system had crashed or "done something mysterious." They established a "Commando Squad" to respond to the steady stream of problems.

Team B started very small and grew, though not as much as Team A. By the targeted completion date, Team B had a working but incomplete system. They required two more months to deliver the finished system, which put them 20 percent over schedule and 10 percent over budget. The system worked well and generated only a few undramatic enhancement suggestions.

Several months later, an audit discovered that System A's mysterious problems were due to a massively corrupted database, which had been accumulating bad information for months. A manual cleansing proved futile. The database was soon corrupt again; no one knew why. Team A did an ugly reversion to the legacy system they were attempting to replace while they totally overhauled their new system. Within a few months, though, their system wouldn't restart at all; the company finally scrapped it as irreparable. They launched a new project to rebuild System A—with Team B's manager at the helm!

The Analysis

Team A rushed a poorly designed and hastily built system into production on schedule without using solid software engineering practices. The team spent months on both pre- and post-delivery rework before the company finally abandoned its investment in the system. Management had expected the people from Team A to be available after delivery to work on the next project, but their Commando Squad was busy chasing down problems and patching in fixes. Because their system was discarded, Team A's ultimate productivity was zero. Poor quality throughout the project cost the company a great deal of time and money.

Meanwhile, Team B took a little more time to build a high-quality system that required little rework effort and freed up most of the team to move on to the next project. I'll take Team B over Team A every time.

The Scourge of Rework

There are two major classes of software rework: fixing defects and paying off technical debt. The previous lesson described how defect-correction costs grow over time. Similarly, the longer that shortcomings linger in the code, the more technical debt that accrues, and the more work it will take to improve the design. (See Lesson 50, "Today's 'gotta get it out right away' development project is tomorrow's maintenance nightmare.") Refactoring makes code easier to maintain and extend, but sometimes code needs to be refactored because it was generated in haste from a less-than-ideal design. Excessive, unanticipated rework is waste that distracts developers from delivering more customer value.

Too often, organizations implicitly accept rework as a normal part of software development and don't give it much thought. A certain amount of software rework is inevitable. It's the nature of knowledge work, imperfect human communication, and our inability to see the future clearly. Reworking a design to accommodate unexpected new functionality is preferable to overdesigning a system to permit potential growth that never materializes. However, each team should strive to minimize *avoidable* rework by improving their initial work quality.

Call out rework as discrete project tasks instead of burying it inside the defect-detection tasks.

Project teams don't always factor the likelihood of rework effort into their planning. Even if their estimates are accurate for the development work, those estimates will be low once rework raises its ugly head. I've seen this problem show up in project plans that didn't allocate any time for fixing errors found during quality control activities like testing or peer review. I suggest explicitly calling out rework as discrete project tasks instead of burying it inside the defect-detection tasks. Making rework effort visible is the first step toward reducing it.

Organizations that track how much of their software effort goes into rework can get some frightening numbers. A bank determined that it spent between $1 million and $1.5 million *per month* on automated retesting (McAllister 2017). Various studies have shown that software teams may spend 40 percent to 50 percent of their time on avoidable rework (Charette 2005). Just think of how your team's productivity would jump if they had one-third or more of their time back for new development work!

If you're recording any software work effort metrics, try to separate defect-finding effort from defect-fixing effort. Learn how much time you spend on rework, when, and why. That data reveals the high-leverage opportunities for increasing productivity. Here's a hint: up to 85 percent of rework costs can be attributed to defects in requirements (Marasco 2007). Having some baseline data regarding your rework burden would let you set improvement targets and see whether better software processes and practices drive down your rework levels (Hossain 2018, Nussbaum 2020). When my software team did this, we reduced our defect-correction maintenance work from 13.5 percent of our total effort down to a sustained level of about 2 percent (Wiegers 1996).

The Cost of Quality

Perhaps you've heard that quality is free. That was the title of a classic 1979 book by Philip B. Crosby. "Quality is free" means that the additional incremental effort needed to do a job properly the first time is a smart investment. It takes more time and money to fix a problem than to prevent one. Poorly done work is a hassle for anyone downstream in the workflow and has unpleasant side consequences like these:

- Accumulating technical debt that makes it harder and harder to enhance a product

- Lost opportunities and delays in other projects when rework diverts development staff

- Customer service outages and the ensuing problem reports, loss of trust, and perhaps lawsuits

- Warranty claims, refunds, and disgruntled customers

The term *cost of quality* refers to the total price a company pays to deliver products and services of acceptable quality. The cost of quality consists of four components (Crosby 1979, American Society for Quality 2021c):

Defect Prevention:	Quality planning, training, process improvement activities, root cause analysis
Quality Appraisal:	Evaluating work products and processes for quality issues
Internal Failure:	Failure analysis and rework to fix problems before releasing the product
External Failure:	Failure analysis and rework to fix problems after delivery; handling customer complaints, product repairs, and replacements

Skimping on defect prevention and quality appraisal leads to skyrocketing failure costs. Besides the rework costs in time and money, external failures can incur business downsides such as compromised business efficiency (as with Team A earlier) and disappearing customers. There are plenty of horror stories about companies that suffered massive monetary losses and a loss of public trust following high-profile software failures (McPeak 2017, Krasner 2018).

Software organizations would find it insightful to understand their total cost of quality and how those costs are distributed across the various quality activities. That assessment requires data collection and analysis, but it shows organizations exactly where they're spending money on quality. The data lets the organization decide whether that's where they *want* to be spending their money.

I built a cost-of-quality spreadsheet model for one of my consulting clients. The model let them calculate just how much a requirement or design error cost them on average. Once they knew what percentage of their budget was spent on new software development versus defect prevention, quality appraisal, and internal and external failure, they could reallocate their effort on quality activities for maximum benefit. This sort of analysis reveals the return on investment an organization is getting from defect prevention and early defect discovery.

Ordinary human errors and some rework are inescapable. Rework can add value if it makes the product more capable, efficient, reliable, or usable. A company's managers might elect to tolerate some rework as an acceptable trade-off between being speedy and spending a little more up front. That business decision might look good on the accounting books, but it could cause more expensive future problems. The techniques described at the end of Lesson 43 also cut down on excessive rework, thereby reducing the organization's overall cost of quality and boosting productivity.

Did I mention that I hate rework?

Lesson 45	Organizations never have time to build software right, yet they find the resources to fix it later.

The preceding lesson described two legacy-system replacement projects that a company conducted at the same time. One project succeeded, albeit a little over schedule and budget. The other substantially overran its budget and delivered, on time, a badly flawed system that ultimately was discarded. When the company abandoned the failed system, they didn't say, "Well, that didn't work out. Let's move on to the next project." They still needed to replace the legacy system for business purposes. Therefore, they had to try it again, this time using sound software engineering approaches.

I've marveled at this great mystery of the software business for a long time. Many project teams work under unrealistic schedule and budget pressures that force them to cut quality corners. The result is often a product that must be extensively—and expensively—repaired or even abandoned. Somehow, though, the organization finds the time, money, and people to perform the repair or replacement work.

My high school chemistry class had a sign on the wall that asked, "If you don't have time to do it right, when will you have time to do it over?"

Why Not the First Time?

You'd think that if a system were so vital and urgent that management placed great pressure on the IT staff to rush it out, it would be worth building it properly. My high school chemistry class had a sign on the wall that asked, "If you don't have time to do it right, when will you have time to do it over?" I internalized that message and have carried it with me ever since. When software teams aren't provided with the time, skilled staff, processes, or tools to do the job right, they'll inevitably have to do at least parts of it over. As we saw in the preceding lesson, such rework is a productivity sinkhole.

Unfortunately, too many people don't appreciate the value of taking some additional time to build the software right instead of fixing it later. Time for effective quality practices such as technical peer reviews often isn't built into the schedule. As a result, people hold reviews only if they've personally internalized the value. Even if reviews are planned as part of the development process, projects with overly aggressive schedules might skip them because no one has time to participate. Omitting reviews and other quality practices doesn't mean the defects aren't there; it just means that someone's going to find them later, when the consequences are greater.

Large-scale failures often are more the result of management problems than technical issues. Underestimated scope, coupled with an unrealistic hope that developers can work faster than they have in the past, leads to schedule slips and quality shortfalls. Both at the individual practitioner and management levels, people need to take the actions and time needed for success to avoid wasting potentially huge amounts of time and money.

The $100 Million Syndrome

It seems that the only time disastrous projects are completely abandoned is when a failed government system costs more than $100 million. Corporations need their new systems to conduct business, so they'll tackle them again; governments sometimes throw in the towel or switch to Plan B. As one example among many, the Federal Aviation Administration's Advanced Automation Program was launched in 1982 as a sweeping program to modernize its air traffic control (ATC) system. The project's centerpiece was the Advanced Automation System, which was estimated to cost $2.5 billion by its planned completion in 1996.

The project suffered many delays and cost overruns, partly attributable to requirement changes that triggered extensive rework. The project was dramatically restructured in 1994 after the estimated final cost had risen to around $7 billion. Some major components were estimated to be as much as eight years behind schedule (Barlas 1996). Some of the project work was salvaged for later ATC modernization efforts, but the federal government experienced a net loss of about $1.5 billion (DOT 1998).

A more recent massive project failure strikes close to home for me. After the U.S. Congress enacted the Affordable Care Act—also known as Obamacare—in 2010, states established health-care exchanges as marketplaces for residents to procure health insurance. Some states built their own exchanges, others established state–federal partnerships, and still others relied on the federal exchange, HealthCare.gov. My state of Oregon attempted to build its own, excessively complex health insurance exchange, called Cover Oregon. The state engaged a huge software contractor for the implementation. After investing about three years and spending some $305 million of taxpayer money, the state abandoned the project and switched to HealthCare.gov (Wright 2016). Cover Oregon was a colossal failure that generated colossal lawsuits.

Striking the Balance

Nearly all technical people want to do good work and deliver high-quality products and services. Sometimes that desire clashes with outside factors, such as ridiculously short deadlines dictated by management or regulations imposed by governing bodies. Technical practitioners don't always know about the business motivation or rationale behind those pressures. Quality—and integrity—need to be part of the discussion when a team contemplates what they can deliver that meets deadlines, achieves business objectives, and includes the right functionality, built in a sustainable way.

Like many people, I have a personal and professional philosophy to "Strive for perfection; settle for excellence." Not everything's going to be perfect, but I do my work as well as I can the first time to avoid the cost, time, embarrassment, and potential legal consequences of having to do it over. If that means taking more time to get it right up front, so be it. The long-term payoff is worth the up-front investment.

Lesson 46	Beware the crap gap.

The difference between quality and not-quality—also known as crap—often is surprisingly small. Hold up your hand with your thumb and index finger about an inch apart. I call that little separation the crap gap (Wiegers 2019e). In many cases, doing just a little additional analyzing, asking, checking, or testing makes the difference between a quality product and one that customers perceive as crap. When I talk about the crap gap, I don't refer to the ordinary mistakes that all human beings make occasionally, but rather to problems that result from haste, sloppiness, or inattention to details.

The Crap Gap Illustrated

Here's an example of the crap-gap scenarios we all encounter in daily life (Wiegers 2021). Last year I bought a major home appliance. I had a question, so I went to the contact form on the manufacturer's website. The form required me to choose a topic and then a subtopic. However, no subtopics were displayed. No matter which major topic I chose, the only option available on the subtopic list was the default prompt: "Please select a topic." When I tried to submit the form anyway, I got an error message that a subtopic is required. Because that was impossible, I couldn't submit the form. I had to call the manufacturer, with all the attendant hassles of trying to reach a helpful support person.

Did no one find this problem while testing the website? Perhaps the function worked just fine in development, but the appropriate tables of options weren't populated for the production version. Or maybe testing revealed the problem, but someone decided not to fix it then. Many months after I reported the problem, the web page now finally provides subtopic lists customized for each major topic. Maybe it didn't cost the company much more to correct the code later than it would have during initial implementation. But how much customer time was wasted before the company finally fixed that bug? Businesses shouldn't regard their customers' time as being free.

Management must shape a culture in which team members are expected, empowered, and enabled to do the job well the first time.

As I mentioned earlier, I dislike performing rework, revisiting something that I thought was done because some problem reared its ugly head. An organization's leaders set the standard by avoiding the crap gap in their own work and not tolerating it in others' work. Management must shape a culture in which team members are expected, empowered, and enabled to do the job well the first time.

Crap-Gap Scenarios in Software

Avoiding the crap gap often is just a matter of thinking a little bit more before proceeding. I encounter too many software products with errors that should have been caught during testing or designs that don't reflect a proper focus on the user experience. For instance, when I login to a popular financial services website, it reports that I have one notification. But when I click on the notification icon, a message says, "You don't have any notifications." As another example, I recently saw a printed report whose final page said, "Page 5 of 4." These kinds of defects puzzle me and often waste my time.

Here are some categories in which software teams might encounter issues that could lead to an avoidable quality shortfall.

- **Assumptions.** A business analyst might make an inaccurate assumption or record an assumption that customers are making but then neglect to verify whether the assumption is valid.

- **Solution Ideas.** Customers often provide input to BAs in the form of solution ideas, not requirements. Unless the BA looks past the proposed solution to understand the real need, it's easy to solve the wrong problem or specify an inadequate solution, which must be rectified later.

- **Regression Testing.** If a developer doesn't run a regression test after making a quick code change, they might miss an error in the modified code—a bad fix. Even a small change can unexpectedly break something else.

- **Exception Handling.** Implementations might focus so much on the "happy path" of expected system behavior that they fail to handle common error conditions. Missing, erroneous, or incorrectly formatted data input will cause unexpected results or even a system failure.

- **Change Impacts.** People sometimes implement a change without considering whether it will affect other, unobvious parts of the system or related products. Changing one aspect of a system's behavior generates an inconsistent user experience if similar functionality that appears elsewhere isn't modified correspondingly.

Lesson 44, "High quality naturally leads to higher productivity," described the cost of quality and the notion that quality is free. Quality isn't truly free in the sense of costing you nothing. Defect prevention, detection, and correction all consume resources. Nonetheless, shrinking the crap gap will pay off as you sidestep avoidable quality problems and their associated costs.

Lesson 47	Never let your boss or your customer talk you into doing a bad job.

A software developer named Chizuko said that her project manager had told her, "To save time, I don't want you to do any unit testing." She was shocked at this directive. As an experienced developer, Chizuko knew that unit testing was important to verify that a program was implemented correctly. Chizuko felt that her manager was demanding she take a quality shortcut in the faint hope that it would somehow speed her progress. Perhaps it would save Chizuko some time, but skipping unit testing would doubtless lead to defects being found later than they should. To her credit, she opted to proceed with unit testing anyway.

We should each commit to following the best professional practices we know, adapting them to be effective in each situation.

I have long believed that we should never let our managers, customers, or colleagues talk us into doing a bad job (Wiegers 1996). It's a matter of personal and professional integrity to stick to our principles. We should each commit to following the best professional practices we know, adapting them to be effective in each situation. If you're pressured into a situation that makes you professionally uncomfortable, try to describe what you need so that you're able to deliver something that won't constitute doing a bad job. As with so many things, it's possible to take this philosophy to a no-longer-useful extreme. Seek suitable balance points of achieving professional excellence while not being overly dogmatic or inflexible.

Power Plays

People in positions of power can attempt to influence you in various ways to do what you might consider to be a bad job. Suppose someone to whom you present an estimate for upcoming work doesn't like your numbers. They might pressure you to reduce your estimate to help them, a senior manager, or a customer achieve their own budgetary or delivery goals. It's an understandable motivation, but that's not a good reason to change an estimate.

Someone who pushes back against an estimate might feel pressures you're not aware of. They're entitled to an explanation of how you derived the estimate and a discussion about whether it could be adjusted. (See Lesson 28, "Don't change an estimate based on what the recipient wants to hear.") However, changing an estimate simply because someone doesn't care for it denies your interpretation of reality. It doesn't change the likely project outcome.

Rushing to Code

Suppose you work in an internal corporate IT department and a new project comes along. Your business stakeholders might pressure your software team to begin writing code immediately, even without a sound business case and clear requirements. Perhaps they have project funding that they want to spend right away before they lose it. The IT staff also might be eager to get started. Maybe they don't want to spend time discussing requirements because those will probably change anyway.

As a consequence, a lot of aimless coding gets done toward an obscure outcome. Too often, nobody is held accountable for the missed target, because no target was clearly defined anyway. Might it not be better for the IT department to resist the business pressure to begin the journey until some destination is established?

Lack of Knowledge

People who lean on you to do something you consider inappropriate might not understand the software development practices you advocate. For example, someone might regard holding technical peer reviews of work products as unnecessary. Maybe they don't think it's worthwhile to spend time on requirements elicitation discussions or writing down requirements. Managers or customers could press for the product's delivery even if it hasn't satisfied all of its release criteria. Customers don't always appreciate that taking quality shortcuts might let you deliver something sooner, but that "something" could require extensive patching to be usable.

A colleague once proposed a technical approach for a particular program to his project manager. The manager was himself an experienced software developer, but he didn't recognize the merits of the approach and shot down the idea. My colleague had three options.

1. Explain the approach so that the technique and its benefits were clear.

2. Use the strategy that he proposed anyway, despite the manager's rejection of it.

3. Follow the less-informed manager's direction and take a suboptimal approach.

Which do you think would be the best choice? I suggest trying option 1 (education) first. If that doesn't succeed, then go with option 2 and do the right thing. Depending on the manager's pettiness, there's some risk in that approach, but I think that's the better decision for the project.

I once had a manager who didn't understand how I could write the user documentation for a new application before we finished the software. He was a scientist who had done some programming, so he thought he understood software development. I explained that I knew what the system would do, thanks to our requirements and design work. Therefore, I wasn't wasting time writing help screens and a user manual before we implemented the final line of code.

A customer told me he didn't understand why a project would take as long as my team anticipated. Based on his limited experience with computers, he declared that the work was a SMOP—a simple matter of programming. I hadn't heard that expression before, but it certainly didn't apply to that project, as I attempted to explain to him. People who don't do it for a living don't appreciate the considerable difference between cranking out some code and software engineering.

Shady Ethics

Independent consultants and contractors can be subjected to various kinds of bad-job pressure. A prospective consulting client once asked me to come into his company under false pretenses. He wanted our contract to state that I'd be performing certain work, although I'd actually be doing something different. The client couldn't get funding for the activity he had in mind, but he had money available for the other service. I viewed his request as unethical, so I declined both the engagement and the client. Accepting the conditions would have constituted professional malpractice on my part and could have exposed me to legal problems if this client's managers found out what was going on.

Circumventing Processes

Sensible processes are in place for a reason. When users asked me about making a change in some application when I worked at Kodak, I would direct them to our very simple change-request tool. The information the user submitted would let the appropriate people make good business decisions about requested changes. Some users didn't want to bother submitting a request; couldn't I just work the change in? Well, no—sorry. Bypassing reasonable, practical processes for convenience constitutes a bad job in my view.

You might need to explain why the approach you're advocating is necessary. Point out how it adds quality and value to the project. That information will help the other person understand why you're resisting their entreaty. However, some people are simply unreasonable. Even with your best efforts to convince them otherwise, they might pressure you to cut corners or follow an inadvisable approach.

Suppose you resist acting in a way that you regard as unprofessional or unethical. The other party might complain to your manager that you're wasting time on unnecessary activities or being uncooperative. The manager could back you up, or they could exert additional pressure on you to comply. In the second case, it becomes your choice. Will you succumb to the pressure, with its potential negative impacts on the project and your psyche? Or will you continue to work in the best professional way you know? There's a risk in there, but I vote for the latter.

Lesson 48	Strive to have a peer, rather than a customer, find a defect.

I made a serious error in the manuscript for a book I wrote recently—I got something exactly backward. Fortunately, one of my sharp-eyed peer reviewers caught the error. I was very grateful. It would have been awkward had the book gone to press with that mistake in it.

Even the most skilled writers, business analysts, programmers, and other professionals make mistakes. No matter how good your work is, having others look it over makes it better. Many years ago, I adopted the routine practice of asking colleagues to review my code and other deliverables I created for a software project.

I always feel silly when a reviewer spots a mistake I made, but the phrase "good catch" immediately pops into my mind.

Presenting your creation to other people and asking them to tell you what's wrong with it is not an instinctive behavior—it's a learned behavior. It's human nature to be embarrassed or even resentful when people find problems in what we've done. I always feel silly when a reviewer spots a mistake I made, but the phrase "good catch" immediately pops into my mind. When I say "Thanks, good catch" to the reviewer, the tone of the conversation gets more pleasant because I'm expressing gratitude for the finding instead of acting hurt or defensive. I would far prefer to have a friend or colleague discover one of my errors before release than to have a customer find it afterward.

Some people think their work doesn't need to be reviewed, but the best software developer I've ever known felt uncomfortable unless someone else had reviewed his code. He knew how valuable the input from other smart developers was. Different reviewers raise different kinds of issues and provide varying levels of feedback, ranging from superficially obvious to deeply insightful. That's true whether you're reviewing a textual manuscript, a requirements specification, or code. All of the perspectives are helpful.

Peer reviews are a true software engineering best practice. After experiencing their benefits for decades, I wouldn't want to work in an organization where reviews weren't embedded in the culture.

Benefits of Peer Reviews

Technical peer reviews are a proven technique for improving both quality and productivity. They improve quality by revealing defects earlier than they might otherwise be detected. As we've seen, those early discoveries increase productivity because team members spend less time fixing defects later in development or following delivery.

People often wait until they've finished an item to ask others to look at it. However, reviewing a work product *before* it's complete lets its consumers assess how well the item will meet their needs. It's frustrating to receive some deliverable like a requirements document, only to discover that it doesn't contain all the information you need, includes material that's not useful, or isn't organized effectively for your purposes. Providing feedback on a deliverable before it's finished lets the author adjust it to be more useful to its audience.

Other than when pair programming, we rarely see the internals of someone else's work unless we have to fix a bug or add an enhancement. Because people other than the original programmer often must modify code in the future, it helps if they've had some exposure to it through reviews. If you bring in reviewers from outside the project team, they can learn about some aspects of the product and also see how another team operates. This cross-fertilization helps to disseminate effective practices throughout an organization.

I see a lot of discussion about code reviews in the software literature these days. I'm always delighted to see people take reviews seriously, and code reviews are certainly important. However, software teams generate many other artifacts that also are candidates for review. That's why I prefer to use the more general term *peer review*. This term doesn't mean we are reviewing our peers, but that we're inviting some of our professional peers to review pieces of our work. Besides code, a project team might create plans, requirements in various forms, several types of designs, test plans and scripts, help screens, documentation, and more. Anything that a person creates could contain errors and would benefit from having other people look it over,

Varieties of Software Reviews

You can perform reviews in various ways: with or without a meeting, online or in person, and with varying degrees of rigor. All the approaches have their advantages and limitations. Review meetings can yield a synergistic effect, in which one person's comment triggers another to spot a problem that no one saw on their own. But reviews with meetings cost more and are harder to schedule than those without meetings. Here are some of the ways that people can examine a colleague's work product (Wiegers 2002a).

- **Peer deskcheck.** Ask one coworker to look over something you created and to offer suggestions for improvements or corrections. The key here is to pair up with someone who has a sharp eye and the time to help out. Offer to return the favor—it's only fair.

- **Passaround.** Distribute the item to several of your peers and ask them to give you feedback individually. Review tools are available that let reviewers see and discuss one another's comments. The passaround is a good approach for conducting asynchronous or distributed reviews when it's either inconvenient or unnecessary for participants to meet.

- **Walkthrough.** The author leads the discussion, explaining the work product a chunk at a time and soliciting feedback. Walkthroughs are often used for design reviews when brainstorming with colleagues is merited.

- **Team review.** The author distributes the work product and any supporting materials to a few reviewers in advance so that they have time to examine it independently and note any issues. During a meeting, the reviewers bring up their observations. A moderator keeps the discussion on track and ensures that the group covers the work product at a reasonable pace. Going too quickly misses defects; going too slowly takes longer and bores people. A recorder can collect the issues raised on standard forms.

- **Inspection.** The most formal type of review includes several roles that participants perform during a structured meeting: author, moderator, recorder, inspector, and sometimes a reader (Gilb and Graham 1993, Radice 2002). Although inspections are the most expensive review method, considerable research indicates that they're the most effective at revealing defects. Inspections are most appropriate for higher-risk work products.

Even if you don't perform any of these structured peer reviews, simply inviting a colleague to look over your shoulder and help find a coding error or improve a bit of your design is an excellent idea. Any review is better than no review. Software engineers at Google suggested several code review best practices, including these: be polite and professional, write small changes, write good change descriptions, and keep reviewers to a minimum (Winters et al. 2020).

The Soft Side: Cultural Implications of Reviews

Peer reviews are both a technical activity and an interpersonal interaction. How an organization practices reviews—or doesn't—reveals its attitudes toward quality and teamwork. If team members hesitate to share their work for fear of being criticized, that's a red flag. If reviewers criticize the author for making mistakes—or just for doing the work differently from how they would have done it—that's another red flag. Reviews handled poorly can be damaging to a software team's culture (Wiegers 2002b).

In a healthy software engineering culture, team members both offer and accept constructive criticism. They aren't territorial, guarding their work against prying eyes. They willingly spend part of their time looking over someone else's work because they recognize the benefits. It's a mutual back-scratching mindset: you help me, I help you, and everyone wins.

One of my consulting clients had a review program in place. The participants referred to holding a review as "going into the shark tank." This is not positive imagery. Who would want to go into a shark tank, unprotected, with bait in their hand? Any author who walks out of a review session feeling insulted or attacked will never again voluntarily invite others to look over their work. Those scars can linger for years.

Reviews can enhance collaborative teamwork when they're performed properly at the right time by the right people. They can also be harmful if the participants aren't considerate about how they provide feedback. The following guidelines can help reviewers contribute to a constructive activity that people perceive as worthwhile.

- Focus your comments on the work product, not on the author. Reviewers aren't there to show how smart they are but to improve the team's collective efforts.

- Phrase comments as observations, not accusations. Say "I" more than "you." "I didn't see where these variables are initialized" is easier to hear than "You didn't initialize these variables."

- Focus on substance over style by hunting for major defects. The author can help by eliminating easy-to-find issues like typographical errors before the review. Follow standard document templates and code formatting conventions (for example, use pretty-print) so that stylistic matters don't become distracting topics for debate.

- As an author, set aside your ego enough to be receptive to improvement suggestions. You're ultimately responsible for the quality of your work, but consider the input your coworkers offer.

You needn't wait for your organization to establish a review program or a review culture—just ask for a little help from your friends. The basic success factor for any review is the mindset that you'd rather have your colleagues uncover defects than assume that your work is error free. If you don't share this philosophy, just pass your work on to the next development stage or to the user, and then wait for the phone to ring.

Lesson 49	Software people love tools, but a fool with a tool is an amplified fool.

My friend Norm is an expert woodworker. He designed and built his woodshop, including the building itself. His shop contains countless hand and power tools, and he knows how and when to use each of them properly and safely. Expert software engineers also know the right tools to use and how to apply them effectively.

Perhaps you've heard that "A fool with a tool is still a fool," a saying sometimes attributed to software engineer Grady Booch. That's too generous. A tool gives someone who doesn't quite know what they're doing a way to do it more quickly and perhaps more dangerously. That leverage just amplifies their ineffectiveness. All tools have benefits and limitations. To reap the full benefit, practitioners need to understand the tool's concepts and methods so that they can apply it correctly to appropriate problems. When I say "tool" here, I'm referring both to software packages that facilitate or automate some project work (estimation, modeling, testing, collaboration) and to specialized software development techniques, such as use cases.

If people don't understand a technique and know when—and when not—to use it, a tool that lets them do it faster and prettier won't help.

Tools can make skilled team members more productive, but they don't make untrained people better. Providing less capable developers with tools can actually inhibit their productivity if they don't use them wisely. If people don't understand a technique and know when—and when not—to use it, a tool that lets them do it faster and prettier won't help.

A Tool Must Add Value

A software team's tools can help them build the right product correctly by saving time or boosting quality, but I've seen numerous examples of ineffective tool use. My software group once adopted Microsoft Project for project planning. Most of us found Project helpful for recording and sequencing tasks, estimating their duration, and tracking progress. One team member got carried away, though. She was the sole developer on a project with three-week development iterations. She spent a couple of days at the start of each iteration creating a detailed Microsoft Project plan for the iteration, down to one-hour resolution. I'm in favor of planning, but her use of this tool was time-wasting overkill.

I know of a government agency that purchased a high-end requirements management (RM) tool but benefited little from it. They recorded hundreds of requirements for their project in a traditional requirements specification document. Then they imported those requirements into the RM tool, but the document remained the definitive repository. Whenever the requirements changed, the BA had to update both the document and the contents stored in the RM tool's database. The only major tool feature that the team exploited was to define a complex network of traceability links between requirements. That's useful, but later they discovered that no one ever used the extensive traceability reports they generated! This agency's ineffective tool use consumed considerable time and money while yielding little value.

Modeling tools are easily misused. Analysts and designers sometimes spend excessive effort perfecting models. I'm a big fan of visual modeling to facilitate iterative thinking and reveal errors, but people should create models selectively. Modeling portions of the system that are already well understood and drilling down to the finest details don't add proportionate value to the project.

Besides automated tools, specialized software practices also can be applied inappropriately. As an example, use cases help me understand what users need to do with a system so that I can then deduce the necessary functionality to implement. But I've known some people who tried to force-fit every known bit of functionality into a use case simply because that's the requirements technique their project employed. If you already know about some needed functionality, I see little value in repackaging it just to say you have a complete set of use cases.

A Tool Must Be Used Sensibly

I was at a consulting client's site the same day that one of their team members was configuring a change-request tool they'd just purchased. I endorse sensible change control mechanisms, including using a tool to collect change requests and track their status over time. However, the team member configured the tool with no fewer than *twenty* possible change-request statuses: submitted, evaluated, approved, deferred, and so forth. Even if they're logically sensible, nobody's going to use twenty statuses; around seven should suffice. Making it so complex imposes an excessive and unrealistic burden on the tool users. It could even discourage them from using the tool at all, making them think it's more trouble than it's worth.

While teaching a class on software engineering best practices one time, I asked the students whether they used any static code analysis tools, such as lint. The project manager said, "Yes, I have ten copies of PC-lint in my desk." My first thought was, "You might want to distribute those to the developers, as they aren't doing any good in your desk." Software tools often become shelfware, products that people have available but don't use for some reason. If people don't understand how to apply a tool effectively, it's worthless to them.

I asked the same question about static code analysis at another company. One student said that when his team ran lint on their system's codebase, it reported about 10,000 errors and warnings, so they didn't use it again. If a sizable program has never been passed through an automated checker, it will probably trigger many alerts. Many of the reports were false positives, inconsequential warnings, or issues the team will decide to ignore. But there were likely some real problems in there, lost in the noise. When the option exists, configure the tools so that you can focus on items of real concern and not be overwhelmed by distracting minor issues.

I've run into the same false-positive problem with a commercial grammar checker I recently began to use in my writing. I disregard more than half of the issues it reports, because they're inappropriate for what I'm writing, inconsistent with my writing style, or simply wrong. It takes considerable time to wade through all the reported issues to find the valuable nuggets. Unfortunately, this tool lacks useful configuration options that would improve the signal-to-noise ratio.

A Tool Is Not a Process

People sometimes think that using a good tool means the problem is solved. However, a tool is not a substitute for a process; a tool supports a process. When one of my clients told me that they used a problem-tracking tool, I asked some questions about the process that the tool supported. I learned that they had no defined process for receiving and processing problem reports; they only had a tool. Without an accompanying practical process, a tool can increase chaos if people don't use it appropriately.

Tools can lead people to think that they're doing a better job than they are. Automated testing tools aren't any better than the tests stored in them. Just because you can run automated regression tests quickly doesn't mean the tests it executes find errors effectively. A code coverage tool could report a high percentage of statement coverage, but that doesn't guarantee that all the important code was executed. Even a high statement coverage percentage doesn't tell you what will happen when the untested code is executed, whether all the logic branches were tested in both directions, what will happen with different input data values, or whether any necessary paths were missing from the implemented code. Nor do tools replace people. Humans who test software will find issues beyond those that are programmed into testing tools.

I've spoken to people who claimed their project was doing a fine job on requirements because they stored them in a requirements management tool. RM tools do offer many valuable capabilities. However, the ability to generate nice reports doesn't mean that the requirements stored in the database are any good. RM tools are a vivid illustration of the old computing expression GIGO: garbage in, garbage out. The tool won't know whether the requirements are accurate, clearly written, or complete. It won't detect missing requirements.

You need to know both the capabilities and the limitations of each tool. Some tools can scan a set of requirements for conflicts, duplicates, and ambiguous words, but that assessment doesn't tell you whether the requirements are logically correct or even necessary. A team that uses a requirements tool first needs to learn how to do a good job of eliciting, analyzing, and specifying requirements. Buying an RM tool doesn't make you a skilled BA. You should learn how to use a technique manually and prove to yourself that it works for you before automating it (Davis 1995).

Properly applied tools and practices can add great value to a project, increasing quality and productivity, improving planning and collaboration, and bringing order out of chaos. But even the best tools won't overcome weak processes, untrained team members, challenging change initiatives, or cultural issues in the organization (Costello 2019). And always remember one of Wiegers's Laws of Computing: "Artificial intelligence is no substitute for the real thing" (Wiegers 1989).

| Lesson 50 | Today's "gotta get it out right away" development project is tomorrow's maintenance nightmare. |

After a system is released into production, it enters a maintenance status. There are four major categories of software maintenance (Merrill 2019):

Adaptive	Modifying the system to work in a changed operating environment
Corrective	Diagnosing and repairing defects
Perfective	Making changes to increase customer value, such as adding new functionality, improving performance, and enhancing usability
Preventive	Optimizing and restructuring code to make it more efficient, easier to understand, more maintainable, and more reliable

For systems that are developed incrementally, adding new, planned functionality and extending existing functionality don't count as perfective maintenance. That's just part of the development cycle. However, delivered increments can still require corrective maintenance to fix defects.

This chapter's previous lessons showed why corrective maintenance gets more expensive over time and how quality problems sap a team's productivity. Beyond requirements defects and code defects, software with design problems will continue to eat up resources as developers and maintainers improve the codebase over time through preventive maintenance.

Technical Debt and Preventive Maintenance

In the interest of speed, development teams sometimes take quality shortcuts that generate technical debt. They might not practice good defensive programming, such as input data validations and exception handling. Code that's written expeditiously could have a haphazard design that works for now but isn't structured for the long haul. It might not execute efficiently or be easily understandable by someone who must work with it in the future. Perhaps the developers didn't design the software or a database to accommodate future extensions easily. New functionality that's quickly pasted onto an otherwise solid demo version or prototype can make it into the production codebase, adding to the technical debt.

Quick code patches can have unexpected side effects. Brittle code shatters when someone changes it, triggering a cascade of modifications needed to keep it working. A future developer might opt to rebuild a troublesome module entirely rather than struggling to incorporate new functionality or make it work in a changed environment.

As with other debts, technical debt must be repaid eventually—with interest. The longer the debt lingers unaddressed in the system, the more interest it accrues. Repaying software technical debt involves refactoring, restructuring, or rewriting code (there's that ugly *re-* prefix again). As Ward Cunningham (1992) explains:

> A little debt speeds development so long as it is paid back promptly with a rewrite... The danger occurs when the debt is not repaid. Every minute spent on not-quite-right code counts as interest on that debt. Entire engineering organizations can be brought to a stand-still under the debt load of an unconsolidated implementation.

Much preventive maintenance effort is devoted to erasing technical debt. Whether you're refactoring code from a previous iteration on the current project or working on a fragile legacy system, your goal should be to leave the code in better shape than you found it. That's more constructive than merely cursing those earlier developers who created the mess that confronts you.

The decision boils down to consciously accepting some technical debt, with the full expectation that you'll need to spend more time on preventive maintenance later.

Conscious Technical Debt

There are times that it's reasonable to accrue some technical debt, provided the team fully appreciates that it will cost more to rework the deficient design in the future. If you expect the code to have a short lifetime, you might decide that it's not worth taking the time for thoughtful design. Too often, though, that expectation fits in the famous-last-words category. So-called temporary code, like you might build into a prototype, too often finds its way into production software, where it bedevils future maintainers.

If you're aware that you're doing expedient design and plan time in future iterations to address the shortcomings—instead of just hoping they won't cause problems—it might make sense to defer thorough design thinking. Or maybe you're doing something novel, uncertain, or exploratory. You find a design that more or less works, and that's good enough for now. You'll need to improve the design eventually, though, so make sure that you do.

The decision boils down to *consciously* accepting some technical debt for good reasons, with the full expectation that you'll need to spend more time on preventive maintenance later as a result. That is, there's deliberate technical debt, and there's accidental technical debt (Soni 2020). Failing to rectify design and code shortcomings makes it harder and harder to work with the system in subsequent iterations or during operation. Those accumulated problems slow down continued development now, and they consume excessive maintenance effort later.

Erasing technical debt adds its own risks to the project. It may feel as though you're just tuning up something that already works, but those improvements need the same level of verification and approval as other project code. Regression testing and other quality practices to catch bad fixes consume time beyond the code revisions themselves. The more extensive the code and design rework, the greater the risk of inadvertently breaking something else.

Designing for Quality, Now or Later

There's always something more pressing to work on than fixing up existing code. A manager can find it difficult to commit resources to paying down technical debt while customers demand more software *now*. Managers need to bite the bullet. Many software applications live on for decades with an ever-growing—and increasingly crumbly—codebase. As David Rice (2016) points out:

> The primary pain point for working with legacy code is how long it takes to make changes. So if you intend for your code to be long-lived, you need to ensure that it will be entirely pleasurable for future developers to make changes to it.

Perhaps "entirely pleasurable" is too much to expect. Still, strive to build software that lets future developers work on it without agony.

Make preventive maintenance a part of your daily development work, improving designs and code whenever you touch them. Don't work around the quality shortcomings you encounter—minimize them. Incremental preventive maintenance is like brushing your teeth daily; performing rework to reduce built-up technical debt is like going to the dentist periodically for a cleaning. I spend a few minutes scrubbing and flossing every day to give my dental hygienist as little as possible to do. Both dental work and software development are less painful if you deal with issues as you go along instead of letting them accumulate.

Next Steps: Quality

1. Revisit your definition of quality from the First Steps. Would you change your definition? If so, would you also change your perception of your product's quality?

2. Identify which of the lessons described in this chapter are relevant to your experiences with software quality.

3. Can you think of any other quality-related lessons from your own experience that are worth sharing with your colleagues?

4. Identify any practices described in this chapter that might be solutions to the quality-related problems you identified in the First Steps at the beginning of the chapter. How could each practice improve the quality of your products?

5. How could you tell whether each practice from Step 4 was yielding the desired results? What would those results be worth to you?

6. Identify any barriers that might make it difficult to apply the practices from Step 4. How could you break down those barriers or enlist allies to help you implement the practices?

7. Put into place process descriptions, templates, guidance documents, and other aids to help future project teams apply your local quality best practices effectively.

Chapter 7

Lessons About Process Improvement

Introduction to Process Improvement

You might recall that the first sentence in this book was: "I've never known anyone who could truthfully say, 'I am building software today as well as software could ever be built.'" Unless you can legitimately make this claim, you should always look for better ways to conduct your software projects. That's what software process improvement (SPI) is all about.

Software Process Improvement: What and Why

The objective of SPI is to reduce the cost of developing and maintaining software. It's not to generate a shelf full of processes and procedures. It's not to comply with the dictates of the process improvement model or project management framework that's currently the most fashionable. Process improvement is a means to an end, the end being superior business results, however you define that. Your goal might be to deliver products more quickly, incur less rework, better satisfy customer needs, reduce support costs, or all of the above. Something needs to change in the way your teams work so that you can achieve the goal. That change is software process improvement. Whenever your team holds a retrospective to get ideas for doing their work better the next time, they're laying the foundation for process improvement. Each time you apply a new technique to make your project work more efficient and effective, you're practicing process improvement.

Process improvement is a means to an end,
the end being superior business results,
however you define that.

Beginning in the late 1980s, many organizations undertook systematic improvement efforts across their departments and project teams, with varying degrees of success. These approaches often followed an established SPI model, such as the Capability Maturity Model for Software or CMM (Paulk et al. 1995) or its successor, the Capability Maturity Model Integration or CMMI (Chrissis et al. 2003). Thousands of organizations worldwide, particularly government suppliers in the United States, still conduct formal CMMI process capability appraisals each year (CMMI Institute 2017). Many companies have found that a systematic SPI approach helped them achieve superior results.

In part, the agile development movement was a reaction to the often comprehensive processes embodied in many maturity-model-driven SPI efforts. In fact, some early agile approaches were called lightweight methodologies. The twelfth principle behind the Manifesto for Agile Software Development states, "At regular intervals, the team reflects on how to become more effective, then tunes and adjusts its behavior accordingly" (Agile Alliance 2021c). That's the essence of process improvement.

Don't Fear the Process

The word *process* has a negative connotation in some circles. Sometimes people don't realize that they already have a process for software development, even if it's ill defined or undocumented. Some developers are afraid that having to follow defined procedures will cramp their style or stifle their creativity. Managers might fear that conforming to a particular process will slow the project down. Sure, it's possible to apply inappropriate processes in a dogmatic fashion that doesn't add value or allow for variations in projects and people. But this is not a requirement! When it works properly, organizations succeed *because* of their processes, not in spite of them.

Sensible and appropriate processes help software organizations be successful consistently, not just when the right people unite to pull off a difficult project through heroic efforts. Process and creativity are not incompatible. I follow a process for writing books, but that process doesn't constrain the words I put on the page in the least. My process is a structure that saves me time, keeps my work organized, and lets me continuously track progress toward my goal of completing a good book on schedule. When I can rely on an existing process, I can concentrate my mental resources on the problem at hand instead of on managing the effort.

Despite its conceptual simplicity, SPI is challenging. It's not easy to get people to acknowledge shortcomings in their current ways of working. With project work always pressing, how do you coax teams to spend the time it takes to identify and address improvement areas? Persuading managers to invest in future strategic benefits when they face looming deadlines is an uphill battle. And it's a challenge to alter an organization's culture, yet SPI involves culture change along with modifications in technical and management practices.

Making SPI Stick

Many SPI programs fail to yield effective and sustained results. Big, shiny new change initiatives are introduced with fanfare, but they quietly disappear with no announcement or retrospective. The organization abandons the effort and tries something different later on. I think you get only two failed attempts at strategic improvement before people conclude that the organization isn't serious about change. After two failures, few team members will take the next change initiative seriously.

Successful process improvement takes time. Organizations need to stick with it long enough to reap the benefits. Almost any systematic improvement approach can yield better results. If you bail out partway through the process, though, after you've invested in assessment and learning but before the changes pay off, you'll lose your investment. Because large-scale process change is not quick, learn to take satisfaction from small victories. Try to spot improvements you can put into place quickly that will address known problems, as well as the longer-term, systemic changes.

Consistency in management leadership also is essential. One of my consulting clients was frustrated. His organization had been making excellent progress on a CMM-based improvement strategy for some time. A new senior manager decided to go in a different direction. He abandoned the CMM effort and switched to an ISO 9001-based quality management system approach. Those who had worked diligently on the CMM strategy were disheartened when the fruits of all their hard work were tossed aside. Flailing on SPI activities can disillusion those practitioners who are genuinely interested in doing better. Unless the organization has a compelling need to comply with a specific standard, such as for certification purposes, any framework for developing high-quality processes should be acceptable.

When I began a new job leading the SPI program in a large corporate division, I met a woman who had held the corresponding position for a year in a similar division in the company. I asked my counterpart what attitude the software developers in her division held toward the program. She thought for a moment and then replied, "They're just waiting for it to go away." If SPI is viewed simply as the latest management fad, most practitioners will just ride it out, trying to get their real work done despite the distraction. That's not a formula for successful change.

This chapter presents nine lessons I've learned in many years of software process improvement work in my organizations and those of my consulting clients. Perhaps they'll help your SPI initiative to succeed.

First Steps: Software Process Improvement

I suggest you spend a few minutes on the following activities before reading the process improvement-related lessons in this chapter. As you read the lessons, contemplate to what extent each of them applies to your organization or project team.

1. What business outcomes have you not yet achieved that might indicate the need for some improved software development or management processes?

2. How successful has your organization been in the past with its SPI initiatives? If you've had some success, what actions and attitudes made those efforts pay off? Did you get better results by applying an established improvement model or with homegrown approaches?

3. Identify any shortcomings or problems in how your organization works to improve its software development and management processes.

4. State the impacts that each problem has on your ability to identify, design, implement, and roll out better processes and practices. How do the problems impede your ability to continuously improve the way you build software or your success in product delivery?

5. For each problem from Step 3, identify the root causes that contribute to the problem. Problems, impacts, and root causes can blur together, so try to tease them apart and see their connections. You might find multiple root causes that contribute to the same problem, as well as several problems that arise from a single root cause.

6. As you read this chapter, list any practices that would be useful to your team.

Lesson 51	Watch out for "Management by Businessweek."

Frustration with disappointing results is a powerful motivation for trying a different approach. However, you need to be confident that any new strategy you adopt has a good chance of solving your problem. Organizations sometimes turn to the latest buzzword solution, the hot new thing in software development, as the magic elixir for their software challenges.

A manager might read about a promising—but possibly overhyped—methodology and insist that his organization adopt it immediately to cure their ills. I've heard this phenomenon called "Management by Businessweek." Perhaps a developer is enthused after hearing a conference presentation about a new way of working and wants his team to try it. The drive to improve is laudable, but you need to direct that energy toward the right problem and assess how well a potential solution fits your culture before adopting it.

Over the years, people have leaped onto the bandwagons of countless new software engineering and management paradigms, methodologies, and frameworks. Among others, we've gone through

- Structured systems analysis and design
- Object-oriented programming
- Information engineering
- Rapid application development
- Spiral model
- Test-driven development
- Rational Unified Process
- DevOps

More recently, agile software development in numerous variations—Extreme Programming, Adaptive Software Development, Feature-Driven Development, Scrum, Lean, Kanban, Scaled Agile Framework, and others—has exemplified this pursuit of ideal solutions.

Alas, as Frederick P. Brooks, Jr. (1995) eloquently informs us, there are no silver bullets: "There is no single development, in either technology or management technique, which by itself promises even one order-of-magnitude improvement within a decade in productivity, in reliability, in simplicity." All of the approaches in the preceding list have their merits and limitations; all must be applied to appropriate problems by properly prepared teams and managers. I'll use a hypothetical new software development approach called Method-9 as an example for this discussion.

Before you settle on any new development approach, ask yourself, "What's preventing us from achieving those better results today?"

First Problem, Then Solution

The articles and books that its inventors and early adopters wrote about Method-9 praised its benefits. Some companies are drawn to Method-9 because they want their products to satisfy customer needs better. Maybe you want to deliver useful software faster (and who doesn't?). Method-9 can get you there. Perhaps you wish to reduce the defects that annoy customers and drain the team's time with rework (again, who doesn't?). Method-9 to the rescue! This is the essence of process improvement: setting goals, identifying barriers, and choosing techniques you believe will address them.

Before you settle on any new development approach, though, ask yourself, *"What's preventing us from achieving those better results today?"* (Wiegers 2019f). If you want to deliver useful products faster, what's slowing you down? If your goal is fewer defects and less rework, why do your products contain too many bugs today? If your ambition is to respond faster to changing needs, what's standing in your way?

In other words, if Method-9 is the answer—at least according to that article you read—what was the question?

I suspect that not all organizations perform a careful root cause analysis before they latch on to what sounds like a promising solution. Setting improvement goals is a great start, but you must also understand the current obstacles to achieving those goals. You need to treat real causes, not symptoms. If you don't understand those problems, choosing any new approach is just a hopeful shot in the dark.

A Root Cause Example

Suppose you want to deliver software products that meet customers' needs better than in the past. You've read that Method-9 teams include a role called the Vision Guru, who's responsible for ensuring the product achieves the desired outcome. "Perfect!" you think. "The Vision Guru will make sure we build the right thing. Happy customers are guaranteed." Problem solved, right? Maybe, but I suggest that, before making any wholesale process changes, your team should understand why your products don't thrill your customers already.

Root cause analysis is a process of thinking backward, asking "why" several times until you get to issues that you can target with thoughtfully selected improvement actions. The first contributing cause suggested might not be directly actionable; nor might it be the ultimate root cause. Therefore, addressing that initial cause won't solve the problem. You need to ask "why" another time or two to ensure that you're getting to the tips of the analysis tree.

Figure 7.1 shows a portion of a fishbone diagram—also called an Ishikawa or cause-and-effect diagram—which is a convenient way to work through a root cause analysis. The only tools you need are a few interested stakeholders, a whiteboard, and some markers. Let's walk through that diagram.

Your goal is to better meet customer needs with the initial release of your software products. Write that goal on a long horizontal line. Alternatively, you could phrase it as a problem statement: "Initial product release does not meet customer needs." In either case, that long horizontal line—the backbone in the fishbone diagram—represents your target issue.

Next, ask your group, "Why are we not already meeting our customer needs?" Now the analysis begins. One possible answer is that the team doesn't get adequate input to the requirements from end users—a common situation. Write that cause on a diagonal line coming off the goal statement line. That's a good start, but you need a deeper understanding to know how to solve the problem. You ask, "Why not?"

One member of the group says, "We've tried to talk to real users, but their managers say they're too busy to work with the software team." Someone else complains that the surrogate customer representatives who work with the team don't do a good job of presenting the ultimate users' real needs. Write those second-level causes on horizontal lines coming off the parent problem's diagonal line.

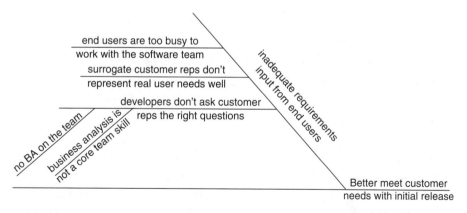

Figure 7.1 *Root cause analysis often is depicted as a fishbone diagram.*

A third participant points out that the developers who attempt to elicit requirements aren't skilled at asking customer reps the right questions. Then comes the usual follow-up question: "Why not?" There could be multiple reasons, including a lack of education or interest in requirements on the developers' part. It might be that business analysis is neither a core team skill nor a dedicated team role. Each cause goes onto a new diagonal line attached to its parent.

Now you're getting to actionable barriers that stand between your team's current performance and where you all want to be. Continue this layered analysis until the participants agree that they understand why they aren't already achieving the desired results. I've found this technique to be remarkably efficient at focusing the participants' thinking and quickly reaching a clear understanding of the situation. The diagram might get messy; consider writing the causes on sticky notes so that you can shuffle them around as the exploration continues.

Diagnosis Leads to Cure

In subsequent brainstorming sessions, team members can explore practical solutions to address those root causes. Then you are well on your way toward achieving superior performance. You might conclude that adding experienced business analysts (BAs) to your teams could be more valuable than adopting Method-9 with its Vision Guru. Or maybe the combination of the two will prove to be the secret sauce. You just don't know until you think it through.

As you contemplate whether a new development method will work for you, look past the hype and the fads. Understand the prerequisites and risks associated with the new approach, and then balance those against a realistic appraisal of the potential payoff. Good questions to explore include these.

- Will your team need training, tools, or consulting assistance to get started and sustain progress?

- Would the solution's cost yield a high return on investment?

- What possible cultural impacts would the transition have on your team, your customers, and their respective organizations and businesses?

- How ugly could the learning curve be?

The insights from a root cause analysis can point you toward better practices to address each problem you discover. Without exploring the barriers between where you are today and your goals, don't be surprised if the problems are still there after you switch to a different development strategy. Try a root cause analysis instead of chasing after the Hottest New Thing someone read in a headline.

Root cause analysis takes less time than you might fear. It's a sound investment in focusing your improvement efforts effectively. Any doctor will tell you that it's a good idea to understand the disease before prescribing a treatment.

| Lesson 52 | Ask not, "What's in it for me?" Ask, "What's in it for us?" |

When people are asked to use a new development approach, follow a different procedure, or undertake an unexpected task, their instinctive reaction is to wonder, "What's in it for me?" That's a natural human reaction, but it's not quite the proper question. The right question is, "What's in it for us?" The *us* in this question could refer to the rest of the team, the IT organization, the company, or even humanity as a whole—anyone beyond the individual. Effective change initiatives must consider the team's collective results, not just the impact on each individual's productivity, effectiveness, or comfort level. The people involved with leading an improvement effort should be able to answer the question "What's in it for us?" persuasively. If there's some important value in it for *us*, then there's also something in it for me, considering that I am part of the *us*.

Asking a busy project team member to do something extra, like reviewing a colleague's work, might not seem to provide any immediate benefit for that individual. However, that effort could collectively save the team more time than the individual invested, thereby providing a net positive contribution to the project. Enlisting colleagues to examine some of your requirements or code for errors does consume their time. A code review could involve two or three hours of work per participant. Those are hours that the reviewers aren't spending on their own responsibilities. However, an effective review reveals defects, and we've seen that it's always cheaper to correct defects earlier rather than later.

The people involved with leading an improvement effort should be able to answer the question "What's in it for us?" persuasively.

The Team Payoff

To illustrate the idea of team versus individual payoffs, let's work through a hypothetical example to see how a peer review can yield a substantial collective benefit. Suppose that my team's BA, Ari, has written several pages of requirements, accompanied by some visual analysis models and a state table. Ari asks two other colleagues and me to review her requirements. The four of us each spend one hour examining the material before a team review meeting, which also lasts an hour:

Preparation effort = 1 hour/reviewer × 4 reviewers = 4 hours

Review meeting effort = 1 hour/reviewer × 4 reviewers = 4 hours

Total review effort = 4 hours + 4 hours = 8 hours

Let's assume that our review discovers 24 defects of varying severity and that it takes Ari an average of 5 minutes to correct each one:

Actual rework effort = 24 defects × 0.0833 hour/defect = 2 hours

Now, imagine that Ari didn't solicit this review. Those defects would remain in the requirements set, only to be discovered later in the development cycle. Ari would still need to correct the requirements, and other team members would have to redo any designs, code, tests, and documentation based on the erroneous requirements. This work could easily take ten times as long as quickly fixing the bad requirements. The rework cost could be far greater if those defects made it into the final product to be discovered by customers. This tenfold effort multiplication factor lets us estimate the potential rework had Ari and company not held the review:

Potential rework effort = 24 defects × 0.833 hour/defect = 20 hours

Thus, this hypothetical requirements review prevented perhaps 18 hours of late-stage rework:

Rework effort prevented = 20 hours potential rework – 2 hours actual rework = 18 hours

This simple analysis suggests a minimum return on investment from the review of 225 percent:

ROI from peer review = 18 avoided rework hours ÷ 8 hours review effort = 2.25 = 225%

That's a tangible benefit for the project team as a whole. There's something in it for *us,* even if there isn't something in it for each participant.

Numerous companies that have measured the benefits of performing the type of rigorous peer review called *inspection* have reported results more dramatic than this example. For instance, Hewlett-Packard measured a return on investment of ten to one from its inspection program (Grady and Van Slack 1994). IBM found that an hour of inspection on average saved eighty-two hours of rework effort compared to finding defects in the released product (Holland 1999). As with all technical practices, your mileage may vary, but few individual software engineering practices can potentially yield a tenfold return on investment.

The Personal Payoff

Suppose you explain this analysis to a reluctant team member who doesn't see what's in it for him if he spends his valuable time reviewing your work. He might buy your reasoning and recognize that his two hours of review time could contribute to a significant payoff for the team. However, he still sees nothing in it for himself. How can you convince him otherwise? As a frequent reviewer myself, I've found many benefits from the time I spent examining someone else's work, including these.

- I learn something every time I look over a colleague's shoulder. They might be using some coding technique I'm not familiar with, or perhaps they've found a way to communicate requirements that's better than my method.

- I better understand certain aspects of the project, which could help me perform my part of the work better. It also helps to ensure against critical knowledge loss when a particular developer leaves the organization.

- A review disseminates knowledge across a project team, which enhances the whole team's performance. It's reasonable to expect all team members to share their knowledge with their colleagues; reviews are one way to do that.

Are these benefits worth the hours I invested in reviewing someone else's work? Maybe not. But there's yet another payoff. At some point, I'll ask some colleagues to review my work. As a software developer and as an author, I've learned the great value of having a diverse group of colleagues examine my work. The errors they find and their improvement suggestions invariably help me create a superior product.

Review input from others makes me aware of the kinds of errors I make. This knowledge, in turn, helps me do a better job from the outset on all my future deliverables. The bottom line is that my participation in a collective quality-improvement activity always pays off for both my colleagues and me.

Take One for the Team

The next time a colleague or a manager asks you to do something on the project that doesn't appear to benefit you personally, think past your self-interest. Employees have a responsibility to conform to established team and company development practices. It's fair to ask, "What's in it for us if I do this?" The burden is on the requester to explain how your contribution will benefit the team collectively. Then it's up to you to contribute to the team's mutual success.

> **Lesson 53**   The best motivation for changing how people work is pain.

When I was traveling on a consulting job in December of 2000, I slipped on some ice-covered steps and fell, badly injuring my right shoulder. It was the most severe pain I've ever experienced. Three days later, I finally got home and saw a doctor, who informed me that I had a rotator cuff tear. A physical therapist gave me exercises to do at home. The pain powerfully motivated me to do the exercises and try to recover quickly, especially because I'm very dominantly right-handed—my left arm is primarily for visual symmetry.

As with individuals, pain is a powerful change motivator for teams and organizations. I'm not talking about artificial, externally induced pain, such as managers or customers who demand the impossible, but rather the very real pain the team experiences from its current ways of working. One way to encourage people to change is to explain how marvelously green the grass will be when they reach CMMI Level 5 or are fully Scrum-Lean-Kanban agilified. A more compelling motivation to get people moving is to point out that the grass behind them is on fire. Process improvement should emphasize reducing project pain by first extinguishing, and then preventing, fires.

To motivate people to engage in the change initiative, the pain-reduction promise must outweigh the discomfort of the effort itself.

Process improvement activities aren't that much fun. They're a distraction from the project work that interests team members the most and delivers business value. Change efforts can feel like eternally pushing a boulder uphill, as so many factors oppose making sustained organizational alterations. To motivate people to engage in the change initiative, the pain-reduction promise must outweigh the discomfort of the effort itself. And at some point, those involved must feel the pain relief, or they won't get on board the next time. Find the influencers in your organization and their pain points, connect those to the change goals, and you should have a strong foundation on which to build the change effort.

Pain Hurts!

I once led SPI activities in a fast-moving group that built a large corporation's websites. They were overwhelmed with requests for new projects and enhancements to their existing sites. They also had a configuration management problem, using two web servers that had largely duplicate—but not precisely the same—content. Everyone in this group accepted my recommendations for introducing a practical change-request system and more disciplined configuration management practices. They saw how much confusion and wasted effort their current practices caused. The processes we put into place helped considerably to reduce the configuration management pain level.

How would you define "pain" in your organization? What recurrent problems do your projects experience? If you can identify them, you can focus improvement efforts where you know they'll yield great rewards. Common examples of project pain include these:

- Failing to meet planned delivery schedules

- Releasing products with excessive defects or functional deficiencies

- An inability to keep up with change requests

- Creating systems that aren't easily extended without significant rework

- Delivering products that don't adequately meet customer needs

- Dealing with system failures that force the on-call support person to work in the middle of the night

- Dealing with managers who lack a sufficient understanding of current technology issues and software development approaches

- Suffering from risks that weren't identified or mitigated

The purpose of any process assessment activity—a team discussion, a project retrospective, or an appraisal by an outside consultant—is to identify these problem areas. Then you can determine the root causes of the problems and select actions to address them. As a consultant, I rarely give my clients surprising observations, but they haven't yet taken the time to confront and resolve the resultant pain. Outside observers can help us see problems more clearly and motivate action.

Invisible Pain

Long ago, I was the customer working with a developer, Jean, to create a database and a simple query interface. We didn't have written requirements, just frequent discussions about the system's capabilities. At one point, Jean's manager called me, a little angry. "You have to stop changing the requirements so much," he demanded. "Jean can't make any progress, because you request so many changes."

This problem was news to me. Jean had never indicated that our uncertainty about requirements was a problem. The difficulty that my approach caused Jean wasn't visible to me. Had she or her manager explained their preferred process at the outset, I would have been happy to follow it. Jean and I agreed on a more structured approach for specifying my needs from then on, and we made better progress.

This experience taught me that problems that affect certain project participants might not be apparent to others. This highlights the need for clear communication of expectations and issues among all the stakeholders. It also revealed an important corollary to this section's lesson: it's hard to sell a better mousetrap to people who don't know they have mice.

If you aren't aware of your current practices' negative impacts, you probably won't be receptive to suggestions for change. Any proposed change would appear to be a solution in search of a problem. Thus, an important aspect of SPI is identifying the causes and costs of process-related problems and then communicating those to the affected people. That knowledge might encourage everyone involved to do something different.

Sometimes you can stimulate this awareness in small ways. I divide the students in my training classes into small groups to discuss problems their project teams currently experience. Those discussions are most fruitful when the group members represent different project viewpoints: BA, project manager, developer, customer, tester, marketing staff, and so forth. After one such discussion, a customer representative shared an eye-opening insight. "I have more sympathy for the developers now," she said. That sympathy is a good starting point toward better ways of working that benefit everyone.

Lesson 54	When steering an organization toward new ways of working, use gentle pressure, relentlessly applied.

When I was in the SPI business some years ago, a joke circulated through our community:

Q: How many process improvement leaders does it take to change a lightbulb?

A: Only one, but the lightbulb must be willing to change.

I've heard that therapists have an analogous joke.

There's truth in that bit of humor. No one can truly change how someone else thinks, behaves, or works. You can only employ mechanisms that motivate them to behave in some different way. You can explain why making some change is to their—and other people's—advantage, hope they accept your reasoning, and reward those who make the switch. You can even threaten or punish people if they don't get on board, though that's not a recommended SPI motivational technique. Ultimately, though, it's up to each individual to decide that they're willing to operate differently in the future.

Steering

Effectively steering a software organization—be it a small group or an entire company—toward new ways of working requires the change leaders to exert continuous, gentle pressure in the desired direction (The Mann Group 2019). To establish that desired direction, the change initiative's goals must be well defined, clearly communicated, and obviously beneficial for the organization's business success. It's hard for any organization or individual to make quick, radical changes. Incremental change is less disruptive and more readily threaded into everyone's daily routine. It takes time for individuals to absorb both new practices and a fresh mindset.

Leaders must try to get buy-in from an emotional perspective as well. Everyone involved needs to understand how they can contribute to the effort's success. Seek out early adopters who are receptive and can serve as champions who advocate for the change with their peers. People who implement and are affected by the change must feel as though their voices are heard and that the change isn't being shoved down their throats.

If you're a change leader, here are some ways to gently—yet relentlessly—apply pressure to keep the organization moving toward its destination.

- Define the change initiative's objectives, the motivation for it, and the key results being sought. Vague targets, like becoming "world class" or "performance leaders," aren't helpful.

- Select metrics—key performance indicators—that will demonstrate progress toward the objectives and the impact those changes have on project performance. The latter are lagging indicators. You initiate a change activity because you're confident the new ways will yield better results. It takes time for those new practices to have an impact on projects, though. Communicating positive metric trends can help sustain commitment from the participants.

- Set realistic, meaningful goals and expectations. Team members will resist demands to dramatically and instantaneously change how they work. They might go through the motions, but that doesn't mean they're sincerely complying with the initiative or that they acknowledge its value.

The change initiative's goals must be well defined, clearly communicated, and obviously beneficial for business success.

- Treat the change initiative as a project with activities, deliverables, milestones, and responsibilities. Oh, and don't forget resources. Provide the necessary time so that people can work on improvement activities in parallel with their project commitments.

- Keep the change initiative visible. Make it a regular part of status meetings and reports. Track the SPI effort's progress toward its objectives along with your regular project tracking activities.

- Hold people accountable for their commitments to perform certain SPI activities. If project work always takes exclusive priority, the improvement actions will be neglected.

- Aim for some small, early wins to show that the change initiative is already beginning to yield results. Make clear what benefits those wins provide to the organization. Teams that successfully pilot new practices blaze the trail for the others.

- Publicly tout even small successes as evidence that the new ways of working are paying off. Keep the practices visible with this low-key, positive pressure until they become ingrained in team members' individual work styles and organizational operations.

- Provide any needed training in the new ways of working. Observe whether team members are applying the training, but accept the reality of the learning curve. It takes time for people to put what they've learned into effective practice.

Training is an investment in future performance. At a year-in-review meeting with nearly 2,000 people, the director of a corporate research laboratory reported as an achievement that a large number of scientists had taken design-of-experiments training. That's not an achievement—it's an investment. I wish management had followed up with the scientists several months later to see what they were doing better because of that training. Management didn't check to see what return they got from their training investment.

Managing Upward

Process changes affect managers as well as technical team members. Managing upward is a valuable skill for any change leader. If you're a change leader, coach your managers regarding what to say publicly, the behaviors and results to look for, and the outcomes to either reward or correct.

I once had a consulting client who was adept at managing upward. Linda had figured out how to present the value of the change project to each manager in terms that would resonate with them and gain their backing. She knew how to guide her managers to publicly reinforce the importance of the change initiative she led. Linda was skilled at navigating the organizational politics to align key leaders behind the change project without becoming entangled in the politics herself. She had mastered a delicate dance.

One organization with a successful SPI program documented the attitudes and behaviors they expected their managers to exhibit in the future. Figure 7.2 shows just a few of their expectations. Whether you're aiming for a higher maturity level in a process framework such as CMMI or implementing agile development across an entire organization, managers need to understand how their own actions and expectations must change. Managers who lead by example, practicing the new ways of working themselves and publicly reinforcing them, send a continuous, positive signal to everyone else that reinforces the culture change.

My father once told me that if I were ever in a big crowd of people all trying to get through the same door, I should just keep my feet moving, and I would get there. I've tried this technique—it works. The same is true with software process improvement. Keep your feet moving in the desired direction, and you'll make steady progress toward better ways of working and superior outcomes.

- I agree that requirements are a fundamental work product.
- I don't commit to the customer's cost and schedule requests until receiving commitment from the project team.
- I commit to following the project planning process, even if it conflicts with customer demands and pressures.
- I help to resolve conflicting project priorities with project managers and customers.
- I encourage team members to consider commitments made across projects during project planning and not to overcommit.
- I ask to see project status tracking data.
- I assist team members by removing obstacles to the software process.
- I create an environment that is data-driven, using relevant measures to manage the business.
- I consider process improvement needs when setting the budget.
- I support and defend the software process to the customer.

Figure 7.2 *One organization defined some expectations of management behavior associated with improved software processes.*

| Lesson 55 | You don't have time to make each mistake that every practitioner before you has already made. |

As I mentioned in Chapter 1, I have little formal education in software development, just three programming courses I took in college long ago. Since then, though, I learned a great deal more by reading books and articles, taking training courses, and attending conferences and professional society meetings. I judge the value of a learning experience by how many ideas I write down for things that I want to try when I get back to work. (I hope you're doing that as you read this book.) The best learning experiences inform me about techniques that I can share with my coworkers so that we all become more capable.

Picking up knowledge from other people is a lot more efficient than climbing every learning curve yourself. That's the point of this book: sharing insights from my career to save you time as you learn about and try to apply the same practices. All professionals should spend part of their time acquiring knowledge and broadening their skills in this ever-growing field.

One software group I was in held weekly learning sessions. In rotation, each team member would select a magazine article or book chapter and summarize it for the others. We discussed how we could apply the topic to our work. Anyone who attended a conference shared the highlights with the rest of us. Such learning sessions propagated a lot of relevant information throughout the team. It did feel a bit awkward when I joined a new group at Kodak that was going chapter by chapter in this fashion through my own first book, *Creating a Software Engineering Culture*. However, we had some interesting discussions, and they could understand my viewpoint as I worked with them to improve their development processes.

The translation from an idea to a routine practice always involves a learning curve.

Not every method I took home from a conference worked as well as I hoped. One enthusiastic speaker touted his technique for stimulating ideas during requirements elicitation workshops. I gave his suggestion a try after I returned to work; it fell flat on its face. I got excited about use cases when I heard conference speakers praise their potential. The first time I tried to apply use cases, I struggled to explain them to my user representatives and make them work. But I pushed through that initial difficulty and was able to employ use cases successfully after that. I had to persevere through the discomfort of learning a new skill to get to the payoff. The translation from an idea to a routine practice always involves a learning curve.

The Learning Curve

The learning curve describes how proficient someone becomes at performing a new task or technique as a function of their experience with it. We all confront countless learning curves in life. Whenever we try to do anything novel, there's another learning curve. We shouldn't expect a method to yield its full potential from the outset. When project teams attempt unfamiliar techniques, their plans must account for the time it will take them to get up to speed. If they don't succeed in mastering the new practice, the time they invested is lost forever.

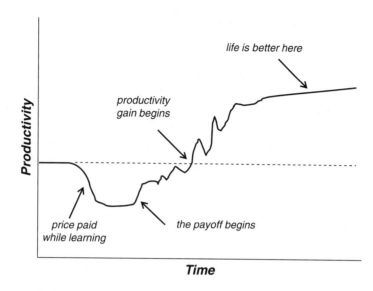

Figure 7.3 *The learning curve reduces your productivity before increasing it.*

You're undoubtedly interested in the overall work performance—productivity, perhaps—that your repertoire of techniques lets you achieve. Figure 7.3 shows that you begin at some initial productivity level, which you want to enhance through an improved process, practice, method, or tool. Your first step is to undertake some learning experience. Your productivity takes an immediate hit because you don't get any work done during the time you invest in learning (Glass 2003).

Productivity decreases further as you take time to create new processes, wrestle to discover how to make a new technique work, acquire and learn to use a new tool, and otherwise get up to speed. As you begin to master some new way of working, you could see gains but also experience some setbacks—the jagged part of the productivity growth curve in Figure 7.3. If all goes well, you eventually reap benefits from your investment and enjoy increased effectiveness, efficiency, and quality. Keep the learning curve's reality in mind as you incorporate new practices into your personal activities, your team, and your organization. And resist the temptation to give up prematurely, before the learning investment begins to pay off.

Good Practices

I find it amusing when someone complains about another person, "He always thinks his way is best." Of course he does! Why would anyone deliberately do something in a way that they knew was not the best option? That would be silly.

The problem doesn't come from thinking your way is best; it comes if you don't consider that others might have better ways and aren't willing to learn from them. I collect good ideas and useful techniques from any source I encounter. It would be foolish to reject something that's demonstrably better than my old way just because of pride.

Peer reviews provide a good opportunity to observe other ways of working. You might see someone using unfamiliar language features, clever coding tricks, or something else that triggers a lightbulb in your brain. During a code review, I saw that the programmer's commenting style was obviously superior to mine. I immediately adopted his style and used it from then on. That's an easy way to learn and improve.

People often talk about industry best practices, which immediately triggers a debate about which practice is best, for what purpose, in what context, and who decided that. An Internet search will produce a vast list of articles and books about software best practices (see [Foord 2017] as one example). Good stuff all, but *best practice* is a strong term.

My advice is to accumulate a toolbox filled with *good practices*. A different technique simply has to be better than what you're doing now to go into your toolbox. For instance, my book *Software Requirements* with coauthor Joy Beatty (2013) describes more than fifty good practices relating to requirements development and management. I believe some of them truly are best practices in their niche, but others might disagree. The point is not worth debating—what works for you might not work for someone else.

As you accumulate tools and techniques, hang onto most of those that you've used successfully in the past. Replace a current technique with a new one only when the new one yields superior results in all cases. Often, the two can coexist, and you can choose between them as the situation dictates. For instance, a UML activity diagram is essentially a flowchart on steroids, but sometimes a basic flowchart shows everything you need to see. So have both tools available, and use the simplest one that gets the job done.

As I've mentioned previously, I'm a proponent of use cases as a requirements elicitation technique. In an otherwise very good book on use cases, the authors recommend that the reader discard certain requirements tools from their repertoire of solutions: "As with requirements lists, we recommend that DFDs [data flow diagrams] be dropped from the requirements analyst's toolbox" (Kulak and Guiney 2004). I consider that poor advice, as I've encountered many situations in which data flow diagrams are useful in requirements analysis. Why not keep a variety of hammers in the toolbox in case you encounter an assortment of nails during your project work?

| Lesson 56 | Good judgment and experience sometimes trump a defined process. |

I knew a project team that tried diligently to conform to the heavy-duty process framework their organization had implemented. They dedicated a person to write a detailed project plan for their six-month project, as that's what they thought the process required. He completed the plan shortly before the project was finished.

This is the kind of story that gives SPI a bad reputation. That team completely missed the point of having a process: it's not to conform to the process, but to get better business results by applying the process than you would otherwise. The process is supposed to work for you, not the reverse. Sensible processes, situationally adjusted based on experience, guide teams to repeated success. People need to select, scale, and adapt processes to yield the maximum benefit for each situation. A process is a structure, not a straitjacket.

Simply having a defined process available is no guarantee that it's sensible, effective, appropriate, or adds value. However, a process often is in place for a good reason. It's always okay to question a process, but it's not always okay to subvert it. Be sure you understand the rationale and intent behind a step that you question before electing to bypass it. In a regulated industry, some process steps are included to achieve mandatory compliance with a quality management system. Skipping a required step could cause problems when you try to get a product certified. Usually, though, the process steps are there simply because some people agreed that they would be beneficial to the team's work and the customer's product.

Processes and Rhythms

Organizations put processes and methodologies in place to try to become more effective. Often the processes contribute significantly to success; sometimes they don't. A process might have made sense when it was written but doesn't serve the current situation well. Even with good intentions, people sometimes create processes that are too elaborate and prescriptive. They seem like a good idea, but if they aren't practical, people will ignore them. A defined process represents good judgment version 1.0, but processes don't replace thinking. The good judgment that grows out of experience helps wise practitioners know when following a process is smart and when it's smarter to bend the process a bit and then improve it based on what they learn.

Whenever people don't follow a process that they claim to be—and should be—using, I see just three possible courses of action.

1. Start following the process, because it's the best way we know to perform that particular activity.

2. If the process doesn't meet your needs, modify it to be more effective and practical—and then follow it.

3. Throw away the process and stop pretending that you follow it.

The word *process* leaves a bad taste in some people's mouths, but it doesn't have to be that way. A process simply describes how individuals and teams get their work done. A process could be random and chaotic, highly structured and disciplined, or anywhere in between. The project situation should dictate how rigorous the process should be.

I don't care how you build a little website or app, provided it works right for the customer, but I care a lot about how people build medical devices and transportation systems.

One of my consulting clients told me, "We didn't have a process, but we had a rhythm." That's a nice way to describe an informal process. He meant that their team didn't have documented procedures, but everyone knew what activities they were expected to perform and how they meshed together so that they could collaborate smoothly.

The other extreme from having no documented process at all is to apply a systematic process improvement framework, such as the five-level CMMI (Chrissis et al. 2003). At maturity level 1, people perform their work in whatever way they think they should at that moment. Higher maturity levels gradually introduce more structured processes and measurements in the spirit of continuous improvement. Level 5 organizations have a comprehensive set of processes in place that teams consistently perform and enhance.

An interesting thing sometimes happens as organizations move to high maturity levels. A friend who worked in a level 5 organization said, "We're not really following a process. This is just how we work." They did indeed have a collection of well-defined processes, but my friend and her colleagues had internalized the process elements. They weren't consciously following each stepwise procedure. Instead, they applied the process automatically and effectively based on years of collected, recorded, and shared experience. That's the ideal objective.

Being Nondogmatic

I believe in sensible processes, but it's important not to adhere dogmatically to overly prescriptive processes or methodologies. As mentioned in the preceding lesson, I like to accumulate a rich toolbox of techniques for diverse problems rather than following a script. I work within a general process framework that's populated with selected good practices that I've found valuable. Over the years, the software world has created many development and management methodologies that claim to solve all your problems. Rather than following any of those strictly, I like to choose the best bits from many and apply them situationally.

Agile software development methods have exploded since the late 1990s. Wikipedia (2021b) identifies no fewer than fourteen significant agile software development frameworks and twenty-one commonly used agile practices. The developers of those frameworks have packaged various practices together, expecting that a particular grouping of techniques and activities will yield the best results.

I encounter some purists who seem highly concerned about conforming to, say, Scrum. There's a worry that dropping or replacing certain practices means that a Scrum team isn't really doing Scrum anymore. That's true, per "The Scrum Guide" (Schwaber and Sutherland 2020):

> The Scrum framework, as outlined herein, is immutable. While implementing only parts of Scrum is possible, the result is not Scrum. Scrum exists only in its

entirety and functions well as a container for other techniques, methodologies, and practices.

No software development approach is so perfect that teams dare not customize it in a way that they believe adds value.

Those who invent a method get to define what constitutes that method—but so what? Is the goal to be Scrum (or whatever) compliant, or is it to get the project work done well and expeditiously? I've heard people complain that certain practices are "not very compliant with the agile way of doing things" or "against agile fundamental principles." Again, I ask, "So what?" Does that particular practice help the project and organization achieve business success, or does it not? That should be the determining factor in deciding whether to use it. No software development approach is so perfect that teams dare not customize it in a way that they believe adds value. I'm a pragmatist, not a purist.

Agile—like all processes and methods—is not an end in itself. It's a means to the end of achieving business success. I propose that all team members accumulate tools and practices to perform their own work and to work well with others toward their common objective. It's not important to me whether a particular practice is compliant with a specific development or management philosophy. However, the practice must be the best way to get the job done in a particular situation when you consider all of its implications. If it's not, then do something else.

| Lesson 57 | Adopt a shrink-to-fit philosophy with document templates. |

After I learned to appreciate the value of creating a written set of requirements, I would compile a simple list of the functionality my customers had requested. That was a good start, but I always had other important pieces of requirements-related knowledge beyond functionality. It wasn't clear where I should put them. Then I discovered the software requirements specification (SRS) template described in the now-obsolete IEEE Standard 830, "IEEE Recommended Practice for Software Requirements Specifications." I adopted this template, as it contained many sections that helped me organize my diverse requirements information. With experience, I modified the template to be more suitable for the systems that my teams developed. Figure 7.4 shows the SRS template I ultimately created with my colleague, Joy Beatty (Wiegers and Beatty 2013).

1. **Introduction**
   1.1   Purpose
   1.2   Document Conventions
   1.3   Project Scope
   1.4   References
2. **Overall Description**
   2.1   Product Perspective
   2.2   User Classes and Characteristics
   2.3   Operating Environment
   2.4   Design and Implementation Constraints
   2.5   Assumptions and Dependencies
3. **System Features**
   3.x   System Feature X
         3.x.1 Description
         3.x.2 Functional Requirements
4. **Data Requirements**
   4.1   Logical Data Model
   4.2   Data Dictionary
   4.3   Reports
   4.4   Data Integrity, Retention, and Disposal
5. **External Interface Requirements**
   5.1   User Interfaces
   5.2   Software Interfaces
   5.3   Hardware Interfaces
   5.4   Communications Interfaces
6. **Quality Attributes**
   6.1   Usability
   6.2   Performance
   6.3   Security
   6.4   Safcty
   6.x   [others]
7. **Internationalization and Localization Requirements**
8. **Other Requirements**
   Appendix A: Glossary
   Appendix B: Analysis Models

Figure 7.4 *A rich software requirements specification template contains sections for many types of information.*

Document templates offer several benefits. They define consistent ways to organize sets of information from one project to the next and from individual to individual. Consistency makes it easier for people who work with those deliverables to find the information they need. A template also can reveal potential gaps in a document author's project knowledge, reminding them of information that perhaps should be included. I've used or developed templates for many types of project documents, including these:

- Request for proposal

- Vision and scope document

- Use cases

- Software requirements specification

- Project charter

- Project management plan

- Risk management plan and risk list

- Configuration management plan

- Test plan

- Lessons learned

- Process improvement action plan

Suppose I'm using the template in Figure 7.4 to structure requirements information about a new system. I don't complete the template from top to bottom; I populate specific sections as I accumulate the pertinent information. After a while, maybe I notice that Section 2.5, Assumptions and Dependencies, is empty. This hole prompts me to wonder whether there's some missing information I should track down regarding assumptions and dependencies. Maybe there are conversations I haven't had yet with certain stakeholders. Perhaps no one has yet pointed out any assumptions or dependencies, but there could be some out there that we should identify. Some assumptions or dependencies might have been recorded someplace else—should I move them to this section or put pointers to them in there? Or maybe there really aren't any known assumptions or dependencies—I should find out. The empty section reminds me that there's work to be done.

I should also consider what to do if a particular template section isn't relevant to my project. One option is to simply delete the section from my requirements document when I'm done. But that absence might raise a question in a reader's mind: "I didn't see anything about assumptions and dependencies here. Are there any? I'd better ask somebody." Or I could leave the heading in place but leave the section blank. That might make a reader wonder whether the document was completed yet. I prefer to leave the heading in place and put an explanation in that section: "No assumptions or dependencies have been identified for this project." Explicit communication causes less confusion than implicit communication.

Developing a suitable template from a blank sheet of paper is slow and haphazard. I like to begin with a rich template and then mold it to each project's size, nature, and needs. That's what I mean by shrink-to-fit. Many established technical standards describe document templates. Organizations that issue technical standards relevant to software development include the following:

- Institute of Electrical and Electronics Engineers (IEEE)
- International Organization for Standardization (ISO)
- International Electrotechnical Commission (IEC)

For instance, international standard ISO/IEC/IEEE 29148 includes suggested outlines—along with descriptive guidance information—for software, stakeholder, and system requirements specifications (ISO/IEC/IEEE 2018). An online search will reveal many sources of downloadable templates for various software project deliverables to help you get started.

Because such generic templates are intended to cover a wide range of projects, they might not be just right for you. But they will provide many ideas regarding the types of information that you should include and reasonable ways to organize that information. The shrink-to-fit concept implies that you can tailor those templates to your situation in the following ways.

- Delete sections that your projects don't need.
- Add sections the template doesn't already contain that would help your projects.
- Simplify or consolidate template sections where that won't cause confusion.
- Change the terminology to suit your project or culture.
- Reorganize the template's contents to meet your audiences' needs better.
- Split or merge templates for related deliverables when appropriate to avoid overly massive documents, document proliferation, and redundancy.

If your organization works on multiple classes or sizes of projects, create sets of templates that are suitable for each class. That's better than expecting every project to start with standard templates that aren't a good fit for what they're doing. A consulting client asked me to create numerous processes and accompanying deliverable templates for their complex systems engineering projects, which worked well for them. That client later requested a parallel set of process assets appropriate for their newer—and smaller—agile projects. Agile projects still must record necessary project information while minimizing their documentation effort, so I simplified the original processes and templates.

As with other sensible process components, a good template will support your work, not impede it.

Companies aren't successful because they write great specifications or plans. They're successful because they build high-quality information systems or commercial applications. Well-crafted key documents can contribute to that success. Some people are leery of templates, perhaps fearing that they'll impose an overly restrictive structure on the project. They could be concerned that the team will focus on completing the template instead of building the product. Unless you have a contractual requirement to do so, you're not obligated to populate every section of a template. And you're certainly not obligated to complete a template before you can proceed with development work. As with other sensible process components, a good template will support your work, not impede it.

Even if your organization doesn't use documents to store information, projects still need to record certain knowledge in some persistent form. You might prefer to use checklists instead of templates to avoid overlooking some important category of information. Like a template, a checklist helps you assess how complete your information set is, but it doesn't help you organize the information in a consistent fashion.

Many organizations store requirements and other project information in a tool. The tools will let you define templates for stored data objects analogous to the sections in a traditional document. Users can create documents when needed as reports generated from the contents of the tool's database. It's important for everyone who uses the tool to recognize that the tool is the ultimate repository of current information. A generated document represents a snapshot in time of the database contents, which could be obsolete tomorrow.

I value simple tools like templates, checklists, and forms that save me from reinventing how to do my work on each project. I don't want to create documents for their own sake or spend time on process overhead that doesn't add proportionate value to the work. Thoughtfully designed templates remind my colleagues and me how we can contribute to the project most effectively. That seems like a reasonable degree of structured process to me.

Lesson 58	Unless you take the time to learn and improve, don't expect the next project to go any better than the last one.

The city in which I live suffered a major ice storm recently. My all-electric house with no fireplace or generator got quite chilly while the power was out. My wife and I were well prepared, so we got through it okay. However, once the lights came back on, I contemplated how we could be even better prepared for the next emergency. I bought several items that would keep us safer and more comfortable during an extended power outage, updated my food storage and preparation plans, and tuned up my emergency planning checklist.

The process of reflecting on an event to learn how to weather—in this case, literally—the next one better is called a *retrospective*. All software project teams should perform retrospectives at the end of a development cycle (a release or an iteration), at the project's conclusion, and when some surprising or disruptive event occurs.

Looking Back

A retrospective is a learning and improvement opportunity. It's a chance for the team to look back at what happened, identify what worked well and what did not, and incorporate the resultant wisdom into future work. An organization that doesn't invest the time for this reflection is basing its desire for better future performance on hope, not on experience-guided improvement.

Also called post-project reviews, after-action reviews, and postmortems (even when the project survived!), the term *retrospective* is well established in the software world. The seminal resource in the field is *Project Retrospectives*, by Norman L. Kerth (2001). A retrospective seeks to answer four questions.

1. What went well for us that we'd like to repeat?

2. What didn't go so well that we should do differently next time?

3. What happened that surprised us and might be a risk to consider in the future?

4. Is there anything that we don't yet understand and should investigate further?

Another way to frame this discussion is to ask the retrospective participants, "If I'm starting a new project that's similar to the one you just completed, what recommendations could you give me?" That sage advice from people who have gone before should help answer the preceding four questions.

A retrospective must be conducted with consideration and respect for all participants.

A retrospective is more of an interpersonal interaction than a technical activity. As such, it must be conducted with consideration and respect for all participants. A retrospective is not an opportunity for laying blame, but rather a mechanism for learning how we can all do better the next time (Winters et al. 2020). It's important to explore what happened objectively and without repercussions. Everyone who participates in a retrospective should remember Kerth's Prime Directive:

> Regardless of what we discover, we must understand and truly believe that everyone did the best job he or she could, given what was known at the time, his or her skills and abilities, the resources available, and the situation at hand.

The agile development community has embraced the idea of continual learning, growth, and adaptation by incorporating retrospectives into each iteration (Scaled Agile 2021d). Recall that one of the principles behind the Manifesto for Agile Software Development states, "At regular intervals, the team reflects on how to become more effective, then tunes and adjusts its behavior accordingly" (Agile Alliance 2021c). Agile's short iteration cycle time provides frequent opportunities to enhance performance on upcoming iterations. Teams that are relatively new to agile or transitioning to a different agile framework will learn a lot from their early iterations. The book *Agile Retrospectives,* by Esther Derby and Diana Larsen (2006), describes a palette of thirty activities from which you can select to craft a retrospective experience that's just right for your team.

Scale the time you invest in a retrospective to the size of the project work, how well it went, and how much there is to learn. An agile team might take thirty to sixty minutes to reflect at the end of a two-week sprint. Kerth (2001) proposes spending up to three days on a retrospective with a large project team that hasn't held one before and encountered significant issues that need exploring. I've facilitated several retrospectives that lasted a half-day. The greater the prospective leverage for improving future performance, the more worthwhile it is to spend the time looking back.

Retrospective Structure

A retrospective is not a free-form gripe session. It involves a structured and time-boxed sequence of activities: planning, kicking off the event, gathering information, prioritizing issues, analyzing issues, and deciding what to do with the information (Wiegers 2007, Wiegers 2019g). Figure 7.5 illustrates the major inputs to and outputs from a retrospective. Team members contribute their recollections of their project experience: what happened when and how it went. It's a good idea to solicit input from everyone involved with the project, as each participant's perspective is unique. I like to begin with the positive: let's remember—with pride—the things we did effectively and how we helped one another succeed.

In a safe and nonjudgmental environment, the retrospective participants also can share their emotional ups and downs. Someone might have been frustrated because the delayed delivery of part of the project affected their ability to make good on their commitments. Another team member might have been grateful for the extra assistance a colleague provided. Perhaps people felt super-stressed because the already optimistic schedule was reduced to even more unrealistic levels, and they had to work to exhaustion in an attempt to deliver on time. The team's well-being is a significant contributor to project success. Addressing the emotional factor during the retrospective yields ideas for elevating everyone's happiness and job satisfaction.

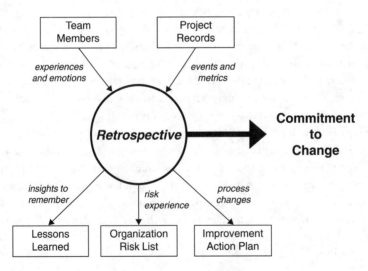

Figure 7.5 *A retrospective collects project experiences and metrics to yield lessons learned, new risks, improvement actions, and a team commitment to make valuable changes.*

The retrospective participants can bring any data the team collected in the usual software metrics dimensions:

- Size: counts and sizes for requirements, user stories, and other items
- Effort: planned and actual labor hours for tasks
- Time: planned and actual calendar duration for tasks
- Quality: defect counts and types, system performance, and other quality attribute measures

All of this input provides fodder for the team to gain deep insight into how the work went and how the participants felt about the project.

The retrospective outputs shown in Figure 7.5 fit into several categories. First are lessons learned that you want to remember for subsequent development cycles. You might make lists of things to make sure you do again, things the team should *not* do again, and things they should do differently the next time. If your organization maintains a lessons-learned repository, add selected items from the retrospective to that collection to help future projects.

Unpleasant surprises could feed into your organization's master list of candidate risks that every project should study. (See Lesson 32, "If you don't control your project's risks, they will control you.") Project risks that weren't adequately mitigated and other things that didn't go quite as intended indicate good starting points for process improvement actions. The most important output from a retrospective is the team's commitment to making changes that will improve their work life (Pearls of Wisdom 2014b).

After the Retrospective

A retrospective on its own won't change how things go the next time—it must feed into ongoing SPI activities. Reaching a better future requires an action plan that itemizes the process changes the team should explore before or during the next development cycle. The people who own retrospective action items need to devote time to exploring ways to solve past problems. That time isn't available for them to work on project tasks, so the improvement effort must be added to project schedules. Otherwise, it won't get done. If a project team holds a retrospective but management provides no resources to address the issues identified, the retrospective was useless.

Teams that lack downtime between development cycles won't have a chance to reflect, learn, and retool their capabilities (DeMarco 2001). Therefore, leave some time in your project schedules for the education and experimentation that people require to apply new practices, tools, and methods effectively. If you don't invest this time, you shouldn't expect the next project to run more smoothly. Conducting retrospectives without ever making any changes wastes time and discourages the participants.

A retrospective is not free—it takes time, effort, and maybe money. However, that investment is more than repaid by the improved performance that teams can achieve on all their future work. Retrospectives align with continuous improvement by triggering changes that target known sources of pain. When the management team is committed to ongoing capability improvement, they'll embrace retrospectives as a powerful tool toward that end.

Retrospectives are valuable when the culture invites, listens to, and acts upon candid feedback. The ritual of a retrospective brings a group of people together to view their shared experience from a wider point of view than any single participant can provide. As the group reflects on the work they just concluded, they can design a new way going forward that they expect will lead to a higher plateau of professional work. The ultimate sign of a successful retrospective is that it leads to sustained change. That's a lasting return on investment from the hours the team spends reflecting on past events.

Lesson 59	The most conspicuous repeatability the software industry has achieved is doing the same ineffective things over and over.

When I worked at Kodak, the company held an annual internal software quality conference. One year, I was invited to serve on the conference's planning committee. I asked to see their procedures book for how to plan and conduct the conference. The response was, "We don't have one."

I was floored. Of all the groups that I thought would know to accumulate procedures, checklists, and lessons learned from previous experience, a leadership team of quality and process improvement specialists was at the top of the list. Such a resource is especially valuable when you have a rotating cast of characters with limited continuity from year to year, as we did. Each year's planning team had to reconstruct how to plan and run the conference, filling in any gaps from scratch. How inefficient! (See Lesson 7, "The cost of recording knowledge is small compared to the cost of acquiring knowledge.") We started a procedures book the year that I served on the committee. I can only hope that the people who worked on subsequent conferences referred to that resource and kept it current.

This experience highlighted a phenomenon that's too common in the software industry: repeating the mistakes of the past, project after project (Brössler 2000, Glass 2003). (This is the point in the book where some authors would incorporate philosopher George Santayana's famous quotation, "Those who cannot remember the past are condemned to repeat it," but I'm not going to do that here.) We have countless collections of software industry best practices and books of lessons learned on various topics—including this one. There's a vast body of literature on all aspects of software engineering and project management. Nonetheless, many projects continue to get into trouble because they don't practice some of the activities that we know contribute to project success.

The Merits of Learning

The Standish Group has published its CHAOS report every few years since 1994. (CHAOS is not a description but an aptly crafted acronym for the Comprehensive Human Appraisal for Originating Software.) Based on data from thousands of projects, CHAOS reports indicate the percentages of recent projects that were fully successful, were challenged in some way, or failed. Success is defined as a combination of being completed approximately on time and on budget and delivering customer and user satisfaction (The Standish Group 2015). The CHAOS report results have varied over the years, but the fraction of fully successful projects still struggles to exceed 40 percent. Perhaps more discouragingly, some of the same factors contribute to challenged and failed projects year after year.

Observing patterns of results is one pathway that leads to new paradigms for doing work. For instance, analysis paralysis and requirements that become obsolete on long-term projects helped motivate a push toward incremental development. Some CHAOS report data indicates that agile projects have a higher average success rate than waterfall projects (The Standish Group 2015).

There's a vast gulf between being a small-scale programmer and being a proficient software engineer.

Software development is unlike other technical fields in that it's possible to do useful work with minimal formal education and background, at least up to a point. No one's going to ask an amateur physician to remove their appendix, but many amateur programmers know enough to write small apps. However, there's a vast gulf between being a small-scale programmer and being a proficient software engineer capable of executing large and complex projects by collaborating with others.

Many young professionals enter the industry today through an academic program in computer science, software engineering, information technology, or a related field. Whether formally educated or self-taught, every software professional should continue to absorb the ever-growing body of knowledge and learn how to apply it effectively. Many facets of the software domain change quickly. Keeping up with the current technologies can feel like running on a treadmill. Fortunately, insights like those I've collected here are durable over time.

Every software organization accumulates an informal collection of local, experience-based knowledge. Rather than passing folklore around the campfire in an oral tradition, I suggest that organizations record that painfully gained knowledge in a lessons-learned collection (Wiegers 2007). Prudent project managers and software developers will refer to this collected wisdom when they're launching a new endeavor.

The Merits of Thinking

When I was a research scientist early in my career, I knew a fellow scientist named Amanda. When Amanda began a new research project, I would sometimes find her leaning back in her office chair, staring at the ceiling. She was thinking. Amanda diligently studied the company's internal technical literature about similar projects. She learned all she could about the problem domain and approaches that had—and had not—worked in the past before she began doing experiments. Amanda's experiments were time consuming and expensive; she didn't want to go off in the wrong direction. Her study of previous research made her a highly efficient scientist. Observing Amanda reinforced the importance of learning from history, both across the industry and from local experience, before diving headlong into a new project.

This chapter is about software process improvement. Individuals, project teams, and organizations all need to enhance their software engineering and management skills continuously. The initial goal of five-level process maturity models was to establish processes that could lead to repeatable success from project to project and from one team to another. Regardless of the specific methodology or framework an organization chooses to structure its improvement efforts, I'm confident that every software development organization wants to be repeatedly successful.

Next Steps: Software Process Improvement

1. Identify which of the lessons described in this chapter are relevant to your experiences with software process improvement.

2. Can you think of any other lessons related to SPI from your own experience that are worth sharing with your colleagues?

3. Identify three of your greatest points of pain and conduct root cause analyses to reveal factors toward which you can direct some initial improvement activities.

4. Identify any practices described in this chapter that might be solutions to the process improvement problems you identified in the First Steps at the beginning of the chapter. How could each practice improve your project teams' efficiency and effectiveness?

5. How could you tell whether each practice from Step 4 was yielding the desired results? What would those results be worth to you?

6. Identify any barriers that might make it difficult to apply the practices from Step 4. How could you break down those barriers or enlist allies to help you implement the practices effectively?

7. What training, materials, guidance, or other resources would help your organization pursue its process improvement activities more successfully?

Chapter 8

What to Do Next

We've covered a lot of ground up to this point. I've shared with you fifty-nine lessons about software engineering and project management that I've accumulated since I began programming five decades ago. These lessons fall into six domains: requirements, design, project management, culture and teamwork, quality, and process improvement. There are certainly other vital aspects of software development that I haven't addressed here, including coding, testing, and configuration management. Now I have just one question for you:

What are you going to do differently after reading this book?

If you worked through the First Steps and Next Steps in each chapter, you should have a list of your project team's or organization's issues in those six domains. Perhaps you analyzed each problem to understand its root causes and impacts. You might have identified the benefits that addressing those issues could provide. I hope you've written down many ideas of practices that could address those issues and add value for your projects and your products' customers.

Whenever someone undertakes a learning experience but doesn't do anything differently, they get no value from their learning investment. I want you to get a high return from the time you invested in reading this book. That means you need to select your next actions. As we work through some thoughts about how to do that, keep one final lesson in mind.

| Lesson 60 | You can't change everything at once. |

No matter how many points of pain, improvement ideas, or desirable destinations you identify, people and organizations can absorb change at only a limited rate. I knew a highly motivated, twenty-person project team that tackled seven major improvement activities simultaneously. Priorities weren't clear; resources were spread thin. Despite their enthusiasm, this team accomplished little on their change journey. Also, changing too many things simultaneously—a multivariable experiment—makes it hard to tell what alteration produced the observed outcome.

All individuals have the power to improve their results at their own pace. However, a management-imposed, large-scale change initiative can overwhelm those affected. Attempting to change too much at once can make it hard for people to get their project work done as they try to understand and conform to the new direction. It's easier to manage the rate of change with a bottom-up improvement initiative.

Although grassroots efforts can work well at the team level, they hit a ceiling beyond which it's hard to influence related groups without management assistance. As Mary Lynn Manns and Linda Rising (2005) explain in their book *Fearless Change*:

> The emphasis in bottom-up change is on participation and on keeping people informed about what is going on, so uncertainty and resistance are minimized. Based on our experience, we believe that change is best introduced bottom-up with support at appropriate points from management—both local and at a higher level.

As with personal growth, software process improvement is a journey, not a destination. It's a cycle, not a straight line. There are many ways to depict a change cycle. Perhaps the best known is quality improvement pioneer Dr. W. Edwards Deming's Plan-Do-Check-Act, also known as the Shewhart Cycle (Praxis 2019, American Society for Quality 2021d). Figure 8.1 shows a similar improvement cycle that I prefer over Deming's.

Step 1: Assess. Take stock of where you are today—the results your projects currently achieve and how well things go. Identify the biggest problem areas and greatest improvement opportunities. Completing the First Steps in the preceding six chapters constitutes an informal assessment activity.

Step 2: Plan. Decide where you'd like to be in the future—your objectives for both business and technical improvements. Map out a plan to get from here to there. The Next Steps in this book suggest some starting points for charting your course to a more desirable future.

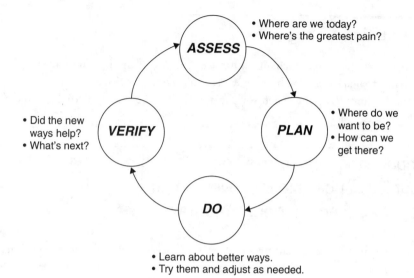

Figure 8.1 *A typical process improvement cycle has four steps: assess, plan, do, and verify.*

Step 3: Do. Now comes the difficult part: doing something different. You'll need to learn about practices and methods that could yield better results, try them out in pilot activities with a receptive team, and adjust to make them work in your environment. Keep what works and modify, replace, or discard that which does not.

Step 4: Verify. Allow the new techniques to take hold, and then check to see whether they're providing the results you hoped for. It takes time to change direction; have patience. The learning curve is unavoidable. Better business outcomes are a long-term, but lagging, indicator of how well your project approaches work. Try to define some interim metrics that could indicate whether whatever you're trying seems to be paying off.

Remember, change is a cycle. There will always be something else to work on. Return to the assessment step at the end of each cycle to examine your new situation and then select the next round of change activities.

Software process improvement is a journey, not a destination. It's a cycle, not a straight line.

Prioritizing Changes

Focus is a keyword in any change initiative. You might think of more changes that you'd like to make than you have time for. You need to prioritize to focus your energy for the maximum benefit. Then you must carve out the time to actually implement each change.

> Choose the most pressing issues from your list of possible improvement areas and begin working on them tomorrow.

There's never a convenient time to work on process or quality improvement activities. Unless you deliberately set time aside, there will never be idle periods when nothing else is going on. But if you don't take the first steps to make changes—as individuals and as organizations—you won't make progress. Everyone should spend some fraction of their time learning how to boost their performance. Choose the most pressing issues from your list of possible improvement areas and begin working on them tomorrow. I'm serious: tomorrow!

Revisit your notes from the First Steps and Next Steps in each chapter of this book. Where would it be most rewarding to see some improvement, to reduce unpleasant outcomes? What changes could deliver the greatest business value for your organization? Which changes seem to be the most achievable with a reasonable investment of energy and money?

Once you've identified the top problem areas, you'll need to select possible solutions that have a high chance of paying off. The dozens of practices described in this book offer some ideas. I've provided many references to other sources where you can learn more about those practices that appear promising. As you prioritize your actions based on their importance, urgency, and cost, begin by addressing changes you can make quickly or those that will have the biggest impact soon. Look for the low-hanging fruit, the quick successes—and celebrate those successes. It's motivating when the team sees that they're making progress and beginning to reap the benefits. It proves that change is possible in their world.

Reality Check

As you consider actions that you think will yield better results, keep in mind a philosophy I adopted as a consultant. Before I give a client advice, I run a little mental check to confirm that the action I'm proposing satisfies two criteria.

1. It must have a high probability of solving the client's problem.

2. It must be practical and achievable in the client's environment.

This reality check ensures that I'm giving sensible advice, not suggesting something that's inappropriate for the client's projects or culture. I suggest you apply that same filter to any changes you recommend for yourself or your organization.

Think about which changes the organization might be ready to accept and which ones should await some cultural or technical evolution before tackling them. Chapter 5 points out some characteristics of both healthy and less-healthy software engineering cultures. Because cultural change takes longer than implementing new technical practices, leaders should start steering the culture in the preferred direction early on. That will lay the foundation for teams to absorb larger transitions later.

I suggest you take a systematic approach, even at the personal level. When I began a new development project, I would always identify two areas of software engineering or project management in which I wanted to improve. It could be unit testing, estimation, algorithm design, peer reviews, build management, or anything else. As I worked on each project, I would allocate part of my time to reading about my chosen topics. I might take a training course or attend a conference. I would hunt for opportunities to apply what I'd learned, recognizing that it would take some effort to determine how to make it work effectively. I do the same thing now with my hobby of recording songs. With each song, I try to learn more about playing something on the guitar, recording and production techniques, and using the vast array of features in my recording software. That way, each song I produce is a bit better than the previous one.

Recall from Lesson 55, "You don't have time to make each mistake that every practitioner before you has already made," that the learning curve isn't a smooth, continuous transition. You'll experience ups and downs as you wrestle with the topic. But you'll get there.

Action Planning

Change doesn't happen by itself. Prioritizing issues and selecting improvement actions aren't enough. If you're serious about change, you must treat it as a project with goals, plans, resources, status tracking, and accountability. Depending on the scope of the change you're exploring, you can create action plans for yourself, the project team, or the organization as a whole. Anyone who's responsible for leading an organization-wide improvement initiative would find the book *Making Process Improvement Work* helpful (Potter and Sakry 2002). Simpler—yet still structured—approaches work well at the individual and team levels.

Figure 8.2 shows a simple action-planning template. Look into the future just one week, about a month, and about six months. List the new technical or management practices you want to try in each of those time frames. Describe the situation you think you could apply them to and the benefits you're looking for. Perhaps you'll need more resources to help you learn how to apply these new practices, such as training, tools, books, or consulting assistance. Some practices apply only to your personal work, but others affect multiple communities, so consider whose cooperation you'll need for each change. It's also helpful to consider barriers that might stand in the way of successfully implementing something new. Then try to identify allies who could help break down those barriers.

	Next Week	Next Month	In Six Months
New practices to try			
Situation you might apply them to			
Benefits you hope to gain			
Help or additional information you might need			
Whose cooperation you might need			
Barriers that might prevent you from succeeding			
Who could break down those barriers			

Figure 8.2 *A simple action-planning template helps you plan improvement actions for the near-term, mid-term, and longer-term time frames.*

Doing some planning greatly increases the chance that you can implement changes successfully. There's a trap to watch out for, though. Look back at the change cycle in Figure 8.1: Assess, Plan, Do, Verify. I've seen too many organizations do a thorough job of assessing their current reality, targeting an improved future state, and planning how to get there, only to stall out at the Do step. That's the hardest part, forcing yourself away from project work to implement items from your action plan and carry them through to completion. Regardless of one's good intentions, improvement action plans that don't turn into actions aren't useful. So, beware of the temptation to take the easy path of continuing to work the way you and your team members always have. That's not a route to better business results.

Your Own Lessons

Every seasoned software professional has accumulated a set of lessons from their experience. This book contains many learnings I have gathered; I'm sure you have your own beyond these. Consider having your team put their heads together and pool their key insights along the lines of this book's lessons. Think about how you could share those lessons across your organization to accelerate everyone's learning process. Your next step would be to choose practices based on those collected lessons that could give your team better results.

Building a learning, improving organization begins with individuals who have internalized the value of gleaning pearls of wisdom from their experience and sharing them with others. I hope you'll take this opportunity to put into action selected bits of what you've read here. Invite your teammates to join you. It might be a fun journey.

Appendix

Summary of Lessons

Requirements

#1. If you don't get the requirements right, it doesn't matter how well you execute the rest of the project.

#2. The key deliverables from requirements development are a shared vision and understanding.

#3. Nowhere more than in the requirements do the interests of all the project stakeholders intersect.

#4. A usage-centric approach to requirements will meet customer needs better than a feature-centric approach.

#5. Requirements development demands iteration.

#6. Agile requirements aren't different from other requirements.

#7. The cost of recording knowledge is small compared to the cost of acquiring knowledge.

#8. The overarching objective of requirements development is clear and effective communication.

#9. Requirements quality is in the eye of the beholder.

#10. Requirements must be good enough to let construction proceed at an acceptable level of risk.

#11. People don't simply gather requirements.

#12. Requirements elicitation must bring the customer's voice close to the developer's ear.

#13. Two commonly used requirements elicitation practices are telepathy and clairvoyance. They don't work.

#14. A large group of people can't agree to leave a burning room, let alone agree on exactly how to word some requirement.

#15. Avoid decibel prioritization when deciding which features to include.

#16. Without a documented and agreed-to project scope, how do you know whether your scope is creeping?

Design

#17. Design demands iteration.

#18. It's cheaper to iterate at higher levels of abstraction.

#19. Make products easy to use correctly and hard to use incorrectly.

#20. You can't optimize all desirable quality attributes.

#21. An ounce of design is worth a pound of recoding.

#22. Many system problems take place at interfaces.

Project Management

#23. Work plans must account for friction.

#24. Don't give anyone an estimate off the top of your head.

#25. Icebergs are always larger than they first appear.

#26. You're in a stronger negotiating position when you have data to build your case.

#27. Unless you record estimates and compare them to what actually happened, you will forever be guessing, not estimating.

#28. Don't change an estimate based on what the recipient wants to hear.

#29. Stay off the critical path.

#30. A task is either entirely done or it is not done: no partial credit.

#31. The project team needs flexibility around at least one of the five dimensions of scope, schedule, budget, staff, and quality.

#32. If you don't control your project's risks, they will control you.

#33. The customer is not always right.

#34. We do too much pretending in software.

Culture and Teamwork

#35. Knowledge is not zero-sum.

#36. No matter how much pressure others exert, never make a commitment you know you can't fulfill.

#37. Without training and better practices, don't expect higher productivity to happen by magic.

#38. People talk a lot about their rights, but the flip side of every right is a responsibility.

#39. It takes little physical separation to inhibit communication and collaboration.

#40. Informal approaches that work for a small colocated team don't scale up well.

#41. Don't underestimate the challenge of changing an organization's culture as it moves toward new ways of working.

#42. No engineering or management technique will work if you're dealing with unreasonable people.

Quality

#43. When it comes to software quality, you can pay now or pay more later.

#44. High quality naturally leads to higher productivity.

#45. Organizations never have time to build software right, yet they find the resources to fix it later.

#46. Beware the crap gap.

#47. Never let your boss or your customer talk you into doing a bad job.

#48. Strive to have a peer, rather than a customer, find a defect.

#49. Software people love tools, but a fool with a tool is an amplified fool.

#50. Today's "gotta get it out right away" development project is tomorrow's maintenance nightmare.

Process Improvement

#51. Watch out for "Management by Businessweek."

#52. Ask not, "What's in it for me?" Ask, "What's in it for us?"

#53. The best motivation for changing how people work is pain.

#54. When steering an organization toward new ways of working, use gentle pressure, relentlessly applied.

#55. You don't have time to make each mistake that every practitioner before you has already made.

#56. Good judgment and experience sometimes trump a defined process.

#57. Adopt a shrink-to-fit philosophy with document templates.

#58. Unless you take the time to learn and improve, don't expect the next project to go any better than the last one.

#59. The most conspicuous repeatability the software industry has achieved is doing the same ineffective things over and over.

General

#60. You can't change everything at once.

References

Achimugu, Philip, Ali Selamat, Roliana Ibrahim, and Mohd Naz'ri Mahrin. 2014. "A systematic literature review of software requirements prioritization research." *Information and Software Technology* **56**(6):568–585.

ACM. 1999. "The Software Engineering Code of Ethics and Professional Practice." Association for Computing Machinery and IEEE Computer Society. https://ethics.acm.org/code-of-ethics/software-engineering-code.

Ageling, Willem-Jan. 2020. "Here's Why Many Developers Hate Scrum." https://medium.com/serious-scrum/here-is-why-many-developers-hate-scrum-3a43baa015d1.

Agile Alliance. 2021a. "Definition of Done." https://www.agilealliance.org/glossary/definition-of-done.

_____. 2021b. "Acceptance Testing." https://www.agilealliance.org/glossary/acceptance.

_____. 2021c. "12 Principles Behind the Agile Manifesto." https://www.agilealliance.org/agile101/12-principles-behind-the-agile-manifesto.

Agile Alliance, Jutta Eckstein, and John Buck. 2021. "Changing the Culture by Changing Habits." https://www.agilealliance.org/changing-the-culture-by-changing-habits.

Aleshire, Peter. 2004. *Eye of the Viper: The Making of an F-16 Pilot*. Guilford, CT: Lyons Press.

Ambler, Scott W. 2005. *The Elements of UML™ 2.0 Style*. New York: Cambridge University Press.

_____. 2006. "Why Agile Software Development Techniques Work: Improved Feedback." https://www.ambysoft.com/essays/whyAgileWorksFeedback.html.

American Society for Quality. 2021a. "Quality Glossary - Q." https://asq.org/quality-resources/quality-glossary/q.

_____. 2021b. "Joseph M. Juran." https://asq.org/about-asq/honorary-members/juran.

_____. 2021c. "Cost of Quality (COQ)." https://asq.org/quality-resources/cost-of-quality.

_____. 2021d. "What Is the Plan-Do-Check-Act (PDCA) Cycle?" https://asq.org/quality-resources/pdca-cycle.

Atwood, Jeff. 2006. "The Programmer's Bill of Rights." https://blog.codinghorror.com/the-programmers-bill-of-rights.

Bakker, Jeffrey. 2020. "Top lessons learned from working with a 10x developer." https://levelup.gitconnected.com/top-lessons-learned-from-working-with-a-10x-developer-51de12383e25.

Barlas, Stephen. 1996. "Anatomy of a Runaway: What Grounded the AAS." *IEEE Software* **13**(1):104–106.

Beatty, Joy, and Anthony Chen. 2012. *Visual Models for Software Requirements.* Redmond, WA: Microsoft Press.

Beck, Kent, et al. 2001. "Manifesto for Agile Software Development." https://agile-manifesto.org.

Beck, Kent. 2003. *Test-Driven Development: By Example.* Boston: Addison-Wesley.

Beck, Kent, and Cynthia Andres. 2005. *Extreme Programming Explained: Embrace Change,* 2nd Ed. Boston: Addison-Wesley.

Bentley, Jon. 2000. *Programming Pearls*, 2nd Ed. Boston: Addison-Wesley.

Booch, Grady, James Rumbaugh, and Ivar Jacobson. 1999. *The Unified Modeling Language User Guide.* Reading, MA: Addison-Wesley.

Bright Hub PM. 2009. "Various Kinds of Risks Associated with Software Project Management." https://www.brighthubpm.com/risk-management/47932-risks-involved-in-software-project-management.

Briski, Kari Ann, Poonam Chitale, Valerie Hamilton, Allan Pratt, Brian Starr, Jim Veroulis, and Bruce Villard. 2008. "Minimizing code defects to improve software quality and lower development costs." IBM Development Solutions Whitepaper. ftp://ftp.software.ibm.com/software/rational/info/do-more/RAW14109USEN.pdf.

Brooks Jr., Frederick P. 1995. *The Mythical Man-Month: Essays on Software Engineering, Anniversary Edition.* Reading, MA: Addison-Wesley.

Brosseau, Jim. 2008. *Software Teamwork: Taking Ownership for Success.* Boston: Addison-Wesley.

Brössler, Peter. 2000. "Knowledge management at a software house: An experience report." In: Ruhe G., Bomarius F. (eds) Learning Software Organizations. SEKE 1999. Lecture Notes in Computer Science, vol 1756. Springer, Berlin, Heidelberg. https://doi.org/10.1007/BFb0101419.

Charette, Robert N. 1996. "Large-Scale Project Management *Is* Risk Management." *IEEE Software* **13**(4):110–117.

———. 2005. "Why Software Fails." *IEEE Spectrum.* **42**(9):42–49. https://spectrum.ieee.org/computing/software/why-software-fails.

Chrissis, Mary Beth, Mike Konrad, and Sandy Shrum. 2003. *CMMI: Guidelines for Process Integration and Product Improvement.* Boston: Addison-Wesley.

CMMI Institute. 2017. "Published Appraisal Results." https://cmmiinstitute.com/pars.

Cohen, Esther. 2018. "How to Use the Critical Path Method for Complete Beginners." https://www.workamajig.com/blog/critical-path-method.

Cohn, Mike. 2004. *User Stories Applied: For Agile Software Development*. Boston: Addison-Wesley.

_____. 2006. *Agile Estimating and Planning*. Boston: Addison-Wesley.

_____. 2010. *Succeeding with Agile: Software Development Using Scrum*. Boston: Addison-Wesley.

_____. 2014. "Know Exactly What Velocity Means to Your Scrum Team." https://www.mountaingoatsoftware.com/blog/know-exactly-what-velocity-means-to-your-scrum-team.

Coleman, Ben, and Dan Goodwin. 2017. *Designing UX: Prototyping*. Collingwood, VIC, Australia: SitePoint Pty. Ltd.

Colorado State University. n.d. "Survey Research." https://writing.colostate.edu/guides/guide.cfm?guideid=68.

Constantine, Larry L., and Lucy A.D. Lockwood. 1999. *Software for Use: A Practical Guide to the Models and Methods of Usage-Centered Design*. Reading, MA: Addison-Wesley.

Construx. 2010. "Individual Productivity Variation in Software Development." https://www.construx.com/blog/productivity-variations-among-software-developers-and-teams-the-origin-of-10x.

Cooper, Alan, Robert Reimann, David Cronin, and Christopher Noessel. 2014. *About Face: The Essentials of Interaction Design*, 4th Ed. Indianapolis: John Wiley & Sons, Inc.

Costello, Katie. 2019. "The Secret to DevOps Success." Gartner. https://www.gartner.com/smarterwithgartner/the-secret-to-devops-success.

Covey, Stephen R. 2020. *The 7 Habits of Highly Effective People, 25th Anniversary Edition*. New York: Simon & Schuster.

Crosby, Philip B. 1979. *Quality Is Free: The Art of Making Quality Certain*. New York: McGraw-Hill.

Cunningham, Ward. 1992. "The WyCash Portfolio Management System." OOPSLA '92 Experience Report. http://c2.com/doc/oopsla92.html.

Datt, Priyanka. 2020a. "Difference Between Product Owner & Business Analyst Role." https://premieragile.com/difference-between-product-owner-and-business-analyst.

_____. 2020b. "What is the Definition of Done (DoD) in Agile?" https://premieragile.com/definition-of-done-in-agile.

Davis, Alan M. 1995. *201 Principles of Software Development*. New York: McGraw-Hill.

_____. 2005. *Just Enough Requirements Management: Where Software Development Meets Marketing*. New York: Dorset House Publishing.

DeMarco, Tom. 1979. *Structured Analysis and System Specification*. Upper Saddle River, NJ: Yourdon Press.

_____. 2001. *Slack: Getting Past Burnout, Busywork, and the Myth of Total Efficiency*. New York: Broadway Books.

DeMarco, Tom, and Timothy Lister. 2003. *Waltzing with Bears: Managing Risk on Software Projects*. New York: Dorset House Publishing.

_____. 2013. *Peopleware: Productive Projects and Teams*, 3rd Ed. Boston: Addison-Wesley.

Derby, Esther, and Diana Larsen. 2006. *Agile Retrospectives: Making Good Teams Great*. Pragmatic Bookshelf.

DOT. 1998. "Audit Report: Advance Automation System, Federal Aviation Administration Report Number AV-1998-113." Washington, DC: Office of Inspector General, U.S. Department of Transportation.

Feldmann, Clarence G. 1998. *The Practical Guide to Business Process Reengineering Using IDEF0*. New York: Dorset House Publishing.

Fisher, Roger, William Ury, and Bruce Patton. 2011. *Getting to Yes: Negotiating Agreement Without Giving In*, 3rd Ed. New York: Penguin Books.

~~Foord, Michael. 2017. "30 best practices for software development and testing."~~ https://opensource.com/article/17/5/30-best-practices-software-development-and-testing.

Gamma, Erich, Richard Helm, Ralph Johnson, and John Vlissides. 1995. *Design Patterns: Elements of Reusable Object-Oriented Software*. Reading, MA: Addison-Wesley.

Gilb, Tom. 2005. *Competitive Engineering: A Handbook for Systems Engineering, Requirements Engineering, and Software Engineering Using Planguage*. Oxford, England: Elsevier Butterworth-Heinemann.

Gilb, Tom, and Dorothy Graham. 1993. *Software Inspection*. Reading, MA: Addison-Wesley.

Glass, Robert L. 2003. *Facts and Fallacies of Software Engineering*. Boston: Addison-Wesley.

Goldratt, Eliyahu M. 1997. *Critical Chain*. Great Barrington, MA: The North River Press.

Gottesdiener, Ellen. 2002. *Requirements by Collaboration: Workshops for Defining Needs*. Boston: Addison-Wesley.

Grady, Robert B. 1999. "An Economic Release Decision Model: Insights into Software Project Management." In *Proceedings of the Applications of Software Measurement Conference*, 227–239. Orange Park, FL: Software Quality Engineering.

Grady, Robert B., and Tom Van Slack. 1994. "Key Lessons in Achieving Widespread Inspection Use." *IEEE Software* **11**(4):46–57.

Gray, Mark. 2020. "Is the Way You Use Burndown Charts Helping or Holding You Back?" https://medium.com/better-programming/the-definitive-guide-to-burndown-charts-a176db096294.

Hasan, Mohammad Shabbir, Abdullah Al Mahmood, Md. Jahangir Alam, Sk. Md. Nahid Hasan, and Farin Rahman. 2010. "An Evaluation of Software Requirement Prioritization Techniques." *International Journal of Computer Science and Information Security* **8**(9):83–94.

Haskins, B., J. Stecklein, D. Brandon, G. Moroney, R. Lovell, and J. Dabney. 2004. "Error Cost Escalation through the Project Life Cycle." In *Proceedings of the 14th Annual International Symposium of INCOSE*, 1723–1737. Toulouse, France. International Council on Systems Engineering.

Hatch, Nan. 2019. "10 Critical Culture Change Elements in Agile Transformation." https://www.insight.com/en_US/content-and-resources/blog/10-critical-culture-change-elements-in-agile-transformation.html.

Hilliard, Andy. 2018. "A Look At Software Development Culture." https://www.accelerance.com/blog/software-development-culture.

Holland, Dick. 1999. "Document Inspection as an Agent of Change." *Software Quality Professional* **2**(1):22–33.

Hossain, Md. Shahadat. 2018. "Rework and Reuse Effects in Software Economy." *Global Journal of Computer Science and Technology (C): Software & Data Engineering* **18**(4-C):35–50. https://globaljournals.org/GJCST_Volume18/5-Rework-and-Reuse-Effects.pdf.

IIBA. 2015. *A Guide to the Business Analysis Body of Knowledge (BABOK Guide)*, 3rd Ed. Toronto, ON, Canada: International Institute of Business Analysis.

ISO/IEC. 2011. *ISO/IEC 25010:2011(en) Systems and software engineering—Systems and software Quality Requirements and Evaluation (SQuaRE)—System and software quality models.* https://www.iso.org/obp/ui/#iso:std:iso-iec:25010:ed-1:v1:en.

ISO/IEC/IEEE. 2018. *ISO/IEC/IEEE 29148:2018 Systems and software engineering—Life cycle processes—Requirements engineering.* https://www.iso.org/standard/72089.html.

Jones, Capers. 1994. *Assessment and Control of Software Risks.* Upper Saddle River, NJ: Yourdon Press.

_____. 2006. "Social and Technical Reasons for Software Project Failures." *Cross-Talk* **19**(6):4–9. https://apps.dtic.mil/dtic/tr/fulltext/u2/a487371.pdf.

Juran. 2019. "Features of Quality & Definition of Quality Excellence." https://www.juran.com/blog/features-of-quality-definition-of-quality-excellence.

Kaley, Anna. 2021. "Mapping User Stories in Agile." https://www.nngroup.com/articles/user-story-mapping.

Kaner, Cem, James Bach, and Bret Pettichord. 2002. *Lessons Learned in Software Testing: A Context-Driven Approach.* New York: John Wiley & Sons.

Karten, Naomi. 1994. *Managing Expectations: Working with People Who Want More, Better, Faster, Sooner, NOW!* New York: Dorset House Publishing.

Kerievsky, Joshua. 2005. *Refactoring to Patterns*. Boston: Addison-Wesley.

Kerth, Norman L. 2001. *Project Retrospectives: A Handbook for Team Reviews*. New York: Dorset House Publishing.

Klement, Alan. 2013. "Replacing The User Story With the Job Story." https://jtbd.info/replacing-the-user-story-with-the-job-story-af7cdee10c27.

Koopman, Philip. 2010. *Better Embedded System Software*. Pittsburgh: Drumnadrochit Press.

Krasner, Herb. 2018. "The Cost of Poor Quality Software in the US: A 2018 Report." Consortium for IT Software Quality. https://www.it-cisq.org/the-cost-of-poor-quality-software-in-the-us-a-2018-report/The-Cost-of-Poor-Quality-Software-in-the-US-2018-Report.pdf.

Kukreja, Nupul, Barry Boehm, Sheetal Swaroop Payyavula, and Srinivas Padmanabhuni. 2012. "Selecting an Appropriate Framework for Value-Based Requirements Prioritization." In *Proceedings of the 2012 20th IEEE International Requirements Engineering Conference*, 303–308. Los Alamitos, CA: IEEE Computer Society Press.

Kulak, Daryl, and Eamonn Guiney. 2004. *Use Cases: Requirements in Context*, 2nd Ed. Boston: Addison-Wesley.

Larman, Craig. 2004. *Agile and Iterative Development: A Manager's Guide*. Boston: Addison-Wesley.

Leffingwell, Dean. 2011. *Agile Software Requirements: Lean Requirements Practices for Teams, Programs, and the Enterprise*. Boston: Addison-Wesley.

Leonard, Andrew. 2020. "Committing to collaboration." https://increment.com/remote/committing-to-collaboration-version-control.

Löwe, Nils. 2015. "Our Responsibility as Software Developers." https://www.infoq.com/articles/Responsible-Software-Development.

Lucidchart. 2021. "How to perform a stakeholder analysis." https://www.lucidchart.com/blog/how-to-do-a-stakeholder-analysis.

MacKay, Jory. 2021. "Context switching: Why jumping between tasks is killing your productivity (and what you can do about it)." https://blog.rescuetime.com/context-switching.

Mancuso, Sandro. 2016. "Cohesion—The cornerstone of Software Design." https://www.codurance.com/publications/software-creation/2016/03/03/cohesion-cornerstone-software-design.

Manns, Mary Lynn, and Linda Rising. 2005. *Fearless Change: Patterns for Introducing New Ideas*. Boston: Addison-Wesley.

Marasco, Joe. 2007. "What Is the Cost of a Requirement Error?" https://www.stickyminds.com/article/what-cost-requirement-error.

Mathieson, SA. 2019. "How diversity spurs creativity in software development." https://www.computerweekly.com/feature/How-diversity-spurs-creativity-in-software-development.

McAllister, David. 2017. "Software Waste & The Cost of Rework." https://www.linkedin.com/pulse/software-waste-cost-rework-david-mcallister.

McConnell, Steve. 1996. *Rapid Development: Taming Wild Software Schedules.* Redmond, WA: Microsoft Press.

_____. 2004. *Code Complete: A Practical Handbook of Software Construction,* 2nd Ed. Redmond, WA: Microsoft Press.

_____. 2006. *Software Estimation: Demystifying the Black Art.* Redmond, WA: Microsoft Press.

_____. 2010. "Origins of 10X—How Valid is the Underlying Research?" https://www.construx.com/blog/the-origins-of-10x-how-valid-is-the-underlying-research.

McGreal, Don, and Ralph Jocham. 2018. *The Professional Product Owner: Leveraging Scrum as a Competitive Advantage.* Boston: Addison-Wesley.

McMenamin, Steve, Tom DeMarco, Peter Hruschka, Tim Lister, James Robertson, and Suzanne Robertson. 2021. *Happy to Work Here: Understanding and Improving the Culture at Work.* New Atlantic.

McPeak, Alex. 2017. "What's the True Cost of a Software Bug?" https://smartbear.com/blog/software-bug-cost.

Merrill, Cache. 2019. "Software Maintenance: Understanding the 4 Main Types." https://www.zibtek.com/blog/software-maintenance-understanding-the-4-main-types.

Microsoft. 2017. "SQL Injection." https://docs.microsoft.com/en-us/sql/relational-databases/security/sql-injection.

Miller, Roxanne E. 2009. *The Quest for Software Requirements.* Milwaukee: Maven-Mark Books.

Minott, Zachary. 2020. "How I Outperformed More Experienced Developers as a Junior Developer (and How You Can Too)." https://medium.com/better-programming/how-i-outperformed-more-experienced-developers-as-a-junior-developer-and-how-you-can-too-19bc6206fa68.

Moore, Geoffrey A. 2014. *Crossing the Chasm: Marketing and Selling Disruptive Products to Mainstream Customers,* 3rd Ed. New York: HarperBusiness.

Musa, J.D. 1993. "Operational profiles in software-reliability engineering." *IEEE Software* **10**(2):14–32.

Nagappan, Raj. 2020a. "Moving beyond user story templates." https://uxdesign.cc/moving-beyond-user-story-templates-79a421c6445c.

_____. 2020b. "The iron triangle and Agile." https://uxdesign.cc/the-iron-triangle-and-agile-7b66d3c72a51.

Nichols, Bill. 2020. "Programmer Moneyball: Challenging the Myth of Individual Programmer Productivity." https://insights.sei.cmu.edu/sei_blog/2020/01/programmer-moneyball-challenging-the-myth-of-individual-programmer-productivity.html.

Nielsen, Jakob. 2020. "10 Usability Heuristics for User Interface Design." https://www.nngroup.com/articles/ten-usability-heuristics.

NIST. 2002. "Planning Report 02-3. The Economic Impacts of Inadequate Infrastructure for Software Testing." National Institute of Standards & Technology. https://www.nist.gov/system/files/documents/director/planning/report02-3.pdf.

Nussbaum, Hillary. 2020. "Rework is Costing Your Company Millions—It's Time to Cut Back." https://codeclimate.com/blog/rework-costs-millions.

Page-Jones, Meilir. 1988. *The Practical Guide to Structured Systems Design*, 2nd Ed. Englewood Cliffs, NJ: Prentice Hall.

_____. 2000. *Fundamentals of Object-Oriented Design in UML*. Boston: Addison-Wesley.

Paulk, Mark C., Charles V. Weber, Bill Curtis, and Mary Beth Chrissis. 1995. *The Capability Maturity Model: Guidelines for Improving the Software Process*. Reading, MA: Addison-Wesley.

Pearls of Wisdom. 2014a. "PEARL XIX: Effective steps to reduce technical debt: An agile approach." https://agilepearls.wordpress.com/tag/technical-debt.

_____. 2014b. "PEARL XXIII: Guidelines for Successful and Effective Retrospectives." https://agilepearls.wordpress.com/2014/05/23/pearl-xxii-guidelines-for-successful-and-effective-retrospectives.

PMI. n.d. "What is Project Management?" Project Management Institute. https://www.pmi.org/about/learn-about-pmi/what-is-project-management.

_____. 2017. "PMI's Pulse of the Profession 2017: 9th Global Project Management Survey." http://www.pmi.org/-/media/pmi/documents/public/pdf/learning/thought-leadership/pulse/pulse-of-the-profession-2017.pdf.

Podeswa, Howard. 2009. *The Business Analyst's Handbook*. Boston: Course Technology.

_____. 2021. *The Agile Guide to Business Analysis and Planning: From Strategic Plan to Continuous Value Delivery*. Boston: Addison-Wesley.

Potter, Neil, and Mary Sakry. 2002. *Making Process Improvement Work*. Boston: Addison-Wesley.

Praxis. 2019. "Shewhart cycle." https://www.praxisframework.org/en/library/shewhart-cycle.

Pronschinske, Mitch. 2017. "Lessons from 7 highly successful software engineering cultures." https://techbeacon.com/app-dev-testing/lessons-7-highly-successful-software-engineering-cultures.

Pugh, Ken. 2005. *Prefactoring: Extreme Abstraction, Extreme Separation, Extreme Readability.* Sebastopol, CA: O'Reilly Media, Inc.

_____. 2006. *Interface Oriented Design: With Patterns.* Pragmatic Bookshelf.

Radice, Ronald A. 2002. *High Quality Low Cost Software Inspections.* Andover, MA: Paradoxicon Publishing.

Resologics. 2021. "Team agreements: A key to high-performing, happy teams." https://www.resologics.com/resologics-blog/2017/7/12/team-agreements-a-key-to-high-performing-happy-teams.

Rettig, Marc. 1990. "Software Teams." *Communications of the ACM* **33**(10):23–27.

Rice, David. 2016. "How to Avoid Brittle Code." https://www.gocd.org/2016/03/24/how-to-avoid-brittle-code.

Robertson, Suzanne, and James Robertson. 2013. *Mastering the Requirements Process: Getting Requirements Right,* 3rd Ed. Boston: Addison-Wesley.

Rothman, Johanna. 1999. "How to Use Inch-Pebbles When You Think You Can't." https://www.jrothman.com/articles/1999/01/how-to-use-inch-pebbles-when-you-think-you-cant.

_____. 2000. "What Does It Cost You To Fix A Defect? And Why Should You Care?" https://www.jrothman.com/articles/2000/10/what-does-it-cost-you-to-fix-a-defect-and-why-should-you-care.

_____. 2004. "Using Inch-Pebbles to Track Project State." https://www.jrothman.com/articles/2004/02/using-inch-pebbles-to-track-project-state.

_____. 2012. "Management Myth #1: The Myth of 100% Utilization." https://www.jrothman.com/articles/2012/01/management-myth-1-the-myth-of-100-utilization.

Rozanski, Nick, and Eoin Woods. 2005. *Software Systems Architecture: Working with Stakeholders Using Viewpoints and Perspectives.* Boston: Addison-Wesley.

St. Augustine's College. n.d. "Rights and responsibilities of software developers." https://sddhsc.wordpress.com/hsc/9-1-development-and-impact-of-software-solutions/9-1-1-social-and-ethical-issues/rights-and-responsibilities-of-software-developers.

Sanket. 2019. "The exponential cost of fixing bugs." https://deepsource.io/blog/exponential-cost-of-fixing-bugs.

Sas, Darius, and Paris Avgeriou. 2020. "Quality attribute trade-offs in the embedded systems industry: an exploratory case study." *Software Quality Journal* **28**(2):505–534. https://doi.org/10.1007/s11219-019-09478-x.

Scaled Agile. 2021a. "Iteration Planning." https://www.scaledagileframework.com/iteration-planning.

_____. 2021b. "Agile Architecture in SAFe." https://www.scaledagileframework.com/agile-architecture.

_____. 2021c. "Nonfunctional Requirements." https://www.scaledagileframework.com/nonfunctional-requirements.

_____. 2021d. "Iteration Retrospective." https://www.scaledagileframework.com/iteration-retrospective.

Schwaber, Ken, and Jeff Sutherland. 2020. "The Scrum Guide: The Definitive Guide to Scrum: The Rules of the Game." https://www.scrumguides.org/docs/scrumguide/v2020/2020-Scrum-Guide-US.pdf.

SEI. 2020. "SEI CERT Coding Standards." https://wiki.sei.cmu.edu/confluence/display/seccode/SEI+CERT+Coding+Standards.

Senycia, Tristan. 2020. "8 Collaboration Tools You Need To Work With Remote Developers." https://youteam.io/blog/8-tools-you-need-to-work-with-remote-developers.

Shore, James. 2010. "The Art of Agile Development: The Planning Game." https://www.jamesshore.com/v2/books/aoad1/the_planning_game.

Simmons, Erik. 2001. "Quantifying Quality Requirements Using Planguage." http://understandingrequirements.com/resources/2.23%20%20Quantifying%20Quality%20Requirements.pdf.

Sliger, Michele. 2012. "Agile estimation techniques." Paper presented at PMI® Global Congress 2012—North America, Vancouver, BC, Canada. Newtown Square, PA: Project Management Institute. https://www.pmi.org/learning/library/agile-project-estimation-techniques-6110.

Soni, Vishal. 2020. "A Practical Prioritization Approach for Technical Debt." https://productcoalition.com/a-practical-prioritization-approach-for-technical-debt-f1eb31b8e409.

Spolsky, Joel. 2001. "Human Task Switches Considered Harmful." https://www.joelonsoftware.com/2001/02/12/human-task-switches-considered-harmful.

StackExchange. n.d. "The Programmers Bill of Responsibilities." https://softwareengineering.stackexchange.com/questions/29177/the-programmers-bill-of-responsibilities.

Stretton, Alan. 2018. "Relating causes of project failure to an organizational strategic business framework." *PM World Journal*, Vol VII, Issue I, January. https://pmworldlibrary.net/wp-content/uploads/2018/01/pmwj66-Jan2018-Stretton-relating-project-failures-to-strategic-framework-featured-paper.pdf.

The American Heritage Dictionary of the English Language. 2020. https://www.ahdictionary.com.

The Mann Group. 2019. "Gentle Pressure, Relentlessly Applied: Agreement on Approach." https://www.manngroup.net/gentle-pressure-relentlessly-applied-agreement-on-approach.

The Standish Group. 2014. "Exceeding Value." The Standish Group International, Inc. https://www.standishgroup.com/sample_research_files/Exceeding%20Value_Layout.pdf.

_____. 2015. "CHAOS Report 2015." The Standish Group International, Inc. https://standishgroup.com/sample_research_files/CHAOSReport2015-Final.pdf.

Thomas, Steven. 2008a. "Agile Project Scope." https://itsadeliverything.com/agile-project-scope.

_____. 2008b. "Agile Project Planning." https://itsadeliverything.com/agile-project-planning.

TutorialsPoint. 2021. "Software Design Basics." https://www.tutorialspoint.com/software_engineering/software_design_basics.htm.

280 Group. 2021. "Product Manager Roles and Responsibilities." https://280group.com/what-is-product-management/roles/product-manager.

Visual Paradigm. 2020. "Daily Scrum Meeting—A Quick Guide." https://www.visual-paradigm.com/scrum/daily-scrum-meeting-quick-guide.

Walker, Bryan, and Sarah A. Soule. 2017. "Changing Company Culture Requires a Movement, Not a Mandate." https://hbr.org/2017/06/changing-company-culture-requires-a-movement-not-a-mandate.

Weinberg, Gerald. 2012. "Agile and the Definition of Quality." https://secretsofconsulting.blogspot.com/2012/09/agile-and-definition-of-quality.html.

Weinberger, Matt. 2019. "Where Are They Now? What happened to the people in Microsoft's iconic 1978 company photo." https://www.businessinsider.com/microsoft-1978-photo-2016-10.

Wiegers, Karl E. 1989. "The Laws of Computing." *ST-Log*, no. 31 (May):97–98. https://www.atarimagazines.com/st-log/issue31/097_1_FOOTNOTES_THE_LAWS_OF_COMPUTING.php.

_____. 1996. *Creating a Software Engineering Culture.* New York: Dorset House Publishing.

_____. 1998a. "Know Your Enemy: Software Risk Management." *Software Development* **6**(10):38–42.

_____. 1998b. "Improve Your Process with Online 'Good Practices'." *Software Development* **6**(12):45–50.

_____. 2002a. *Peer Reviews in Software: A Practical Guide.* Boston: Addison-Wesley.

_____. 2002b. "Karl Wiegers on Humanizing Peer Reviews." *STQE* **4**(2):22–28. http://www.processimpact.com/articles/humanizing_reviews.pdf.

_____. 2003. "See You in Court." *Software Development* **11**(1):36–40.

_____. 2006a. *More About Software Requirements: Thorny Issues and Practical Advice.* Redmond, WA: Microsoft Press.

_____. 2006b. "Estimation Safety Tips." https://www.stickyminds.com/article/estimation-safety-tips.

_____. 2007. *Practical Project Initiation: A Handbook with Tools.* Redmond, WA: Microsoft Press.

Wiegers, Karl. 2019a. "Why Modeling Is an Essential Business Analysis Technique." https://www.modernanalyst.com/Resources/Articles/tabid/115/ID/5438/Why-Modeling-Is-an-Essential-Business-Analysis-Technique.aspx.

———. 2019b. "Why Is Software Always Ninety Percent Done?" https://medium.com/swlh/why-is-software-always-ninety-percent-donc-38e125c8b35c.

———. 2019c. "Rethinking the Triple Constraint: Five Project Dimensions." https://medium.com/swlh/rethinking-the-triple-constraint-five-project-dimensions-b3593c364b11.

———. 2019d. "Negotiating Achievable Commitments." https://medium.com/swlh/negotiating-achievable-commitments-6575b3d73b20.

———. 2019e. "Mind the Crap Gap." https://karlwiegers.medium.com/mind-the-crap-gap-61f314fe9678.

———. 2019f. "The Core Question about Building Better Software." https://www.modernanalyst.com/Resources/Articles/tabid/115/ID/5315/categoryId/35/The-Core-Question-about-Building-Better-Software.aspx.

———. 2019g. "Project Retrospectives: Looking Back to Look Ahead." https://medium.com/swlh/project-retrospectives-looking-back-to-look-ahead-f77ab9d4591c.

———. 2021. *The Thoughtless Design of Everyday Things*. Plantation, FL: J. Ross Publishing.

Wiegers, Karl, and Joy Beatty. 2013. *Software Requirements,* 3rd Ed. Redmond, WA: Microsoft Press.

———. 2016. "Agile Requirements: What's the Big Deal?" https://www.modernanalyst.com/Resources/Articles/tabid/115/ID/3573/Agile-Requirements-Whats-the-Big-Deal.aspx.

Wikic2. 2006. "Developer Bill Of Responsibilities." https://wiki.c2.com/?DeveloperBillOfResponsibilities.

———. 2008. "Developer Bill Of Rights." https://wiki.c2.com/?DeveloperBillOfRights.

Wikipedia. 2021a. "Design for X." Last modified July 3, 2021. https://en.wikipedia.org/wiki/Design_for_X.

———. 2021b. "Agile software development." Last modified July 8, 2021. https://en.wikipedia.org/wiki/Agile_software_development.

Winters, Titus, Tom Manshreck, and Hyrum Wright. 2020. *Software Engineering at Google: Lessons Learned from Programming Over Time*. Sebastopol, CA: O'Reilly Media, Inc.

Wright, Elizabeth. 2016. "The Cover Oregon Debacle." Citizens Against Government Waste. https://www.cagw.org/thewastewatcher/cover-oregon-debacle.

Index

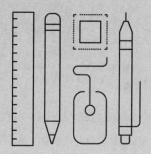

Register Your Product at informit.com/register

Access additional benefits and **save 35%** on your next purchase

- Automatically receive a coupon for 35% off your next purchase, valid for 30 days. Look for your code in your InformIT cart or the Manage Codes section of your account page.

- Download available product updates.

- Access bonus material if available.*

- Check the box to hear from us and receive exclusive offers on new editions and related products.

Registration benefits vary by product. Benefits will be listed on your account page under Registered Products.

InformIT.com—The Trusted Technology Learning Source

InformIT is the online home of information technology brands at Pearson, the world's foremost education company. At InformIT.com, you can:

- Shop our books, eBooks, software, and video training
- Take advantage of our special offers and promotions (informit.com/promotions)
- Sign up for special offers and content newsletter (informit.com/newsletters)
- Access thousands of free chapters and video lessons

Connect with InformIT—Visit informit.com/community

inform IT®
the trusted technology learning source

Addison-Wesley • Adobe Press • Cisco Press • Microsoft Press • Pearson IT Certification • Que • Sams • Peachpit Press

 Pearson